D1065509

The World's Best Poetry

Volume V

Nature

Poetry Anthology Press

The World's Best Poetry

Volume	I	Home and Friendship
	II	Love
	III	Sorrow and Consolation
	IV	The Higher Life
	V	Nature
	VI	Fancy and Sentiment
	VII	Descriptive and Narrative
	VIII	National Spirit
	IX	Tragedy and Humor
	X	Poetical Quotations; General Indexes
Supplement	I	Twentieth Century English and American Verse, 1900-1929
	II	Twentieth Century English and American Verse, 1930-1950
	III	Critical Companion

Survey of American Poetry

Volume	I	Colonial Period, 1607-1765
	II	Revolutionary Era, 1766-1799
	III	Early 19th Century, 1800-1829
	IV	First Great Period, 1830-1860
	V	Civil War and Aftermath, 1861-1889
	VI	Twilight Interval, 1890-1912
	VII	Poetic Renaissance, 1913-1919
	VIII	Interval Between World Wars, 1920-1939
	IX	World War II and Aftermath, 1940-1950
	X	Midcentury to Present; General Indexes

The World's Best Poetry

Volume V

Nature

Edited by Bliss Carman

Prepared by
The Editorial Board, Granger Book Co., Inc.

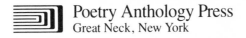 Poetry Anthology Press
Great Neck, New York

TABLE OF CONTENTS.

INTRODUCTORY ESSAY:

"THE POETRY OF NATURE."

PAGE

By *Charles George Douglas Roberts* . ix

POEMS OF NATURE:

NATURE'S INFLUENCE 3
LIGHT: DAY: NIGHT 30
THE SEASONS. 70
INLAND WATERS: HIGHLANDS 193
TREES: FLOWERS: PLANTS 218
ANIMATE NATURE 287
THE SEA 374

INDEX: AUTHORS AND TITLES 443

Preface

The publications of **Poetry Anthology Press** constitute a comprehensive conspectus of international verse in English designed to form the core of a library's poetry collection. Covering the entire range of poetic literature, these anthologies encompass all topics and national literatures.

Each collection, published in a multivolume continuing series format, is devoted to a major area of the whole undertaking and contains complete author, title, and first line indexes. Biographical data is also provided.

The World's Best Poetry, with coverage through the 19th century, is topically classified and arranged by subject matter. Supplements keep the 10 volume foundation collection current and complete.

Survey of American Poetry is an anthology of American verse arranged chronologically in 10 volumes. Each volume presents a significant period of American poetic history, from 1607 to date.

THE POETRY OF NATURE.

BY CHARLES GEORGE DOUGLAS ROBERTS.

WHEN Keats wrote, " The Poetry of Earth is never dead," he enunciated a truth which the world of his own day was hardly ready to accept in its fulness. To-day, none would seriously question it. Regarded subjectively, the poetry of earth, or, in other words, the quality which makes for poetry in external nature, is that power in nature which moves us by suggestion, which excites in us emotion, imagination, or poignant association which plays upon the tense-strings of our sympathies with the fingers of memory or desire. This power may reside not less in a bleak pasture-lot than in a paradisal close of bloom and verdure, not less in a roadside thistle-patch than in a peak that soars into the sunset. It works through sheer beauty or sheer sublimity; but it may work with equal effect through austerity or reticence or limitation or change. It may use the most common scenes, the most familiar facts and forms, as the vehicle of its most penetrating and most illuminating message. It is apt to make the drop of dew on a grass-glade as significant as the starred concave of the sky.

The poetry of nature, by which I mean this

"poetry of earth" expressed in words, may be roughly divided into two main classes: that which deals with mere description, and that which treats of nature in some one of its many relations with humanity. The latter class is that which alone was contemplated in Keats's line. It has many subdivisions; it includes much of the greatest poetry that the world has known; and there is little verse of acknowledged mastery that does not depend upon it for some portion of its appeal.

The former class has but a slender claim to recognition as poetry, under any definition of poetry that does not make metrical form the prime essential. The failures of the wisest to enunciate a satisfactory definition of poetry make it almost presumptuous for a critic now to attempt the task; but from an analysis of these failures one may educe something roughly to serve the purpose. To say that *poetry is the metrical expression in words of thought fused in emotion,* is of course incomplete; but it has the advantage of defining. No one can think that anything other than poetry is intended by such a definition; and nothing is excluded that can show a clear claim to admittance. But the poetry of mere enumerative description might perhaps not pass without challenge, so faint is the flame of its emotion, so imperfect the fusion of its thought. It is verse of this sort that is meant by undiscriminating critics when they inveigh against "nature-poetry," and declare that the only poetry worth man's attention is that which has to do with the heart of man.

Merely descriptive poetry is not very far re-
moved from the work of the reporter and the
photographer. Lacking the selective quality of
creative art, it is in reality little more than a
representation of some of the raw materials of
poetry. It leaves the reader unmoved, because
little emotion has gone to its making. Poetry of
this sort, at its best, is to be found abundantly in
Thomson's "Seasons." At less than its best it
concerns no one.

Nature becomes significant to man when she
is passed through the alembic of his heart. Ir-
relevant and confusing details having been
purged away, what remains is single and vital.
It acts either by interpreting, recalling, suggesting, or symbolizing some phase of human feeling.
Out of the fusing heat born of this contact comes
the perfect line, luminous, unforgettable, with
something of mystery in its beauty that eludes
analysis. Whatever it be that is brought to the
alembic,—naked hill, or barren sand-reach, sea
or meadow, weed or star,—it comes out charged
with a new force, imperishable and active wherever it finds sympathies to vibrate under its currents.

In the imperishable verse of ancient Greece
and Rome, nature-poetry of the higher class is
generally supposed to play but a small part. In
reality, it is nearly always present, nearly always
active in that verse; but it appears in such a
disguise that its origin is apt to be overlooked.
The Greeks—and the Romans, of course, following their pattern—personified the phenomena of

nature till these, for all purposes of art, became
human. The Greeks made their anthropomorphic
gods of the forces of nature which compelled their
adoration. Of these personifications they sang,
as of men of like passions with themselves; but
in truth it was of external nature that they
made their songs. Bion's wailing "Lament for
Adonis," human as it is throughout, is in its final
analysis a poem of nature. By an intense, but
perhaps unconscious, subjective process, the an-
cients supplied external nature with their own
moods, impulses, and passions.

The transitions from the ancient to the modern
fashion of looking at nature are to be found prin-
cipally in the work of the Celtic bards, who,
rather than the cloistered students of that time,
kept alive the true fire of poetry through the long
darkness of the Middle Ages.

The modern attitude toward nature, as distin-
guished from that of the Greeks, begins to show
itself clearly in English song very soon after the
great revivifying movement which we call the
Renaissance. At first, it is a very simple matter
indeed. Men sing of nature because nature is
impressing them directly. A joyous season calls
forth a joyous song:—

> " Sumer is icumen in
>   Lhude sing, cuccu.
>   Groweth sed and bloweth med
>   And springth the wude nu."

This is the poet's answering hail, when the
spring-time calls to his blood. With the fall of

the leaf, his singing has a sombre and foreboding note; and winter in the world makes winter in his song.

This is nature-poetry in its simplest form,—the form which it chiefly took with the spontaneous Elizabethans. But it soon became more complex, as life and society became entangled in more complex conditions. The artificialities of the Queen Anne period delayed this evolution; but with Gray and Collins we see it fairly in process. Man, looking upon external nature, projects himself into her workings. His own wrath he apprehends in the violence of the storm; his own joy in the loveliness of opening blossoms; his own mirth in the light waves running in the sun; his own gloom in the heaviness of the rain and wind. In all nature he finds but phenomena of himself. She becomes but an expression of his hopes, his fears, his cravings, his despair. This intense subjectivity is peculiarly characteristic of the nature-poetry produced by Byron and his school. When that Titan of modern song apostrophizes the storm thundering over Jura, he speaks to the tumult in the deeps of his own soul. When he addresses the stainless tranquillities of " clear, placid Leman," what moves him to utterance is the contemplation of such a calm as his vexed spirit often craved.

When man's heart and the heart of nature had become thus closely involved, the relationship between them and, consequently, the manner of its expression in song became complex almost beyond the possibilities of analysis. Wordsworth's

best poetry is to be found in the utterances of
the high-priest in nature's temple, interpreting
the mysteries. The function of the " Lines Composed a Few Miles Above Tintern Abbey " is to
convey to a restless age, troubled with small
cares seen in too close perspective, the large, con-
templative wisdom which seemed to Wordsworth
the message of the scene which moved him.

Keats, his soul aflame with the worship of
beauty, was impassioned toward the manifesta-
tions of beauty in the world about him; and, at
the same time, he used these freely as symbols to
express other aspects of the same compelling
spirit. Shelley, the most complex of the group,
sometimes combined all these methods, as in the
" Ode to the West Wind." But he added a new
note,—which was yet an echo of the oldest,—the
note of nature-worship. He saw continually in
nature the godhead which he sought and adored,
youthful protestations and affectations of atheism
to the contrary notwithstanding. Most of Shelley's nature-poetry carries a rich vein of panthe-
ism, allied to that which colors the oldest verse
of time and particularly characterizes ancient
Celtic song. With this significant and stimulat-
ing revival, goes a revival of that strong sense of
kinship, of the oneness of earth and man, which
the Greeks and Latins felt so keenly at times,
which Omar knew and uttered, and which under-
lies so much of the verse of these later days.

That other unity—the unity of man and God,
which forms so inevitable a corollary to the
pantheistic proposition—comes to be dwelt upon

more and more insistently throughout the nature-poetry of the last fifty years.

The main purpose of these brief suggestions is to call attention to the fact that nature-poetry is not mere description of landscape in metrical form, but the expression of one or another of many vital relationships between external nature and " the deep heart of man." It may touch the subtlest chords of human emotion and human imagination not less masterfully than the verse which sets out to be a direct transcript from life. The most inaccessible truths are apt to be reached by indirection. The divinest mysteries of beauty are not possessed exclusively by the eye that loves, or by the lips of a child, but are also manifested in some bird-song's unforgotten cadence, some flower whose perfection pierces the heart, some ineffable hue of sunset or sunrise that makes the spirit cry out for it knows not what. And whosoever follows the inexplicable lure of beauty, in color, form, sound, perfume, or any other manifestation,—reaching out to it as perhaps a message from some unfathomable past, or a premonition of the future,—knows that the mystic signal beckons nowhere more imperiously than from the heights of nature-poetry.

Charles G. D. Roberts

The World's Best Poetry

Volume V

Nature

POEMS OF NATURE.

I.

NATURE'S INFLUENCE.

THE WORLD IS TOO MUCH WITH US.

SONNET.

THE World is too much with us; late and soon,
Getting and spending, we lay waste our powers;
Little we see in nature that is ours;
We have given our hearts away, a sordid boon!
This sea that bares her bosom to the moon;
The winds that will be howling at all hours,
And are up-gathered now like sleeping flowers;
For this, for everything, we are out of tune;
It moves us not.—Great God! I'd rather be
A Pagan suckled in a creed outworn,
So might I, standing on this pleasant lea,
Have glimpses that would make me less forlorn;
Have sight of Proteus rising from the sea,
Or hear old Triton blow his wreathèd horn.

WILLIAM WORDSWORTH.

3

EARTH, OCEAN, AIR.

FROM " ALASTOR "; PREFACE.

" Nondum amabam, et amare amabam, quærebam quid amarem, amans amare."—*Confessions of Saint Augustine.*

EARTH, ocean, air, belovèd brotherhood!
If our great mother has imbued my soul
With aught of natural piety to feel
Your love, and recompense the boon with mine;
If dewy morn, and odorous noon, and even,
With sunset and its gorgeous ministers,
And solemn midnight's tingling silentness;
If autumn's hollow sighs in the sere wood,
And winter robing with pure snow and crowns
Of starry ice the gray grass and bare boughs;
If spring's voluptuous pantings when she
    breathes
Her first sweet kisses, have been dear to me;
If no bright bird, insect, or gentle beast
I consciously have injured, but still loved
And cherished these my kindred; then forgive
This boast, belovèd·brethren, and withdraw
No portion of your wonted favor now!

Mother of this unfathomable world!
Favor my solemn song, for I have loved
Thee ever, and thee only; I have watched
Thy shadow, and the darkness of thy steps,
And my heart ever gazes on the depth
Of thy deep mysteries. I have made my bed
In charnels and on coffins, where black death

Keeps record of the trophies won from thee,
Hoping to still these obstinate questionings
Of thee and thine, by forcing some lone ghost,
Thy messenger, to render up the tale
Of what we are. In lone and silent hours,
When night makes a weird sound of its own still-
    ness,
Like an inspired and desperate alchemist
Staking his very life on some dark hope,
Have I mixed awful talk and asking looks
With my most innocent love, until strange tears
Uniting with those breathless kisses, made
Such magic as compels the charmèd night
To render up thy charge: and, tho' ne'er yet
Thou hast unveiled thy inmost sanctuary,
Enough from incommunicable dream,
And twilight phantasms, and deep noonday
    thought,
Has shone within me, that serenely now
And moveless, as a long-forgotten lyre
Suspended in a solitary dome
Of some mysterious and deserted fane,
I wait thy breath, Great Parent, that my strain
May modulate with murmurs of the air,
And motions of the forests and the sea
And voice of living beings, and woven hymns
Of night and day, and the deep heart of man.

              PERCY BYSSHE SHELLEY.

ON A BEAUTIFUL DAY.

O UNSEEN Spirit! now a calm divine
    Comes forth from thee, rejoicing earth and air!
Trees, hills, and houses, all distinctly shine,
    And thy great ocean slumbers everywhere.

The mountain ridge against the purple sky
    Stands clear and strong, with darkened rocks
        and dells,
And cloudless brightness opens wide and high
    A home aerial, where thy presence dwells.

The chime of bells remote, the murmuring sea,
    The song of birds in whispering copse and wood,
The distant voice of children's thoughtless glee,
    And maiden's songs, are all one voice of good.

Amid the leaves' green mass a sunny play
    Of flash and shadow stirs like inward life:
The ship's white sail glides onward far away,
    Unhaunted by a dream of storm or strife.

JOHN STERLING.

GOD IN NATURE.

FROM "PARACELSUS."

I KNEW, I felt, (perception unexpressed,
Uncomprehended by our narrow thought,
But somehow felt and known in every shift
And change in the spirit,—nay, in every pore
Of the body, even,)—what God is, what we are,
What life is—how God tastes an infinite joy

In infinite ways—one everlasting bliss,
From whom all being emanates, all power
Proceeds; in whom is life forevermore,
Yet whom existence in its lowest form
Includes; where dwells enjoyment there is he;
With still a flying point of bliss remote,
A happiness in store afar, a sphere
Of distant glory in full view; thus climbs
Pleasure its heights forever and forever.
The centre-fire heaves underneath the earth,
And the earth changes like a human face;
The molten ore bursts up among the rocks,
Winds into the stone's heart, outbranches bright
In hidden mines, spots barren river-beds,
Crumbles into fine sand where sunbeams bask—
God joys therein. The wroth sea's waves are
    edged
With foam, white as the bitten lip of hate,
When, in the solitary waste, strange groups
Of young volcanos come up, cyclops-like,
Staring together with their eyes on flame—
God tastes a pleasure in their uncouth pride.
Then all is still; earth is a wintry clod:
But spring-wind, like a dancing psaltress, passes
Over its breast to waken it, rare verdure
Buds tenderly upon rough banks, between
The withered tree-roots and the cracks of frost,
Like a smile striving with a wrinkled face;
The grass grows bright, the boughs are swoln
    with blooms
Like chrysalids impatient for the air,
The shining dorrs are busy, beetles run
Along the furrows, ants make their ado;

Above, birds fly in merry flocks, the lark
Soars up and up, shivering for very joy;
Afar the ocean sleeps; white fishing-gulls
Flit where the strand is purple with its tribe
Of nested limpets; savage creatures seek
Their loves in wood and plain—and God renews
His ancient rapture. Thus he dwells in all,
From life's minute beginnings, up at last
To man—the consummation of this scheme
Of being, the completion of this sphere
Of life: whose attributes had here and there
Been scattered o'er the visible world before,
Asking to be combined, dim fragments meant
To be united in some wondrous whole,
Imperfect qualities throughout creation,
Suggesting some one creature yet to make,
Some point where all those scattered rays should
    meet
Convergent in the faculties of man.

ROBERT BROWNING.

MY HEART LEAPS UP.

My heart leaps up when I behold
    A rainbow in the sky;
So was it when my life began,
So is it now I am a man,
So be it when I shall grow old,
    Or let me die!
The Child is father of the Man;
And I could wish my days to be
Bound each to each by natural piety.

WILLIAM WORDSWORTH.

EACH AND ALL.

LITTLE thinks, in the field, yon red-cloaked
    clown,
Of thee from the hill-top looking down;
The heifer that lows in the upland farm,
Far-heard, lows not thine ear to charm;
The sexton tolling his bell at noon,
Deems not that great Napoleon
Stops his horse, and lists with delight,
Whilst his files sweep round yon Alpine height;
Nor knowest thou what argument
Thy life to thy neighbor's creed has lent.
All are needed by each one;
Nothing is fair or good alone.
I thought the sparrow's note from heaven,
Singing at dawn on the alder bough;
I brought him home, in his nest, at even;
He sings the song, but it pleases not now,
For I did not bring home the river and sky;—
He sang to my ear,—they sang to my eye.
The delicate shells lay on the shore;
The bubbles of the latest wave
Fresh pearls to their enamel gave;
And the bellowing of the savage sea
Greeted their safe escape to me.
I wiped away the weeds and foam,
I fetched my sea-born treasures home;
But the poor, unsightly, noisome things
Had left their beauty on the shore,
With the sun and the sand and the wild uproar.

The lover watched his graceful maid,
As mid the virgin train she strayed,
Nor knew her beauty's best attire
Was woven still by the snow-white choir.
At last she came to his hermitage,
Like the bird from the woodlands to the cage;—
The gay enchantment was undone,
A gentle wife, but fairy none.
Then I said, " I covet truth;
Beauty is unripe childhood's cheat;
I leave it behind with the games of youth."—
As I spoke, beneath my feet
The ground-pine curled its pretty wreath,
Running over the club-moss burrs;
I inhaled the violet's breath;
Around me stood the oaks and firs;
Pine-cones and acorns lay on the ground;
Over me soared the eternal sky,
Full of light and of deity;
Again I saw, again I heard,
The rolling river, the morning bird;—
Beauty through my senses stole;
I yielded myself to the perfect whole.

RALPH WALDO EMERSON.

THE COUNTRY FAITH.

HERE in the country's heart
Where the grass is green,
Life is the same sweet life
As it e'er hath been.

Trust in a God still lives,
And the bell at morn
Floats with a thought of God
O'er the rising corn.

God comes down in the rain,
And the crop grows tall—
This is the country faith,
And the best of all!

NORMAN GALE.

TINTERN ABBEY.

FIVE years have past; five summers, with the
    length
Of five long winters! and again I hear
These waters,* rolling from their mountain-
    springs
With a soft inland murmur.—Once again
Do I behold these steep and lofty cliffs,
That on a wild, secluded scene impress
Thoughts of more deep seclusion, and connect
The landscape with the quiet of the sky.
The day is come when I again repose
Here, under this sycamore, and view
These plots of cottage-ground, these orchard-
    tufts,
Which, at this season, with their unripe fruits,
Are clad in one green hue, and lose themselves
Mid groves and copses. Once again I see
These hedge-rows, hardly hedge-rows, little lines
Of sportive wood run wild: these pastoral farms,

* The River Wye.

Green to the very door; and wreaths of smoke
Sent up, in silence, from among the trees!
With some uncertain notice, as might seem
Of vagrant dwellers in the houseless woods,
Or of some hermit's cave, where by his fire
The hermit sits alone.
               These beauteous forms,
Through a long absence, have not been to me
As is a landscape to a blind man's eye;
But oft, in lonely rooms, and mid the din
Of towns and cities, I have owed to them,
In hours of weariness, sensations sweet,
Felt in the blood, and felt along the heart;
And passing even into my purer mind,
With tranquil restoration:—feelings too
Of unremembered pleasure: such, perhaps,
As have no slight or trivial influence
On that best portion of a good man's life,
His little, nameless, unremembered acts
Of kindness and of love. Nor less, I trust,
To them I may have owed another gift,
Of aspect more sublime; that blessèd mood,
In which the burden of the mystery,
In which the heavy and the weary weight
Of all this unintelligible world,
Is lightened,—that serene and blessèd mood,
In which the affections gently lead us on,
Until, the breath of this corporeal frame
And even the motion of our human blood
Almost suspended, we are laid asleep
In body, and become a living soul:
While with an eye made quiet by the power
Of harmony, and the deep power of joy,

We see into the life of things.
                                    If this
Be but a vain belief, yet, O, how oft—
In darkness and amid the many shapes
Of joyless daylight; when the fretful stir
Unprofitable, and the fever of the world,
Have hung upon the beatings of my heart—
How oft, in spirit, have I turned to thee,
O sylvan Wye! thou wanderer through the woods,
How often has my spirit turned to thee!

  And now, with gleams of half-extinguished
      thought,
With many recognitions dim and faint,
And somewhat of a sad perplexity,
The picture of the mind revives again:
While here I stand, not only with the sense
Of present pleasure, but with pleasing thoughts
That in this moment there is life and food
For future years.   And so I dare to hope,
Though changed, no doubt, from what I was when
      first
I came among these hills; when like a roe
I bounded o'er the mountains, by the sides
Of the deep rivers, and the lonely streams,
Wherever nature led: more like a man
Flying from something that he dreads, than one
Who sought the thing he loved.   For nature then
(The coarser pleasures of my boyish days
And their glad animal movements all gone by)
To me was all in all.—I cannot paint
What then I was.   The sounding cataract
Haunted me like a passion: the tall rock,

The mountain, and the deep and gloomy wood,
Their colors and their forms, were then to me
An appetite; a feeling and a love,
That had no need of a remoter charm
By thought supplied, nor any interest
Unborrowed from the eye.—That time is past,
And all its aching joys are now no more,
And all its dizzy raptures. Not for this
Faint I, nor mourn nor murmur; other gifts
Have followed; for such loss, I would believe,
Abundant recompense. For I have learned
To look on nature, not as in the hour
Of thoughtless youth; but hearing oftentimes
The still, sad music of humanity,
Nor harsh nor grating, though of ample power
To chasten and subdue. And I have felt
A presence that disturbs me with the joy
Of elevated thoughts; a sense sublime
Of something far more deeply interfused,
Whose dwelling is the light of setting suns,
And the round ocean, and the living air,
And the blue sky, and in the mind of man:
A motion and a spirit, that impels
All thinking things, all objects of all thought,
And rolls through all things. Therefore am I
 still
A lover of the meadows and the woods,
And mountains; and of all that we behold
From this green earth; of all the mighty world
Of eye, and ear,—both what they half create,*

---

* " This line has a close resemblance to an admirable
line of Young's, the exact expression of which I do not
recollect."—THE AUTHOR.

And what perceive; well pleased to recognize
In nature and the language of the sense,
The anchor of my purest thoughts, the nurse,
The guide, the guardian of my heart, and soul
Of all my moral being.
                Nor perchance,
If I were not thus taught, should I the more
Suffer my genial spirits to decay:
For thou art with me here upon the banks
Of this fair river; thou my dearest friend,
My dear, dear friend; and in thy voice I catch
The language of my former heart, and read
My former pleasures in the shooting lights
Of thy wild eyes. O, yet a little while
May I behold in thee what I was once,
My dear, dear sister! and this prayer I make,
Knowing that Nature never did betray
The heart that loved her; 't is her privilege,
Through all the years of this our life, to lead
From joy to joy: for she can so inform
The mind that is within us, so impress
With quietness and beauty, and so feed
With lofty thoughts, that neither evil tongues,
Rash judgments, nor the sneers of selfish men,
Nor greetings where no kindness is, nor all
The dreary intercourse of daily life,
Shall e'er prevail against us, or disturb
Our cheerful faith, that all which we behold
Is full of blessings. Therefore let the moon
Shine on thee in thy solitary walk;
And let the misty mountain-winds be free
To blow against thee: and, in after years,
When these wild ecstasies shall be matured

Into a sober pleasure; when thy mind
Shall be a mansion for all lovely forms,
Thy memory be as a dwelling-place
For all sweet sounds and harmonies; O, then,
If solitude or fear or pain or grief
Should be thy portion, with what healing thoughts
Of tender joy wilt thou remember me,
And these my exhortations! Nor, perchance,—
If I should be where I no more can hear
Thy voice, nor catch from thy wild eyes these
        gleams
Of past existence,—wilt thou then forget
That on the banks of this delightful stream
We stood together; and that I, so long
A worshipper of Nature, hither came
Unwearied in that service: rather say
With warmer love,—O, with far deeper zeal
Of holier love. Nor wilt thou then forget
That after many wanderings, many years
Of absence, these steep woods and lofty cliffs,
And this green pastoral landscape, were to me
More dear, both for themselves and for thy sake!
                        WILLIAM WORDSWORTH.

GREAT NATURE IS AN ARMY GAY.

GREAT Nature is an army gay,
Resistless marching on its way;
        I hear the bugles clear and sweet,
I hear the tread of million feet.
        Across the plain I see it pour;
It tramples down the waving grass;

Within the echoing mountain-pass
    I hear a thousand cannon roar.

    It swarms within my garden gate;
My deepest well it drinketh dry.
It doth not rest; it doth not wait;
By night and day it sweepeth by;
Ceaseless it marches by my door;
It heeds me not, though I implore.
I know not whence it comes, nor where
It goes. For me it doth not care—
Whether I starve, or eat, or sleep,
Or live, or die, or sing, or weep.
And now the banners are all bright,
Now torn and blackened by the fight.
Sometimes its laughter shakes the sky,
Sometimes the groans of those who die.
Still through the night and through the livelong
    day
The infinite army marches on its remorseless way.
                RICHARD WATSON GILDER.

COME TO THESE SCENES OF PEACE.

Come to these scenes of peace,
  Where, to rivers murmuring,
  The sweet birds all the summer sing,
Where cares and toil and sadness cease!
Stranger, does thy heart deplore
Friends whom thou wilt see no more?
Does thy wounded spirit prove
Pangs of hopeless, severed love?

2

Thee the stream that gushes clear,
Thee the birds that carol near
Shall soothe, as silent thou dost lie
And dream of their wild lullaby;
Come to bless these scenes of peace,
Where cares and toil and sadness cease.

WILLIAM LISLE BOWLES.

ODE ON THE PLEASURE ARISING FROM VICISSITUDE.

Now the golden Morn aloft
　　Waves her dew-bespangled wing,
With vermeil cheek and whisper soft
　　She woos the tardy Spring:
Till April starts, and calls around
The sleeping fragrance from the ground,
And lightly o'er the living scene
Scatters his freshest, tenderest green.

New-born flocks, in rustic dance,
　　Frisking ply their feeble feet;
Forgetful of their wintry trance
　　The birds his presence greet:
But chief, the skylark warbles high
His trembling thrilling ecstasy;
And lessening from the dazzled sight,
Melts into air and liquid light.

Yesterday the sullen year
　　Saw the snowy whirlwind fly;
Mute was the music of the air,
　　The herd stood drooping by:

Their raptures now that wildly flow
No yesterday nor morrow know;
'T is Man alone that joy descries
With forward and reverted eyes.

Smiles on past misfortune's brow
   Soft reflection's hand can trace,
And o'er the cheek of sorrow throw
   A melancholy grace;
While hope prolongs our happier hour,
Or deepest shades, that dimly lour
And blacken round our weary way,
Gilds with a gleam of distant day.

Still, where rosy pleasure leads,
   See a kindred grief pursue;
Behind the steps that misery treads
   Approaching comfort view:
The hues of bliss more brightly glow
Chastised by sabler tints of woe,
And blended form, with artful strife,
The strength and harmony of life.

See the wretch that long has tost
   On the thorny bed of pain,
At length repair his vigor lost
   And breathe and walk again:
The meanest floweret of the vale,
The simplest note that swells the gale,
The common sun, the air, the skies,
To him are opening Paradise.

          THOMAS GRAY.

NATURE.

THE bubbling brook doth leap when I come by,
Because my feet find measure with its call;
The birds know when the friend they love is nigh,
For I am known to them, both great and small.
The flower that on the lonely hillside grows
Expects me there when spring its bloom has given;
And many a tree and bush my wanderings knows,
And e'en the clouds and silent stars of heaven;
For he who with his Maker walks aright,
Shall be their lord as Adam was before;
His ear shall catch each sound with new delight,
Each object wear the dress that then it wore;
And he, as when erect in soul he stood,
Hear from his Father's lips that all is good.

JONES VERY.

INFLUENCE OF NATURAL OBJECTS.

FROM "THE PRELUDE," I.

WISDOM and Spirit of the universe!
Thou Soul, that art the eternity of thought!
And giv'st to forms and images a breath
And everlasting motion! not in vain,
By day or star-light, thus from my first dawn
Of childhood didst thou intertwine for me
The passions that build up our human soul—
Not with the mean and vulgar works of Man,
But with high objects, with enduring things,
With Life and Nature; purifying thus

The elements of feeling and of thought,
And sanctifying by such discipline
Both pain and fear,—until we recognize
A grandeur in the beatings of the heart.
  Nor was this fellowship vouchsafed to me
With stinted kindness. In November days,
When vapors rolling down the valleys made
A lonely scene more lonesome; among woods
At noon; and 'mid the calm of summer nights,
When, by the margin of the trembling lake,
Beneath the gloomy hills, homeward I went
In solitude, such intercourse was mine.
Mine was it in the fields both day and night,
And by the waters, all the Summer long;
And in the frosty season, when the sun
Was set, and, visible for many a mile,
The cottage windows through the twilight blazed,
I heeded not the summons. Happy time
It was indeed for all of us; for me
It was a time of rapture! Clear and loud
The village-clock tolled six; I wheeled about,
Proud and exulting like an untired horse
That cares not for his home. All shod with steel,
We hissed along the polished ice, in games
Confederate, imitative of the chase
And woodland pleasures,—the resounding horn,
The pack loud-chiming, and the hunted hare.
So through the darkness and the cold we flew,
And not a voice was idle. With the din
Smitten, the precipices rang aloud;
The leafless trees and every icy crag
Tinkled like iron; while far-distant hills
Into the tumult sent an alien sound

Of melancholy, not unnoticed; while the stars,
Eastward, were sparkling clear, and in the west
The orange sky of evening died away.
  Not seldom from the uproar I retired
Into a silent bay, or sportively
Glanced sideway, leaving the tumultuous throng,
To cut across the reflex of a star—
Image, that, flying still before me, gleamed
Upon the glassy plain. And oftentimes,
When we had given our bodies to the wind,
And all the shadowy banks on either side
Came sweeping thro' the darkness, spinning still
The rapid line of motion, then at once
Have I, reclining back upon my heels,
Stopped short; yet still the solitary cliffs
Wheeled by me,—even as if the Earth had rolled
With visible motion her diurnal round!
Behind me did they stretch in solemn train,
Feebler and feebler; and I stood and watched
Till all was tranquil as a summer sea.

WILLIAM WORDSWORTH.

AN INDIAN SONG.

O WANDERER in the southern weather,
  Our isle awaits us; on each lea
The pea-hens dance; in crimson feather
  A parrot swaying on a tree
  Rages at his own image in the enamelled sea.

There dreamy Time lets fall his sickle
  And Life the sandals of her fleetness,

And sleek young Joy is no more fickle,
  And Love is kindly and deceitless,
  And all is over save the murmur and the sweet-
    ness.

There we will moor our lonely ship
  And wander ever with woven hands,
Murmuring softly, lip to lip,
  Along the grass, along the sands—
  Murmuring how far away are all earth's fever-
    ish lands:

How we alone of mortals are
  Hid in the earth's most hidden part,
While grows our love an Indian star,
  A meteor of the burning heart,
  One with the waves that softly round us laugh
    and dart;

One with the leaves; one with the dove
  That moans and sighs a hundred days;
How when we die our shades will rove,
  Dropping at eve in coral bays
  A vapory footfall on the ocean's sleepy blaze.
                              WILLIAM BUTLER YEATS.

THE TABLES TURNED.

Up! up, my friend! and quit your books,
  Or surely you 'll grow double;
Up! up, my friend! and clear your looks!
  Why all this toil and trouble?

The sun, above the mountain's head,
  A freshening lustre mellow
Through all the long green fields has spread,
  His first sweet evening yellow.

Books! 't is a dull and endless strife;
  Come, hear the woodland linnet—
How sweet his music! on my life,
  There 's more of wisdom in it!

And hark! how blithe the throstle sings!
  He, too, is no mean preacher;
Come forth into the light of things—
  Let Nature be your teacher.

She has a world of ready wealth,
  Our minds and hearts to bless,—
Spontaneous wisdom breathed by health,
  Truth breathed by cheerfulness.

One impulse from a vernal wood
  May teach you more of man,
Of moral evil and of good,
  Than all the sages can.

Sweet is the lore which nature brings;
  Our meddling intellect
Misshapes the beauteous forms of things—
  We murder to dissect.

Enough of science and of art;
  Close up those barren leaves;
Come forth, and bring with you a heart
  That watches and receives.
                    WILLIAM WORDSWORTH.

RUS IN URBE.

Poets are singing the whole world over
  Of May in melody, joys for June;
Dusting their feet in the careless clover,
  And filling their hearts with the blackbird's
    tune.
The " brown bright nightingale " strikes with
    pity
  The sensitive heart of a count or clown;
But where is the song for our leafy city,
  And where the rhymes for our lovely town?

" O for the Thames, and its rippling reaches,
  Where almond rushes, and breezes sport!
Take me a walk under Burnham Beeches;
  Give me a dinner at Hampton Court! "
Poets, be still, though your hearts I harden;
  We 've flowers by day and have scents at dark,
The limes are in leaf in the cockney garden,
  And lilacs blossom in Regent's Park.

" Come for a blow," says a reckless fellow,
  Burned red and brown by passionate sun;
" Come to the downs, where the gorse is yellow;
  The season of kisses has just begun!
Come to the fields where bluebells shiver,
  Hear cuckoo's carol, or plaint of dove;
Come for a row on the silent river;
  Come to the meadows and learn to love! "

Yes, I will come when this wealth is over
  Of softened color and perfect tone—
The lilac 's better than fields of clover;
  I 'll come when the blossoming May has flown.

When dust and dirt of a trampled city
   Have dragged the yellow laburnum down,
I 'll take my holiday—more 's the pity—
   And turn my back upon London town.

Margaret! am I so wrong to love it,
   This misty town that your face shines through?
A crown of blossom is waved above it;
   But heart and life of the whirl—*'t is you!*
Margaret! pearl! I have sought and found you;
   And, though the paths of the wind are free,
I 'll follow the ways of the world around you,
   And build my nest on the nearest tree!

CLEMENT SCOTT.

THE FAUN.

A FRAGMENT.

I WILL go out to grass with that old King,
For I am weary of clothes and cooks.
I long to lie along the banks of brooks,
And watch the boughs above me sway and swing.
Come, I will pluck off custom's livery,
Nor longer be a lackey to old Time,
Time shall serve me, and at my feet shall fling
The spoil of listless minutes. I shall climb
The wild trees for my food, and run
Through dale and upland as the fox runs free,
Laugh for cool joy and sleep i' the warm sun,
And men will call me mad, like that old King.

For I am woodland-natured, and have made
Dryads my bedfellows,

And I have played
With the sleek Naiads in the splash of the pools
And made a mock of gowned and trousered fools.
Helen, none knows
Better than thou how like a Faun I strayed.
And I am half Faun now, and my heart goes
Out to the forest and the crack of twigs,
The drip of wet leaves and the low soft laughter
Of brooks that chuckle o'er old mossy jests
And say them over to themselves, the nests
Of squirrels and the holes the chipmunk digs,
Where through the branches the slant rays
Dapple with sunlight the leaf-matted ground,
And the wind comes with blown vestures rustling
    after,
And through the woven lattice of crisp sound
A bird's song lightens like a maiden's face.

O wildwood Helen, let them strive and fret,
Those goggled men with their dissecting-knives!
Let them in charnel-houses pass their lives
And seek in death life's secret! And let
Those hard-faced worldlings prematurely old
Gnaw their thin lips with vain desire to get
Portia's fair fame or Lesbia's carcanet,
Or crown of Cæsar or Catullus,
Apicius' lampreys or Crassus' gold!
For these consider many things—but yet
By land or sea
They shall not find the way to Arcady,
The old home of the awful heart-dear Mother,
Whereto child-dreams and long rememberings
    lull

Far from the cares that overlay and smother
The memories of old woodland out-door mirth
In the dim first life-burst centuries ago,
The sense of the freedom and nearness of Earth—
Nay, this they shall not know;
For who goes thither,
Leaves all the cark and clutch of his soul behind,
The doves defiled and the serpents shrined,
The hates that wax and the hopes that wither;
Nor does he journey, seeking where it be,
But wakes and finds himself in Arcady.

Hist! there 's a stir in the brush.
Was it a face through the leaves?
Back of the laurels a skurry and rush
Hillward, then silence except for the thrush
That throws one song from the dark of the bush
And is gone; and I plunge in the wood, and the
    swift soul cleaves
Through the swirl and the flow of the leaves,
As a swimmer stands with his white limbs bare
    to the sun
For the space that a breath is held, and drops in
    the sea;
And the undulant woodland folds round me, in-
    timate, fluctuant, free,
Like the clasp and the cling of the waters, and
    the reach and the effort is done,—
There is only the glory of living, exultant to be.

O goodly damp smell of the ground!
O rough sweet bark of the trees!
O clear sharp cracklings of sound!

O life that 's a-thrill and a-bound
With the vigor of boyhood and morning, and the
    noontide's rapture of ease!
Was there ever a weary heart in the world?
A lag in the body's urge or a flag of the spirit's
    wings?
Did a man's heart ever break
For a lost hope's sake?
For here there is lilt in the quiet and calm in the
    quiver of things.
Ay, this old oak, gray-grown and knurled,
Solemn and sturdy and big,
Is as young of heart, as alert and elate in his rest,
As the nuthatch there that clings to the tip of the
    twig
And scolds at the wind that buffets too rudely
    its nest.

Oh, what is it breathes in the air?
Oh, what is it touches my cheek?
There 's a sense of a presence that lurks in the
    branches.
But where?
Is it far, is it far to seek?

RICHARD HOVEY.

II.

LIGHT: DAY: NIGHT.

INVOCATION TO LIGHT.

FROM " PARADISE LOST," BOOK III.

HAIL, holy Light, offspring of Heaven first-born!
Or of the Eternal coeternal beam
May I express thee unblamed? since God is light,
And never but in unapproachèd light
Dwelt from eternity, dwelt then in thee,
Bright effluence of bright essence increate!
Or hear'st thou rather pure ethereal stream,
Whose fountain who shall tell? Before the sun,
Before the heavens, thou wert, and at the voice
Of God, as with a mantle, did invest
The rising world of waters dark and deep,
Won from the void and formless infinite.
Thee I revisit now with bolder wing,
Escaped the Stygian pool, though long detained
In that obscure sojourn, while in my flight
Through utter and through middle darkness
     borne,
With other notes than to the Orphean lyre,
I sung of Chaos and eternal Night,
Taught by the heavenly Muse to venture down
The dark descent, and up to reascend,

Though hard and rare: thee I revisit safe,
And feel thy sovereign vital lamp; but thou
Revisitest not these eyes, that roll in vain
To find thy piercing ray, and find no dawn;
So thick a drop serene hath quenched their orbs,
Or dim suffusion veiled. Yet not the more
Cease I to wander where the Muses haunt
Clear spring, or shady grove, or sunny hill,
Smit with the love of sacred song; but chief
Thee, Sion, and the flowery brooks beneath,
That wash thy hallowed feet, and warbling flow,
Nightly I visit: nor sometimes forget
Those other two equalled with me in fate,
So were I equalled with them in renown,
Blind Thamyris and blind Mæonides,
And Tiresias and Phineus, prophets old:
Then feed on thoughts that voluntary move
Harmonious numbers; as the wakeful bird
Sings darkling, and in shadiest covert hid
Tunes her nocturnal note. Thus with the year
Seasons return, but not to me returns
Day, or the sweet approach of even or morn,
Or sight of vernal bloom, or summer's rose,
Or flocks, or herds, or human face divine;
But cloud, instead, and ever-during dark,
Surrounds me, from the cheerful ways of men
Cut off, and for the book of knowledge fair
Presented with a universal blank
Of nature's works, to me expunged and rased,
And wisdom at one entrance quite shut out.
So much the rather thou, celestial Light,
Shine inward, and the mind through all her
    powers

Irradiate; there plant eyes, all mist from thence
Purge and disperse, that I may see and tell
Of things invisible to mortal sight.

MILTON.

LIGHT.

FROM "PARADISE LOST," BOOK VII.

"LET there be light," God said; and forthwith
    Light
Ethereal, first of things, quintessence pure,
Sprung from the deep; and from her native east
To journey through the aery gloom began,
Sphered in a radiant cloud, for yet the Sun
Was not; she in a cloudy tabernacle
Sojourned the while.　God saw the light was
    good;
And light from darkness by the hemisphere
Divided: light the Day, and darkness Night,
He named.

MILTON.

LIGHT.

THOU art the joy of age:
Thy sun is dear when long the shadow falls.
Forth to its friendliness the old man crawls,
And, like the bird hung in his poor cage
To gather song from radiance, in his chair
Sits by the door; and sitteth there
His soul within him, like a child that lies
Half dreaming, with half-open eyes,
At close of a long afternoon in summer—
High ruins around him, ancient ruins, where
The raven is almost the only comer;

Half dreams, half broods, in wonderment
At thy celestial descent,
Through rifted loops alighting on the gold
That waves its bloom in many an airy rent:
So dreams the old man's soul, that is not old,
But sleepy 'mid the ruins that enfold.

What soul-like changes, evanescent moods,
Upon the face of the still passive earth,
Its hills, and fields, and woods,
Thou with thy seasons and thy hours art ever call-
    ing forth!
Even like a lord of music bent
Over his instrument,
Who gives to tears and smiles an equal birth!
When clear as holiness the morning ray
Casts the rock's dewy darkness at its feet,
Mottling with shadows all the mountain gray;
When, at the hour of sovereign noon,
Infinite silent cataracts sheet
Shadowless through the air of thunder-breeding
    June;
And when a yellower glory slanting passes
'Twixt longer shadows o'er the meadow grasses;
When now the moon lifts up her shining shield,
High on the peak of a cloud-hill revealed;
Now crescent, low, wandering sun-dazed away,
Unconscious of her own star-mingled ray,
Her still face seeming more to think than see,
Makes the pale world lie dreaming dreams of
    thee!
No mood of mind, no melody of soul,
But lies within thy silent soft control.

3

Of operative single power,
And simple unity the one emblem,
Yet all the colors that our passionate eyes devour,
In rainbow, moonbow, or in opal gem,
Are the melodious descant of divided thee.
Lo thee in yellow sands! lo thee
In the blue air and sea!
In the green corn, with scarlet poppies lit,
Thy half souls parted, patient thou dost sit.
Lo thee in speechless glories of the west!
Lo thee in dewdrop's tiny breast!
Thee on the vast white cloud that floats away,
Bearing upon its skirt a brown moon-ray!
Regent of color, thou dost fling
Thy overflowing skill on everything!
The thousand hues and shades upon the flowers
Are all the pastime of thy leisure hours;
And all the jewelled ores in mines that hidden be
Are dead till touched by thee.

GEORGE MACDONALD.

THE NORTHERN LIGHTS.

To claim the Arctic came the sun
With banners of the burning zone.
Unrolled upon their airy spars,
They froze beneath the light of stars;
And there they float, those streamers old,
Those Northern Lights, forever cold!

BENJAMIN FRANKLIN TAYLOR.

FROM THE "HYMN TO LIGHT."

S_AY_, from what golden quivers of the sky
    Do all thy wingèd arrows fly?
    Swiftness and Power by birth are thine:
From thy great sire they came, thy sire, the Word
        Divine.

    Thou in the Moon's bright chariot, proud and
        gay,
    Dost thy bright wood of stars survey;
    And all the year dost with thee bring
Of thousand flowery lights thine own nocturnal
        spring.

    Thou, Scythian-like, dost round thy lands
        above
    The Sun's gilt tent forever move,
    And still, as thou in pomp dost go,
The shining pageants of the world attend thy
        show.

    Nor amidst all these triumphs dost thou scorn
    The humble glow-worms to adorn,
    And with those living spangles gild
(O greatness without pride!) the bushes of the
        field.

    Night and her ugly subjects thou dost fright,
    And Sleep, the lazy owl of night;

Ashamed and fearful to appear,
They screen their horrid shapes with the black
    hemisphere.

   .   .   .   .   .   .

At thy appearance, Grief itself is said
    To shake his wings, and rouse his head:
    And cloudy Care has often took
A gentle beamy smile, reflected from thy look.

At thy appearance, Fear itself grows bold;
    The sunshine melts away his cold.
    Encouraged at the sight of thee
To the cheek color comes, and firmness to the
    knee.

When, goddess, thou lift'st up thy wakened
    head
    Out of the morning's purple bed,
    Thy quire of birds about thee play,
And all the joyful world salutes the rising day.

All the world's bravery, that delights our eyes,
    Is but thy several liveries;
    Thou the rich dye on them bestow'st,
Thy nimble pencil paints this landscape as thou
    go'st.

A crimson garment in the rose thou wear'st;
    A crown of studded gold thou bear'st;
    The virgin-lilies, in their white,
Are clad but with the lawn of almost naked
    light.

The violet, Spring's little infant, stands
 Girt in thy purple swaddling-bands;
 On the fair tulip thou dost dote;
Thou cloth'st it in a gay and party-colored coat.

 . . . . . .

Through the soft ways of heaven, and air, and
  sea,
 Which open all their pores to thee,
 Like a clear river thou dost glide,
And with thy living stream through the close
  channels slide.

 . . . . . .

But the vast ocean of unbounded day,
 In the empyrean heaven does stay.
 Thy rivers, lakes, and springs, below,
From thence took first their rise, thither at last
  must flow.

ABRAHAM COWLEY.

DAYBREAK.

A wind came up out of the sea,
And said, " O mists, make room for me! "

It hailed the ships, and cried, " Sail on,
Ye mariners, the night is gone! "

And hurried landward far away,
Crying, " Awake! it is the day! "

It said unto the forest, " Shout!
Hang all your leafy banners out! "

It touched the wood-bird's folded wing,
And said, " O bird, awake and sing ! "

And o'er the farms, " O chanticleer,
Your clarion blow; the day is near ! "

It whispered to the fields of corn,
" Bow down, and hail the coming morn ! "

It shouted through the belfry-tower,
" Awake, O bell ! proclaim the hour."

It crossed the churchyard with a sigh,
And said, " Not yet ! in quiet lie."

HENRY WADSWORTH LONGFELLOW.

DAWN.

THE night was dark, though sometimes a faint
        star
A little while a little space made bright.
The night was long and like an iron bar
Lay heavy on the land: till o'er the sea
Slowly, within the East, there grew a light
Which half was starlight, and half seemed to be
The herald of a greater. The pale white
Turned slowly to pale rose, and up the height
Of heaven slowly climbed. The gray sea grew
Rose-colored like the sky. A white gull flew
Straight toward the utmost boundary of the East,
Where slowly the rose gathered and increased.
It was as on the opening of a door

By one that in his hand a lamp doth hold,
Whose flame is hidden by the garment's fold,—
The still air moves, the wide room is less dim.

More bright the East became, the ocean turned
Dark and more dark against the brightening
    sky,—
Sharper against the sky the long sea line.
The hollows of the breakers on the shore
Were green like leaves whereon no sun doth shine,
Though white the outer branches of the tree.
From rose to red the level heaven burned;
Then sudden, as if a sword fell from on high,
A blade of gold flashed on the horizon's rim.

               RICHARD WATSON GILDER.

MORNING SONG.

Up! quit thy bower! late wears the hour,
Long have the rooks cawed round the tower;
O'er flower and tree loud hums the bee,
And the wild kid sports merrily.
The sun is bright, the sky is clear;
Wake, lady, wake! and hasten here.

Up, maiden fair! and bind thy hair,
And rouse thee in the breezy air!
The lulling stream that soothed thy dream
Is dancing in the sunny beam.
Waste not these hours, so fresh, so gay:
Leave thy soft couch and haste away!

Up! Time will tell the morning bell
Its service-sound has chimed well;

The aged crone keeps house alone,
The reapers to the fields are gone.
Lose not these hours, so cool, so gay:
Lo! while thou sleep'st they haste away!

JOANNA BAILLIE.

MORNING.

In the barn the tenant cock,
　Close to partlet perched on high,
Briskly crows (the shepherd's clock!)
　Jocund that the morning's nigh.

Swiftly from the mountain's brow,
　Shadows, nursed by night, retire:
And the peeping sunbeam now
　Paints with gold the village spire.

Philomel forsakes the thorn,
　Plaintive where she prates at night;
And the lark, to meet the morn,
　Soars beyond the shepherd's sight.

From the low-roofed cottage ridge,
　See the chattering swallow spring;
Darting through the one-arched bridge,
　Quick she dips her dappled wing.

Now the pine-tree's waving top
　Gently greets the morning gale:
Kidlings now begin to crop
　Daisies, on the dewy dale.

From the balmy sweets, uncloyed
   (Restless till her task be done),
Now the busy bee 's employed
   Sipping dew before the sun.

Trickling through the creviced rock,
   Where the limpid stream distils,
Sweet refreshment waits the flock
   When 't is sun-drove from the hills.

Colin 's for the promised corn
   (Ere the harvest hopes are ripe)
Anxious;—whilst the huntsman's horn,
   Boldly sounding, drowns his pipe.

Sweet, O sweet, the warbling throng,
   On the white emblossomed spray!
Nature's universal song
   Echoes to the rising day.
                  JOHN CUNNINGHAM.

PACK CLOUDS AWAY.

PACK clouds away, and welcome day,
   With night we banish sorrow;
Sweet air, blow soft; mount, lark, aloft,
   To give my love good morrow.
Wings from the wind to please her mind,
   Notes from the lark I 'll borrow:
Bird, prune thy wing; nightingale, sing,
   To give my love good morrow.
   To give my love good morrow,
   Notes from them all I 'll borrow.

Wake from thy nest, robin redbreast,
　Sing, birds, in every furrow;
And from each hill let music shrill
　Give my fair love good morrow.
Blackbird and thrush in every bush,
　Stare, linnet, and cock-sparrow,
You petty elves, amongst yourselves,
　Sing my fair love good morrow.
To give my love good morrow,
　Sing, birds, in every furrow.

THOMAS HEYWOOD.

MORNING.

FROM "THE MINSTREL."

BUT who the melodies of morn can tell?
The wild brook babbling down the mountain-
　　side;
The lowing herd; the sheepfold's simple bell;
The pipe of early shepherd dim descried
In the lone valley; echoing far and wide
The clamorous horn along the cliffs above;
The hollow murmur of the ocean-tide;
The hum of bees, the linnet's lay of love,
And the full choir that wakes the universal grove.

The cottage curs at early pilgrim bark;
Crowned with her pail the tripping milkmaid
　　sings;
The whistling ploughman stalks afield; and,
　　hark!
Down the rough slope the ponderous wagon
　　rings;

Through rustling corn the hare astonished
    springs;
Slow tolls the village-clock the drowsy hour;
The partridge bursts away on whirring wings;
Deep mourns the turtle in sequestered bower,
And shrill lark carols clear from her aerial tower.

JAMES BEATTIE.

SUMMER RAIN.

THICK lay the dust, uncomfortably white,
In glaring mimicry of Arab sand.
The woods and mountains slept in hazy light;
The meadows looked athirst and tawny tanned;
The little rills had left their channels bare,
With scarce a pool to witness what they were;
And the shrunk river gleamed 'mid oozy stones,
That stared like any famished giant's bones.

Sudden the hills grew black, and hot as stove
The air beneath; it was a toil to be.
There was a growling as of angry Jove,
Provoked by Juno's prying jealousy—
A flash—a crash—the firmament was split,
And down it came in drops—the smallest fit
To drown a bee in fox-glove bell concealed;
Joy filled the brook, and comfort cheered the field.

HARTLEY COLERIDGE.

THE OASIS OF SIDI KHALED.

How the earth burns! Each pebble under foot
Is as a living thing with power to wound.
The white sand quivers, and the footfall mute
Of the slow camels strikes but gives no sound,
As though they walked on flame, not solid ground!
'T is noon, and the beasts' shadows even have fled
Back to their feet, and there is fire around
And fire beneath, and the sun overhead.
Pitiful Heaven! what is this we view?
Tall trees, a river, pools, where swallows fly,
Thickets of oleander where doves coo,
Shades, deep as midnight, greenness for tired eyes.
Hark, how the light winds in the palm-tops sigh!
Oh, this is rest! oh, this is paradise!

WILFRED SCAWEN BLUNT.

A MIDSUMMER'S NOON IN THE AUSTRALIAN FOREST.

Not a sound disturbs the air,
There is quiet everywhere;
Over plains and over woods
What a mighty stillness broods!
All the birds and insects keep
Where the coolest shadows sleep;
Even the busy ants are found
Resting in their pebbled mound;
Even the locust clingeth now
Silent to the barky bough:
Over hills and over plains

Quiet, vast and slumbrous, reigns.
Only there 's a drowsy humming
From yon warm lagoon slow-coming:
'T is the dragon-hornet—see!
All bedaubed resplendently
Yellow on a tawny ground—
Each rich spot not square nor round,
Rudely heart-shaped, as it were
The blurred and hasty impress there
Of a vermeil-crusted seal
Dusted o'er with golden meal.
Only there 's a droning where
Yon bright beetle shines in air,
Tracks it in its gleaming flight
With a slanting beam of light
Rising in the sunshine higher,
Till its shards flame out like fire.

Every other thing is still,
Save the ever-wakeful rill,
Whose cool murmur only throws
Cooler comfort round repose;
Or some ripple in the sea,
Of leafy boughs, where, lazily,
Tired summer, in her bower
Turning with the noontide hour,
Heaves a slumbrous breath ere she
Once more slumbers peacefully.

Oh, 't is easeful here to lie
Hidden from noon's scorching eye,
In this grassy cool recess
Musing thus of quietness.

CHARLES HARPUR.

NOONTIDE.

BENEATH a shivering canopy reclined,
Of aspen-leaves that wave without a wind,
I love to lie, when lulling breezes stir
The spiry cones that tremble on the fir;
Or wander mid the dark-green fields of broom,
When peers in scattered tufts the yellow bloom;
Or trace the path with tangling furze o'errun,
When bursting seed-bells crackle in the sun,
And pittering grasshoppers, confus'dly shrill,
Pipe giddily along the glowing hill:
Sweet grasshopper, who lov'st at noon to lie
Serenely in the green-ribbed clover's eye,
To sun thy filmy wings and emerald vest,
Unseen thy form, and undisturbed thy rest,
Oft have I listening mused the sultry day,
And wondered what thy chirping song might say,
When naught was heard along the blossomed lea,
To join thy music, save the listless bee.

JOHN LEYDEN.

A SUMMER NOON.

Who has not dreamed a world of bliss
On a bright sunny noon like this,
Couched by his native brook's green maze,
With comrade of his boyish days,
While all around them seemed to be
Just as in joyous infancy?
Who has not loved, at such an hour,

Upon that heath, in birchen bower,
Lulled in the poet's dreamy mood,
Its wild and sunny solitude?
While o'er the waste of purple ling
You mark a sultry glimmering;
Silence herself there seems to sleep,
Wrapped in a slumber long and deep,
Where slowly stray those lonely sheep
Through the tall foxglove's crimson bloom,
And gleaming of the scattered broom.
Love you not, then, to list and hear
The crackling of the gorse-flowers near,
Pouring an orange-scented tide
Of fragrance o'er the desert wide?
To hear the buzzard's whimpering shrill,
Hovering above you high and still?
The twittering of the bird that dwells
Among the heath's delicious bells?
While round your bed, o'er fern and blade,
Insects in green and gold arrayed,
The sun's gay tribes have lightly strayed;
And sweeter sound their humming wings
Than the proud minstrel's echoing strings.

WILLIAM HOWITT.

THE MIDGES DANCE ABOON THE BURN.

THE midges dance aboon the burn;
  The dews begin to fa' ;
The pairtricks down the rushy holm
  Set up their e'ening ca'.
Now loud and clear the blackbird's sang
  Rings through the briery shaw,

While, flitting gay, the swallows play
　Around the castle wa'.

Beneath the golden gloamin' sky
　The mavis mends her lay;
The redbreast pours his sweetest strains
　To charm the lingering day;
While weary yeldrins seem to wail
　Their little nestlings torn,
The merry wren, frae den to den,
　Gaes jinking through the thorn.

The roses fauld their silken leaves,
　The foxglove shuts its bell;
The honeysuckle and the birk
　Spread fragrance through the dell.
Let others crowd the giddy court
　Of mirth and revelry,
The simple joys that nature yields
　Are dearer far to me.

ROBERT TANNAHILL.

———

SUNSET.

FROM " QUEEN MAB."

IF solitude hath ever led thy steps
To the wild ocean's echoing shore,
　And thou hast lingered there
　Until the sun's broad orb
Seemed resting on the burnished wave,
　Thou must have marked the lines
Of purple gold that motionless

Hung o'er the sinking sphere:
Thou must have marked the billowy clouds,
Edged with intolerable radiancy,
    Towering like rocks of jet
    Crowned with a diamond wreath.
    And yet there is a moment,
    When the sun's highest point
Peeps like a star o'er ocean's western edge,
When those far clouds of feathery gold,
    Shaded with deepest purple, gleam
    Like islands on a dark-blue sea;
Then has thy fancy soared above the earth,
    And furled its wearied wing
    Within the Fairy's fane.
    Yet not the golden islands
    Gleaming in yon flood of light,
    Nor the feathery curtains
    Stretching o'er the sun's bright couch,
    Nor the burnished ocean's waves
    Paving that gorgeous dome,
    So fair, so wonderful a sight
As Mab's ethereal palace could afford.
Yet likest evening's vault, that fairy Hall!
  Heaven, low resting on the wave, it spread
    Its floors of flashing light,
    Its vast and azure dome,
    Its fertile golden islands
    Floating on a silver sea;
Whilst suns their mingling beamings darted
Through clouds of circumambient darkness,
    And pearly battlements around
    Looked o'er the immense of heaven.

               PERCY BYSSHE SHELLEY.

4

FANCY IN NUBIBUS.

O, it is pleasant, with a heart at ease,
Just after sunset, or by moonlight skies,
To make the shifting clouds be what you please,
Or let the easily persuaded eyes
Own each quaint likeness issuing from the mould
Of a friend's fancy; or, with head bent low,
And cheek aslant, see rivers flow of gold,
'Twixt crimson banks; and then a traveller go
From mount to mount, through Cloudland, gorgeous land!
Or, listening to the tide with closèd sight,
Be that blind Bard, who on the Chian strand,
By those deep sounds possessed with inward light,
Beheld the Iliad and the Odyssey
Rise to the swelling of the voiceful sea.

　　　　　　　　　SAMUEL TAYLOR COLERIDGE.

DAY IS DYING.

FROM "THE SPANISH GYPSY."

Day is dying! Float, O song,
　Down the westward river,
Requiem chanting to the Day,—
　Day, the mighty Giver.

Pierced by shafts of Time he bleeds,
　Melted rubies sending
Through the river and the sky,
　Earth and heaven bleeding;

All the long-drawn earthy banks
   Up to cloud-land lifting:
Slow between them drifts the swan,
   'Twixt two heavens drifting.

Wings half open, like a flower
   Inly deeper flushing,
Neck and breast as virgin's pure,—
   Virgin proudly blushing.

Day is dying! Float, O swan,
   Down the ruby river;
Follow, song, in requiem
   To the mighty Giver.

       MARIAN EVANS LEWES CROSS (*George Eliot*).

THE END OF THE DAY.

I HEAR the bells at eventide
   Peal softly one by one,
Near and far off they break and glide;
   Across the stream float faintly beautiful
   The antiphonal bells of Hull;
The day is done, done, done,
   The day is done.

The dew has gathered in the flowers,
   Like tears from some unconscious deep:
The swallows whirl around the towers,
   The light runs out beyond the long cloud bars,
   And leaves the single stars;
'T is time for sleep, sleep, sleep,
   'T is time for sleep.

The hermit thrush begins again,—
    Timorous eremite—
That song of risen tears and pain,
    As if the one he loved was far away:
    ' Alas! another day—'
' And now Good Night, Good Night,'
    Good Night.'
DUNCAN CAMPBELL SCOTT.

EVENING.

FROM upland slopes I see the cows file by,
    Lowing, great-chested, down the homeward
        trail,
    By dusking fields and meadows shining pale
With moon-tipped dandelions; flickering high,
A peevish night-hawk in the western sky
    Beats up into the lucent solitudes,
    Or drops with griding wing; the stilly woods
Grow dark and deep, and gloom mysteriously.
Cool night-winds creep and whisper in mine ear;
    The homely cricket gossips at my feet;
    From far-off pools and wastes of reeds I hear
With ebb and change the chanting frogs break
        sweet
    In full Pandean chorus; one by one
Shine out the stars, and the great night comes on.
ARCHIBALD LAMPMAN.

A TWILIGHT FANCY.

I SIT here and the earth is wrapped in snow,
And the cold air is thick with falling night:
I think of the still, dewy summer eves,
When cows came slowly sauntering up the lane,
Waiting to nibble at the juicy grass;
When the green earth was full of changing life,
When the warm wind blew soft, and slowly
        passed,
Caressing now and then some wayside flower,
Stopping to stir the tender maple-leaves,
And breathing all its fragrance on the air!
I think of the broad meadows, daisy-white,
With the long shade of some stray apple-tree
Falling across them,—and the rustlings faint
When evening breezes shook along the grass.
I think of all the thousand summer sounds,—
The cricket's chirp, repeated far and near;
The sleepy note of robins in their nest;
The whippoorwill, whose sudden cry rang out,
Plaintive, yet strong, upon the startled air.
And so it was the summer twilight fell,
And deepened to the darkness of the night:
And now I lift my heart out of my dream
And see instead the pale, cold, dying lights,
The dull gray skies, the barren, snow-clad fields,
That come to us when winter evenings come.

                    DORA READ GOODALE.

TO THE EVENING STAR.

Star that bringest home the bee,
And sett'st the weary laborer free!
If any star shed peace, 't is thou,
    That send'st it from above,
Appearing when heaven's breath and brow
    Are sweet as hers we love.

Come to the luxuriant skies,
Whilst the landscape's odors rise,
Whilst far-off lowing herds are heard,
    And songs when toil is done,
From cottages where smoke unstirred
    Curls yellow in the sun.

Star of love's soft interviews,
Parted lovers on thee muse;
Their remembrancer in heaven
    Of thrilling vows thou art,
Too delicious to be riven
    By absence from the heart.

                    THOMAS CAMPBELL.

THE EVENING WIND.

Spirit that breathest through my lattice: thou
    That cool'st the twilight of the sultry day!
Gratefully flows thy freshness round my brow;
    Thou hast been out upon the deep at play,
Riding all day the wild blue waves till now,

Roughening their crests, and scattering high
      their spray,
And swelling the white sail. I welcome thee
To the scorched land, thou wanderer of the sea!

Nor I alone,—a thousand bosoms round
Inhale thee in the fulness of delight;
And languid forms rise up, and pulses bound
   Livelier, at coming of the wind of night;
And languishing to hear thy welcome sound,
   Lies the vast inland, stretched beyond the sight.
Go forth into the gathering shade; go forth,—
God's blessing breathed upon the fainting earth!

Go, rock the little wood-bird in his nest;
   Curl the still waters, bright with stars; and
     rouse
The wide old wood from his majestic rest,
   Summoning from the innumerable boughs,
The strange deep harmonies that haunt his breast.
   Pleasant shall be thy way where meekly bows
The shutting flower, and darkling waters pass,
And where the. o'ershadowing branches sweep the
     grass.

Stoop o'er the place of graves, and softly sway
   The sighing herbage by the gleaming stone,
That they who near the churchyard willows stray,
   And listen in the deepening gloom, alone,
May think of gentle souls that passed away,
   Like thy pure breath, into the vast unknown,
Sent forth from heaven among the sons of men,
And gone into the boundless heaven again.

The faint old man shall lean his silver head
  To feel thee; thou shalt kiss the child asleep,
And dry the moistened curls that overspread
    His temples, while his breathing grows more
      deep:
And they who stand about the sick man's bed
  Shall joy to listen to thy distant sweep,
And softly part his curtains to allow
Thy visit, grateful to his burning brow.

Go,—but the circle of eternal change,
  Which is the life of nature, shall restore,
With sounds and scents from all thy mighty
    range,
  Thee to thy birthplace of the deep once more.
Sweet odors in the sea air, sweet and strange,
  Shall tell the homesick mariner of the shore;
And, listening to thy murmur, he shall deem
He hears the rustling leaf and running stream.

WILLIAM CULLEN BRYANT.

EVENING IN PARADISE.

FROM "PARADISE LOST," BOOK IV.

Now came still evening on, and twilight gray
Had in her sober livery all things clad;
Silence accompanied; for beast and bird,
They to their grassy couch, these to their nests,
Were slunk, all but the wakeful nightingale;
She all night long her amorous descant sung.
Silence was pleased: now glowed the firmament
With living sapphires; Hesperus, that led

The starry host, rode brightest, till the moon
Rising in clouded majesty, at length
Apparent queen, unveiled her peerless light,
And o'er the dark her silver mantle threw.

MILTON.

EVENING.

FROM "DON JUAN."

Ave Maria! o'er the earth and sea,
That heavenliest hour of heaven is worthiest thee!

Ave Maria! blessèd be the hour,
　The time, the clime, the spot, where I so oft
Have felt that moment in its fullest power
　Sink o'er the earth so beautiful and soft,
While swung the deep bell in the distant tower
　Or the faint dying day-hymn stole aloft,
And not a breath crept through the rosy air,
And yet the forest leaves seemed stirred with
　　prayer.

Ave Maria! 't is the hour of prayer!
　Ave Maria! 't is the hour of love!
Ave Maria! may our spirits dare
　Look up to thine and to thy Son's above!
Ave Maria! O that face so fair!
　Those downcast eyes beneath the Almighty
　　dove,—
What though 't is but a pictured image?—
　　strike,—
That painting is no idol,—'t is too like.

Sweet hour of twilight! in the solitude
　　Of the pine forest, and the silent shore
Which bounds Ravenna's immemorial wood,
　　Rooted where once the Adrian wave flowed o'er
To where the last Cæsarean fortress stood,
　　Evergreen forest; which Boccaccio's lore
And Dryden's lay made haunted ground to me,
How have I loved the twilight hour and thee!

The shrill cicalas, people of the pine,
　　Making their summer lives one ceaseless song,
Were the sole echoes, save my steed's and mine,
　　And vesper bells that rose the boughs along;
The spectre huntsman of Onesti's line,
　　His hell-dogs, and their chase, and the fair
　　　　throng
Which learned from this example not to fly
From a true lover,—shadowed my mind's eye.

O Hesperus! thou bringest all good things,—
　　Home to the weary, to the hungry cheer,
To the young bird the parent's brooding wings,
　　The welcome stall to the o'erlabored steer;
Whate'er of peace about our hearthstone clings,
　　Whate'er our household gods protect of dear,
Are gathered round us by thy look of rest;
Thou bring'st the child, too, to the mother's
　　　　breast.

Soft hour! which wakes the wish and melts the
　　　　heart
　　Of those who sail the seas, on the first day
When they from their sweet friends are torn
　　　　apart;

Or fills with love the pilgrim on his way,
As the far bell of vesper makes him start,
  Seeming to weep the dying day's decay:
Is this a fancy which our reason scorns?
Ah! surely nothing dies but something mourns.

LORD BYRON.

MOONLIGHT ON THE PRAIRIE.

FROM "EVANGELINE."

BEAUTIFUL was the night. Behind the black wall
   of the forest,
Tipping its summit with silver, arose the moon.
   On the river
Fell here and there through the branches a tremu-
   lous gleam of the moonlight,
Like the sweet thoughts of love on a darkened
   and devious spirit.
Nearer and round about her, the manifold flowers
   of the garden
Poured out their souls in odors, that were their
   prayers and confessions
Unto the night, as it went its way, like a silent
   Carthusian.
Fuller of fragrance than they, and as heavy with
   shadows and night-dews,
Hung the heart of the maiden. The calm and
   the magical moonlight
Seemed to inundate her soul with indefinable
   longings,
As, through the garden gate, and beneath the
   shade of the oak-trees,

Passed she along the path to the edge of the
measureless prairie.

Silent it lay, with a heavy haze upon it, and
fireflies

Gleaming and floating away in mingled and infinite numbers.

Over her head the stars, the thoughts of God in
the heavens,

Shone on the eyes of man, who had ceased to
marvel and worship,

Save when a blazing comet was seen on the walls
of that temple,

As if a hand had appeared and written upon
them, " Upharsin."

And the soul of the maiden, between the stars
and the fireflies,

Wandered alone, and she cried, " O Gabriel!
O my beloved!

Art thou so near unto me, and yet I cannot
behold thee?

Art thou so near unto me, and yet thy voice does
not reach me?

Ah! how often thy feet have trod this path to
the prairie!

Ah! how often thine eyes have looked on the
woodlands around me!

Ah! how often beneath this oak, returning from
labor,

Thou hast lain down to rest, and to dream of me
in thy slumbers.

When shall these eyes behold, these arms be
folded about thee? "

Loud and sudden and near the note of a whip-
    poorwill sounded
Like a flute in the woods; and anon, through the
    neighboring thickets,
Farther and farther away it floated and dropped
    into silence.
" Patience! " whispered the oaks from oracular
    caverns of darkness;
And, from the moonlit meadow, a sigh responded,
    " To-morrow! "

               HENRY WADSWORTH LONGFELLOW.

TO DELIA.

CARE-CHARMER Sleep, son of the sable Night,
Brother to Death, in silent darkness born:
Relieve my languish and restore the light;
With dark forgetting of my care, return,
And let the day be time enough to mourn
The shipwreck of my ill-adventured youth:
Let waking eyes suffice to wail their scorn
Without the torment of the night's untruth.
Cease dreams, the images of day desires,
To model forth the passion of the morrow;
Never let rising sun approve you liars,
To add more grief to aggravate my sorrow.
Still let me sleep, embracing clouds in vain,
And never wake to feel the day's disdain.

               SAMUEL DANIEL.

THE CAMP AT NIGHT.

FROM " THE ILIAD," BOOK VIII.

THE winds transferred into the friendly sky
Their supper's savor; to the which they sat de-
  lightfully,
And spent all night in open field; fires round
  about them shined.
As when about the silver moon, when air is free
  from wind,
And stars shine clear, to whose sweet beams,
  high prospects, and the brows
Of all steep hills and pinnacles, thrust up them-
  selves for shows,
And even the lowly valleys joy to glitter in their
  sight,
When the unmeasured firmament bursts to dis-
  close her light,
And all the signs in heaven are seen, that glad
  the shepherd's heart;
So many fires disclose their beams, made by the
  Trojan part,
Before the face of Ilion, and her bright turrets
  showed.
A thousand courts of guard kept fires, and every
  guard allowed
Fifty stout men, by whom their horse eat oats
  and hard white corn,
And all did wishfully expect the silver-thronèd
  morn.

From the Greek of HOMER.
Translation of GEORGE CHAPMAN.

TO NIGHT.

SWIFTLY walk over the western wave,
       Spirit of Night!
Out of the misty eastern cave,
Where, all the long and lone daylight,
Thou wovest dreams of joy and fear
Which make thee terrible and dear,—
       Swift be thy flight!

Wrap thy form in a mantle gray,
       Star-inwrought;
Blind with thine hair the eyes of Day,
Kiss her until she be wearied out;
Then wander o'er city and sea and land,
Touching all with thine opiate wand,—
       Come, long-sought!

When I arose and saw the dawn,
       I sighed for thee;
When light rode high and the dew was gone
And noon lay heavy on flower and tree,
And the weary Day turned to her rest,
Lingering like an unloved guest,
       I sighed for thee!

Thy brother Death came, and cried,
       " Wouldst thou me? "
Thy sweet child Sleep, the filmy-eyed,
       Murmured like a noontide bee,
" Shall I nestle near thy side?
Wouldst thou me? "—And I replied,
       " No, not thee! "

Death will come when thou art dead,
　　Soon, too soon,—
Sleep will come when thou art fled;
Of neither would I ask the boon
I ask of thee, belovèd Night,—
Swift be thine approaching flight,
　　Come soon, soon!

　　　　　　　　PERCY BYSSHE SHELLEY.

———

NIGHT.

MYSTERIOUS Night! when our first parent knew
Thee, from report divine, I heard thy name,
Did he not tremble for this lovely frame,—
This glorious canopy of light and blue?
Yet 'neath a curtain of translucent dew,
Bathed in the rays of the great setting flame,
Hesperus, with the host of heaven, came,
And lo! creation widened in man's view.
Who could have thought such darkness lay con-
　　cealed
Within thy beams, O Sun! or who could find,
Whilst fly and leaf and insect stood revealed,
That to such countless orbs thou mad'st us blind!
Why do we then shun death with anxious strife!
If light can thus deceive, wherefore not life?

　　　　　　　　JOSEPH BLANCO WHITE.

NIGHT.

FROM " CHILDE HAROLD," CANTO II.

'T is night, when Meditation bids us feel
We once have loved, though love is at an end:
The heart, lone mourner of its baffled zeal,
Though friendless now, will dream it had a
 friend.
Who with the weight of years would wish to
 bend,
When Youth itself survives young Love and
 joy?
Alas! when mingling souls forget to blend,
Death hath but little left him to destroy!
Ah! happy years! once more who would not be a
 boy?

Thus bending o'er the vessel's laving side,
To gaze on Dian's wave-reflected sphere,
The soul forgets her schemes of Hope and Pride,
And flies unconscious o'er each backward year.
None are so desolate but something dear,
Dearer than self, possesses or possessed
A thought, and claims the homage of a tear;
A flashing pang! of which the weary breast
Would still, albeit in vain, the heavy heart divest.

To sit on rocks, to muse o'er flood and fell,
To slowly trace the forest's shady scene,
Where things that own not man's dominion
 dwell,

5

And mortal foot hath ne'er or rarely been;
To climb the trackless mountain all unseen,
With the wild flock that never needs a fold;
Alone o'er steeps and foaming falls to lean,—
This is not solitude; 't is but to hold
Converse with Nature's charms, and view her
    stores unrolled.

But midst the crowd, the hum, the shock of
    men
To hear, to see, to feel, and to possess,
And roam along, the world's tired denizen,
With none who bless us, none whom we can
    bless;
Minions of splendor shrinking from distress!
None that, with kindred consciousness endued,
If we were not, would seem to smile the less
Of all that flattered, followed, sought, and
    sued;
This is to be alone; this, this is solitude!

               LORD BYRON.

NIGHT.

FROM "QUEEN MAB."

How beautiful this night! the balmiest sigh
Which vernal zephyrs breathe in evening's ear
Were discord to the speaking quietude
That wraps this moveless scene. Heaven's ebon
    vault,
Studded with stars unutterably bright,
Through which the moon's unclouded grandeur
    rolls,

Seems like a canopy which love has spread
To curtain her sleeping world. Yon gentle hills,
Robed in a garment of untrodden snow:
Yon darksome rocks, whence icicles depend
So stainless that their white and glittering spires
Tinge not the moon's pure beam; yon castle steep,
Whose banner hangeth o'er the time-worn tower
So idly that rapt fancy deemeth it
A metaphor of peace—all form a scene
Where musing solitude might love to lift
Her soul above this sphere of earthliness;
Where silence undisturbed might watch alone,
So cold, so bright, so still.

                 The orb of day
In southern climes o'er ocean's waveless field
Sinks sweetly smiling: not the faintest breath
Steals o'er the unruffled deep; the clouds of eve
Reflect unmoved the lingering beam of day;
And vesper's image on the western main
Is beautifully still. To-morrow comes:
Cloud upon cloud, in dark and deepening mass,
Rolls o'er the blackened waters; the deep roar
Of distant thunder mutters awfully;
Tempest unfolds its pinion o'er the gloom
That shrouds the boiling surge; the pitiless fiend,
With all his winds and lightnings, tracks his
      prey;
The torn deep yawns,—the vessel finds a grave
Beneath its jaggèd gulf.

                PERCY BYSSHE SHELLEY.

HYMN TO THE NIGHT.

Ασπασίη, τρίλλιστος.

I HEARD the trailing garments of the Night
  Sweep through her marble halls!
I saw her sable skirts all fringed with light
  From the celestial walls!

I felt her presence, by its spell of might,
  Stoop o'er me from above;
The calm, majestic presence of the Night,
  As of the one I love.

I heard the sounds of sorrow and delight,
  The manifold, soft chimes,
That filled the haunted chambers of the Night,
  Like some old poet's rhymes.

From the cool cisterns of the midnight air
  My spirit drank repose;
The fountain of perpetual peace flows there,—
  From those deep cisterns flows.

O holy Night! from thee I learn to bear
  What man has borne before!
Thou layest thy finger on the lips of Care,
  And they complain no more.

Peace! Peace! Orestes-like I breathe this prayer!
  Descend with broad-winged flight,
The welcome, the thrice-prayed for, the most fair,
  The best-belovèd Night!

                    HENRY WADSWORTH LONGFELLOW.

IN THE WIDE AWE AND WISDOM OF THE NIGHT.

In the wide awe and wisdom of the night
 I saw the round world rolling on its way,
Beyond significance of depth or height,
 Beyond the interchange of dark and day.
I marked the march to which is set no pause,
 And that stupendous orbit, round whose rim
The great sphere sweeps, obedient unto laws
 That utter the eternal thought of Him.
I compassed time, outstripped the starry speed,
 And in my still Soul apprehended space,
Till weighing laws which these but blindly heed,
 At last I came before Him face to face,—
And knew the Universe of no such span
As the august infinitude of man.

     CHARLES G. D. ROBERTS.

III.

THE SEASONS.

A HYMN.

FROM "THE SEASONS," CONCLUSION.

THESE, as they change, Almighty Father, these
Are but the varied God. The rolling year
Is full of thee. Forth in the pleasing Spring
Thy beauty walks, thy tenderness and love.
Wide flush the fields; the softening air is balm;
Echo the mountains round; the forest smiles;
And every sense and every heart is joy.
Then comes thy glory in the Summer months,
With light and heat refulgent. Then thy sun
Shoots full perfection through the swelling year;
And oft thy voice in dreadful thunder speaks,
And oft at dawn, deep noon, or falling eve,
By brooks and groves in hollow-whispering gales
Thy bounty shines in Autumn unconfined,
And spreads a common feast for all that lives.
In Winter awful thou! with clouds and storms
Around thee thrown, tempest o'er tempest rolled.
Majestic darkness! on the whirlwind's wing
Riding sublime, thou bidd'st the world adore,
And humblest nature with thy northern blast.

Mysterious round! what skill, what force divine,
Deep felt, in these appear! a simple train,
Yet so delightful mixed, with such kind art,
Such beauty and beneficence combined;
Shade, unperceived, so softening into shade;
And all so forming an harmonious whole,
That, as they still succeed, they ravish still.
But wandering oft, with brute unconscious gaze,
Man marks not thee, marks not the mighty hand,
That, ever busy, wheels the silent spheres;
Works in the secret deep; shoots, steaming, thence
The fair profusion that o'erspreads the Spring;
Flings from the Sun direct the flaming day;
Feeds every creature; hurls the tempest forth;
And, as on Earth this grateful change revolves,
With transport touches all the springs of life.

Nature, attend! join every living soul,
Beneath the spacious temple of the sky,
In adoration join; and, ardent, raise
One general song! To Him, ye vocal gales,
Breathe soft, whose spirit in your freshness
   breathes:
O, talk of him in solitary glooms;
Where, o'er the rock, the scarcely waving pine
Fills the brown shade with a religious awe.
And ye whose bolder note is heard afar,
Who shake the astonished world, lift high to
   Heaven
The impetuous song, and say from whom you
   rage.
His praise, ye brooks, attune, ye trembling rills;
And let me catch it as I muse along.
Ye headlong torrents, rapid, and profound;

Ye softer floods, that lead the humid maze
Along the vale; and thou, majestic main,
A secret world of wonders in thyself,
Sound his stupendous praise,—whose greater voice
Or bids you roar, or bids your roarings fall.
Soft roll your incense, herbs, and fruits, and
 flowers,
In mingled clouds to him,—whose Sun exalts,
Whose breath perfumes you, and whose pencil
 paints.
Ye forests bend, ye harvests wave, to him;
Breathe your still song into the reaper's heart,
As home he goes beneath the joyous Moon.
Ye that keep watch in Heaven, as Earth asleep
Unconscious lies, effuse your mildest beams,
Ye constellations, while your angels strike,
Amid the spangled sky, the silver lyre.
Great source of day! best image here below
Of thy Creator, ever pouring wide,
From world to world, the vital ocean round,
On Nature write with every beam his praise.
The thunder rolls: be hushed the prostrate world;
While cloud to cloud returns the solemn hymn.
Bleat out afresh, ye hills; ye mossy rocks,
Retain the sound; the broad responsive low,
Ye valleys, raise; for the great Shepherd reigns,
And his unsuffering kingdom yet will come.
Ye woodlands all, awake: a boundless song
Burst from the groves! and when the restless day,
Expiring, lays the warbling world asleep,
Sweetest of birds! sweet Philomela, charm
The listening shades, and teach the night his
 praise.

Ye chief, for whom the whole creation smiles,
At once the head, the heart, and tongue of all,
Crown the great hymn! in swarming cities vast,
Assembled men to the deep organ join
The long-resounding voice, oft breaking clear,
At solemn pauses, through the swelling bass;
And, as each mingling flame increases each,
In one united ardor rise to Heaven.
Or if you rather choose the rural shade,
And find a fane in every sacred grove,
There let the shepherd's flute, the virgin's lay,
The prompting seraph, and the poet's lyre,
Still sing the God of Seasons as they roll.
For me, when I forget the darling theme,
Whether the blossom blows, the Summer ray
Russets the plain, inspiring Autumn gleams,
Or Winter rises in the blackening east,—
Be my tongue mute, my fancy paint no more,
And, dead to joy, forget my heart to beat!
   Should fate command me to the farthest verge
Of the green earth, to distant barbarous climes,
Rivers unknown to song,—where first the sun
Gilds Indian mountains, or his setting beam
Flames on the Atlantic isles,—'t is naught to me;
Since God is ever present, ever felt,
In the void waste as in the city full;
And where he vital breathes there must be joy.
When even at last the solemn hour shall come,
And wing my mystic flight to future worlds,
I cheerful will obey; there, with new powers,
Will rising wonders sing: I cannot go
Where Universal Love not smiles around,
Sustaining all yon orbs, and all their suns;

From seeming evil still educing good,
And better thence again, and better still,
In infinite progression. But I lose
Myself in him, in Light ineffable!
Come, then, expressive Silence, muse his praise.

JAMES THOMSON.

MARCH.

SLAYER of winter, art thou here again?
O welcome, thou that bring'st the summer nigh!
The bitter wind makes not thy victory vain,
Nor will we mock thee for thy faint blue sky.
Welcome, O March! whose kindly days and dry
Make April ready for the throstle's song,
Thou first redresser of the winter's wrong!

Yea, welcome March! and though I die ere June,
Yet for the hope of life I give thee praise,
Striving to swell the burden of the tune
That even now I hear thy brown birds raise,
Unmindful of the past or coming days;
Who sing, " O joy! a new year is begun!
What happiness to look upon the sun! "

O, what begetteth all this storm of bliss,
But Death himself, who, crying solemnly,
Even from the heart of sweet Forgetfulness,
Bids us, " Rejoice! lest pleasureless ye die.
Within a little time must ye go by.
Stretch forth your open hands, and, while ye live,
Take all the gifts that Death and Life may give."

WILLIAM MORRIS.

WHEN THE HOUNDS OF SPRING.

WHEN the hounds of spring are on winter's traces,
    The mother of months in meadow or plain
Fills the shadows and windy places
    With lisp of leaves and ripple of rain;
And the brown bright nightingale amorous
Is half assuaged for Itylus,
For the Thracian ships and the foreign faces;
    The tongueless vigil, and all the pain.

Come with bows bent and with emptying of
        quivers,
    Maiden most perfect, lady of light,
With a noise of winds and many rivers,
    With a clamor of waters, and with might;
Bind on thy sandals, O thou most fleet,
Over the splendor and speed of thy feet!
For the faint east quickens, the wan west shivers,
    Round the feet of the day and the feet of the
        night.

Where shall we find her, how shall we sing to her,
    Fold our hands round her knees and cling?
O that man's heart were as fire and could spring
        to her,
    Fire, or the strength of the streams that spring!
For the stars and the winds are unto her
As raiment, as songs of the harp-player;
For the risen stars and the fallen cling to her,
    And the southwest-wind and the west-wind sing.

For winter's rains and ruins are over,
    And all the season of snows and sins!

The days dividing lover and lover,
　The light that loses, the night that wins;
And time remembered its grief forgotten,
And frosts are slain and flowers begotten,
And in green underwood and cover
　Blossom by blossom the spring begins.

The full streams feed on flower of rushes,
　Ripe grasses trammel a travelling foot,
The faint fresh flame of the young year flushes
　From leaf to flower and flower to fruit;
And fruit and leaf are as gold and fire,
And the oat is heard above the lyre,
And the hoofèd heel of a satyr crushes
　The chestnut-husk at the chestnut-root.

And Pan by noon and Bacchus by night,
　Fleeter of foot than the fleet-foot kid,
Follows with dancing and fills with delight
　The Mænad and the Bassarid;
And soft as lips that laugh and hide,
The laughing leaves of the trees divide,
And screen from seeing and leave in sight
　The god pursuing, the maiden hid.

The ivy falls with the Bacchanal's hair
　Over her eyebrows shading her eyes;
The wild vine slipping down leaves bare
　Her bright breast shortening into sighs;
The wild vine slips with the weight of its leaves,
But the berried ivy catches and cleaves
To the limbs that glitter, the feet that scare
　The wolf that follows, the fawn that flies.

ALGERNON CHARLES SWINBURNE.

MARCH.

The cock is crowing,
The stream is flowing,
The small birds twitter,
The lake doth glitter,
The green field sleeps in the sun;
The oldest and youngest
Are at work with the strongest;
The cattle are grazing,
Their heads never raising;
There are forty feeding like one!

Like an army defeated
The snow hath retreated,
And now doth fare ill
On the top of the bare hill;
The ploughboy is whooping—anon—anon
There's joy on the mountains;
There's life in the fountains;
Small clouds are sailing,
Blue sky prevailing;
The rain is over and gone!

WILLIAM WORDSWORTH.

SPRING, THE SWEET SPRING.

Spring, the sweet spring, is the year's pleasant
king;
Then blooms each thing, then maids dance in a
ring,
Cold doth not sting, the pretty birds do sing,
Cuckoo, jug-jug, pu-we, to-witta-woo!

The palm and may make country-houses gay,
Lambs frisk and play, the shepherds pipe all day,
And we hear aye birds tune this merry lay,
   Cuckoo, jug-jug, pu-we, to-witta-woo!

The fields breathe sweet, the daisies kiss our feet,
Young lovers meet, old wives a sunning sit,
In every street these tunes our ears do greet,
   Cuckoo, jug-jug, pu-we, to-witta-woo!
         Spring! the sweet spring!

                                   THOMAS NASH.

RETURN OF SPRING.

God shield ye, heralds of the spring!
Ye faithful swallows, fleet of wing,
      Houps, cuckoos, nightingales,
Turtles, and every wilder bird,
That make your hundred chirpings heard
      Through the green woods and dales.

God shield ye, Easter daisies all,
Fair roses, buds, and blossoms small,
      And he whom erst the gore
Of Ajax and Narciss did print,
Ye wild thyme, anise, balm, and mint,
      I welcome ye once more!

God shield ye, bright embroidered train
Of butterflies, that on the plain
      Of each sweet herblet sip;
And ye, new swarms of bees, that go
Where the pink flowers and yellow grow
      To kiss them with your lip!

A hundred thousand times I call
A hearty welcome on ye all!
   This season how I love—
This merry din on every shore—
For winds and storms, whose sullen roar
   Forbade my steps to rove.

From the French of PIERRE RONSARD.

SPRING.

Lo! where the rosy-bosomed Hours,
   Fair Venus' train, appear,
   And wake the purple year!
The Attic warbler pours her throat
Responsive to the cuckoo's note,
The untaught harmony of spring:
While, whispering pleasure as they fly,
Cool zephyrs through the clear blue sky
   Their gathered fragrance fling.

Where'er the oak's thick branches stretch
   A broader, browner shade,
Where'er the rude and moss-grown beech
   O'ercanopies the glade,
Beside some water's rushy brink
With me the Muse shall sit, and think
(At ease reclined in rustic state)
How vain the ardor of the crowd,
How low, how little are the proud,
   How indigent the great!

Still is the toiling hand of care;
   The panting herds repose:

Yet hark, how through the peopled air
  The busy murmur glows!
The insect youth are on the wing,
Eager to taste the honeyed spring
And float amid the liquid noon:
Some lightly o'er the current skim,
Some show their gayly gilded trim
  Quick-glancing to the sun.

To Contemplation's sober eye
  Such is the race of man;
And they that creep, and they that fly,
  Shall end where they began.
Alike the busy and the gay
But flutter through life's little day,
In Fortune's varying colors drest:
Brushed by the hand of rough mischance
Or chilled by age, their airy dance
  They leave, in dust to rest.

Methinks I hear in accents low
  The sportive kind reply:
Poor moralist! and what art thou?
  A solitary fly!
Thy joys no glittering female meets,
No hive hast thou of hoarded sweets,
No painted plumage to display;
On hasty wings thy youth is flown;
Thy sun is set, thy spring is gone,—
  We frolic while 't is May.

THOMAS GRAY.

SUMMER LONGINGS.

Ah! my heart is weary waiting,
  Waiting for the May,—
Waiting for the pleasant rambles
Where the fragrant hawthorn-brambles,
  With the woodbine alternating,
    Scent the dewy way.
  Ah! my heart is weary waiting,
    Waiting for the May.

Ah! my heart is sick with longing,
  Longing for the May,—
Longing to escape from study
To the young face fair and ruddy,
  And the thousand charms belonging
    To the summer's day.
  Ah! my heart is sick with longing,
    Longing for the May.

Ah! my heart is sore with sighing,
  Sighing for the May,—
Sighing for their sure returning,
When the summer beams are burning,
  Hopes and flowers that, dead or dying,
    All the winter lay.
  Ah! my heart is sore with sighing,
    Sighing for the May.

Ah! my heart is pained with throbbing,
  Throbbing for the May,—

6

Throbbing for the seaside billows,
Or the water-wooing willows;
  Where, in laughing and in sobbing,
    Glide the streams away.
  Ah! my heart, my heart is throbbing,
    Throbbing for the May.

Waiting sad, dejected, weary,
    Waiting for the May:
Spring goes by with wasted warnings,—
Moonlit evenings, sunbright mornings,—
    Summer comes, yet dark and dreary
    Life still ebbs away;
  Man is ever weary, weary,
    Waiting for the May!

DENIS FLORENCE MAC CARTHY.

SWEETLY BREATHING, VERNAL AIR.

SWEETLY breathing, vernal air,
That with kind warmth doth repair
Winter's ruins; from whose breast
All the gums and spice of the East
Borrow their perfumes; whose eye
Gilds the morn, and clears the sky.
Whose dishevelled tresses shed
Pearls upon the violet bed;
On whose brow, with calm smiles drest
The halcyon sits and builds her nest;
Beauty, youth, and endless spring
Dwell upon thy rosy wing!

Thou, if stormy Boreas throws
Down whole forests when he blows,
With a pregnant, flowery birth,
Canst refresh the teeming earth.
If he nip the early bud,
If he blast what 's fair or good,
If he scatter our choice flowers,
If he shake our halls or bowers,
If his rude breath threaten us,
Thou canst stroke great Æolus,
And from him the grace obtain,
To bind him in an iron chain.

THOMAS CAREW.

HOME THOUGHTS FROM ABROAD.

I.

Oh, to be in England now that April's there
And whoever wakes in England sees, some morn-
  ing, unaware,
That the lowest boughs and the brushwood sheaf
Round the elm-tree bole are in tiny leaf,
While the chaffinch sings on the orchard bough
In England—now!

II.

And after April, when May follows
And the white-throat builds, and all the swallows!
Hark, where my blossomed pear-tree in the hedge
Leans to the field and scatters on the clover
Blossoms and dewdrops—at the bent spray's
  edge—

That's the wise thrush: he sings each song twice
　　over
Lest you should think he never could recapture
The first fine careless rapture!
And, though the fields look rough with hoary dew,
All will be gay when noontide wakes anew
The buttercups, the little children's dower,
Far brighter than this gaudy melon-flower!

ROBERT BROWNING.

MAY MORNING.

WARM, wild, rainy wind, blowing fitfully,
Stirring dreamy breakers on the slumberous May
　　sea,
What shall fail to answer thee?　What thing shall
　　withstand
The spell of thine enchantment, flowing over sea
　　and land?

All along the swamp-edge in the rain I go;
All about my head thou the loosened locks dost
　　blow;
Like the German goose-girl in the fairy tale,
I watch across the shining pool my flock of ducks
　　that sail.

Redly gleam the rose-haws, dripping with the wet,
Fruit of sober autumn, glowing crimson yet;
Slender swords of iris leaves cut the water clear,
And light green creeps the tender grass, thick-
　　spreading far and near.

Every last year's stalk is set with brown or
    golden studs;
All the boughs of bayberry are thick with scented
    buds;
Islanded in turfy velvet, where the ferns uncurl,
Lo! the large white duck's egg glimmers like a
    pearl!

Softly sing the billows, rushing, whispering low;
Freshly, oh, deliciously, the warm, wild wind doth
    blow!
Plaintive bleat of new-washed lambs comes faint
    from far away;
And clearly cry the little birds, alert and blithe
    and gay.

O happy, happy morning! O dear, familiar
    place!
O warm, sweet tears of Heaven, fast falling on
    my face!
O well-remembered, rainy wind, blow all my care
    away,
That I may be a child again this blissful morn
    of May.

CELIA THAXTER.

SONG.

ON MAY MORNING.

Now the bright morning star, day's harbinger,
Comes dancing from the east, and leads with her
The flowery May, who from her green lap throws
The yellow cowslip and the pale primrose.

Hail, bounteous May! that doth inspire
Mirth and youth and warm desire;
Woods and groves are of thy dressing,
Hill and dale doth boast thy blessing.
Thus we salute thee with our early song,
And welcome thee, and wish thee long.

MILTON.

SPRING IN CAROLINA.

SPRING, with that nameless pathos in the air
Which dwells with all things fair,
Spring, with her golden suns and silver rain,
Is with us once again.

Out in the lonely woods the jasmine burns
Its fragrant lamps, and turns
Into a royal court with green festoons
The banks of dark lagoons.

In the deep heart of every forest tree
The blood is all aglee,
And there's a look about the leafless bowers
As if they dreamed of flowers.

Yet still on every side we trace the hand
Of Winter in the land,
Save where the maple reddens on the lawn,
Flushed by the season's dawn;

Or where, like those strange semblances we find
That age to childhood bind,
The elm puts on, as if in Nature's scorn,
The brown of autumn corn.

As yet the turf is dark, although you know
That, not a span below,
A thousand germs are groping through the gloom,
And soon will burst their tomb.

In gardens you may note amid the dearth,
The crocus breaking earth;
And near the snowdrop's tender white and green,
The violet in its screen.

But many gleams and shadows need must pass
Along the budding grass,
And weeks go by, before the enamored South
Shall kiss the rose's mouth.

Still there 's a sense of blossoms yet unborn
In the sweet airs of morn;
One almost looks to see the very street
Grow purple at his feet.

At times a fragrant breeze comes floating by,
And brings, you know not why,
A feeling as when eager crowds await
Before a palace gate

Some wondrous pageant; and you scarce would
start,
If from a beech's heart,
A blue-eyed Dryad, stepping forth, should say,
" Behold me! I am May!"

HENRY TIMROD.

SPRING.

Again the violet of our early days
Drinks beauteous azure from the golden sun,
And kindles into fragrance at his blaze;
The streams, rejoiced that winter's work is done,
Talk of to-morrow's cowslips, as they run.
Wild apple, thou art blushing into bloom!
Thy leaves are coming, snowy-blossomed thorn!
Wake, buried lily! spirit, quit thy tomb!
And thou shade-loving hyacinth, be born!
Then, haste, sweet rose! sweet woodbine, hymn
      the morn,
Whose dewdrops shall illume with pearly light
Each grassy blade that thick embattled stands
From sea to sea, while daisies infinite
Uplift in praise their glowing hands,
O'er every hill that under heaven expands.

                    EBENEZER ELLIOTT.

DIE DOWN, O DISMAL DAY.

Die down, O dismal day, and let me live;
And come, blue deeps, magnificently strewn
With colored clouds,—large, light, and fugitive,—
By upper winds through pompous motions blown.
Now it is death in life,—a vapor dense
Creeps round my window, till I cannot see
The far snow-shining mountains, and the glens
Shagging the mountain-tops. O God! make free

This barren shackled earth, so deadly cold,—
Breathe gently forth thy spring, till winter flies
In rude amazement, fearful and yet bold,
While she performs her customed charities;
I weigh the loaded hours till life is bare,—
O God, for one clear day, a snowdrop, and sweet
    air!

DAVID GRAY.

MORNING IN MAY.*

FROM " THE CANTERBURY PILGRIMS: THE KNIGHTES
TALE."

THE busy larke, messager of daye,
  Salueth in hire song the morwe graye;
And fyry Phebus ryseth up so brighte,
That al the orient laugheth of the lighte,
And with his stremes dryeth in the greves †
The silver dropes, hongyng on the leeves.
And Arcite, that is in the court ryal
With Theseus, his squyer principal,
Is risen, and loketh on the merye day.
And for to doon his observaunce to May,
Remembryng on the poynt of his desir,
He on his courser, stertyng as the fir, ‡
Is riden, into the feeldes him to pleye, §
Out of the court, were it a myle or tweye.
And to the grove, of which that I yow tolde,
By aventure his wey he gan to holde,
To maken him a garland of the greves,

* Text of the Clarendon Series.
† Groves.   ‡ Fire.   § Play.

Were it of woodebynde or hawethorn leves,
And lowde he song ayens the sonne scheene:
" May, with alle thy floures and thy greene,
Welcome be thou, wel faire fressche May,
I hope that I som greene gete may."

CHAUCER.

CUCKOO SONG.

SUMER is icumen in.
Lhude sing cuccu.
Groweth sed
And bloweth med
And springth the wude nu.
Sing cuccu!

Awe bleteth after lomb,
Lhouth after calve cu;
Bulluc sterteth,
Bucke verteth,
Murie sing cuccu.
Cuccu, cuccu.

Wel singes thu cuccu,
Ne swike thu naver nu.

BURDEN.

Sing cuccu, nu. Sing cuccu,
Sing cuccu, sing cuccu nu!

ENGLISH: THIRTEENTH CENTURY.

lhude, *loud ;* awe, *ewe ;* lhouth, *loweth ;* sterteth, *leapeth ;*
swike, *cease.*

SPRING.

FROM " IN MEMORIAM."

LXXXII.

DIP down upon the northern shore,
  O sweet new-year, delaying long:
  Thou dost expectant Nature wrong;
Delaying long, delay no more.

What stays thee from the clouded noons,
  Thy sweetness from its proper place?
  Can trouble live with April days,
Or sadness in the summer moons?

Bring orchis, bring the foxglove spire,
  The little speedwell's darling blue,
  Deep tulips dashed with fiery dew,
Laburnums, dropping-wells of fire.

O thou, new-year, delaying long,
  Delayest the sorrow in my blood,
  That longs to burst a frozen bud,
And flood a fresher throat with song.

.   .   .   .   .   .

CXIV.

Now fades the last long streak of snow;
  Now bourgeons every maze of quick
  About the flowering squares, and thick
By ashen roots the violets blow.

Now rings the woodland loud and long,
  The distance takes a lovelier hue,
  And drowned in yonder living blue
The lark becomes a sightless song.

Now dance the lights on lawn and lea,
  The flocks are whiter down the vale,
  And milkier every milky sail
On winding stream or distant sea;

Where now the sea-mew pipes, or dives
  In yonder greening gleam, and fly
  The happy birds, that change their sky
To build and brood, that live their lives

From land to land; and in my breast
  Spring wakens too; and my regret
  Becomes an April violet,
And buds and blossoms like the rest.

                    ALFRED, LORD TENNYSON.

BETROTHED ANEW.

THE sunlight fills the trembling air,
  And balmy days their guerdons bring;
The Earth again is young and fair,
  And amorous with musky Spring.

The golden nurslings of the May
  In splendor strew the spangled green,
And hues of tender beauty play,
  Entangled where the willows lean.

Mark how the rippled currents flow;
    What lustres on the meadows lie!
And hark! the songsters come and go,
    And trill between the earth and sky.

Who told us that the years had fled,
    Or borne afar our blissful youth?
Such joys are all about us spread;
    We know the whisper was not truth.

The birds that break from grass and grove
    Sing every carol that they sung
When first our veins were rich with love,
    And May her mantle round us flung.

O fresh-lit dawn! immortal life!
    O Earth's betrothal, sweet and true,
With whose delights our souls are rife,
    And aye their vernal vows renew!

Then, darling, walk with me this morn;
    Let your brown tresses drink its sheen;
These violets, within them worn,
    Of floral fays shall make you queen.

What though there comes a time of pain
    When autumn winds forebode decay?
The days of love are born again;
    That fabled time is far away!

And never seemed the land so fair
    As now, nor birds such notes to sing,
Since first within your shining hair
    I wove the blossoms of the spring.

            EDMUND CLARENCE STEDMAN.

THE PLOUGHMAN.

CLEAR the brown path to meet his coulter's
    gleam!
Lo! on he comes, behind his smoking team,
With toil's bright dew-drops on his sunburnt
    brow,
The lord of earth, the hero of the plough!

First in the field before the reddening sun,
Last in the shadows when the day is done,
Line after line, along the bursting sod,
Marks the broad acres where his feet have trod.
Still where he treads the stubborn clods divide,
The smooth, fresh furrow opens deep and wide;
Matted and dense the tangled turf upheaves,
Mellow and dark the ridgy cornfield cleaves;
Up the steep hillside, where the laboring train
Slants the long track that scores the level plain,
Through the moist valley, clogged with oozing
    clay,
The patient convoy breaks its destined way;
At every turn the loosening chains resound,
The swinging ploughshare circles glistening
    round,
Till the wide field one billowy waste appears,
And wearied hands unbind the panting steers.

These are the hands whose sturdy labor brings
The peasant's food, the golden pomp of kings;
This is the page whose letters shall be seen,
Changed by the sun to words of living green;

This is the scholar whose immortal pen
Spells the first lesson hunger taught to men;
These are the lines that heaven-commanded Toil
Shows on his deed,—the charter of the soil!

O gracious Mother, whose benignant breast
Wakes us to life, and lulls us all to rest,
How thy sweet features, kind to every clime,
Mock with their smile the wrinkled front of Time!
We stain thy flowers,—they blossom o'er the
    dead;
We rend thy bosom, and it gives us bread;
O'er the red field that trampling strife has torn,
Waves the green plumage of thy tasselled corn;
Our maddening conflicts scar thy fairest plain,
Still thy soft answer is the growing grain.
Yet, O our Mother, while uncounted charms
Steal round our hearts in thine embracing arms,
Let not our virtues in thy love decay,
And thy fond sweetness waste our strength away.

No, by these hills whose banners now displayed
In blazing cohorts Autumn has arrayed;
By yon twin summits, on whose splintery crests
The tossing hemlocks hold the eagles' nests;
By these fair plains the mountain circle screens,
And feeds with streamlets from its dark ra-
    vines,—
True to their home, these faithful arms shall toil
To crown with peace their own untainted soil;
And, true to God, to freedom, to mankind,
If her chained ban-dogs Faction shall unbind,
These stately forms, that, bending even now,

Bowed their strong manhood to the humble
    plough,
Shall rise erect, the guardians of the land,
The same stern iron in the same right hand,
Till o'er their hills the shouts of triumph run,—
The sword has rescued what the ploughshare
    won!

OLIVER WENDELL HOLMES.

THE PLOUGH.

ABOVE yon sombre swell of land
    Thou seest the dawn's grave orange hue,
With one pale streak like yellow sand,
    And over that a vein of blue.

The air is cold above the woods;
    All silent is the earth and sky,
Except with his own lonely moods
    The blackbird holds a colloquy.

Over the broad hill creeps a beam,
    Like hope that gilds a good man's brow;
And now ascends the nostril-steam
    Of stalwart horses come to plough.

Ye rigid Ploughmen! bear in mind
    Your labor is for future hours.
Advance! spare not! nor look behind!
    Plough deep and straight with all your pow-
        ers!

RICHARD HENGIST HORNE.

THEY COME! THE MERRY SUMMER MONTHS.

THEY come! the merry summer months of beauty,
    song, and flowers;
They come! the gladsome months that bring thick
    leafiness to bowers.
Up, up, my heart! and walk abroad; fling cark
    and care aside;
Seek silent hills, or rest thyself where peaceful
    waters glide;
Or, underneath the shadow vast of patriarchal
    tree,
Scan through its leaves the cloudless sky in rapt
    tranquillity.

The grass is soft, its velvet touch is grateful to
    the hand;
And, like the kiss of maiden love, the breeze is
    sweet and bland;
The daisy and the buttercup are nodding courte-
    ously;
It stirs their blood with kindest love, to bless and
    welcome thee;
And mark how with thine own thin locks—they
    now are silvery gray—
That blissful breeze is wantoning, and whisper-
    ing, " Be gay!"

There is no cloud that sails along the ocean of yon
    sky
But hath its own winged mariners to give it
    melody;

7

Thou seest their glittering fans outspread, all
    gleaming like red gold;
And hark! with shrill pipe musical, their merry
    course they hold.
God bless them all, those little ones, who, far
    above this earth,
Can make a scoff of its mean joys, and vent a
    nobler mirth.

But soft! mine ear upcaught a sound,—from
    yonder wood it came!
The spirit of the dim green glade did breathe his
    own glad name;—
Yes, it is he! the hermit bird, that, apart from
    all his kind,
Slow spells his beads monotonous to the soft
    western wind;
Cuckoo! Cuckoo! he sings again,—his notes are
    void of art;
But simplest strains do soonest sound the deep
    founts of the heart.

Good Lord! it is a gracious boon for thought-
    crazed wight like me,
To smell again the summer flowers beneath this
    summer tree!
To suck once more in every breath their little
    souls away,
And feed my fancy with fond dreams of youth's
    bright summer day,
When, rushing forth like untamed colt, the reck-
    less, truant boy
Wandered through greenwoods all day long, a
    mighty heart of joy!

I 'm sadder now,—I have had cause; but O, I 'm
    proud to think
That each pure joy-fount, loved of yore, I yet
    delight to drink;—
Leaf, blossom, blade, hill, valley, stream, the calm,
    unclouded sky.
Still mingle music with my dreams, as in the days
    gone by.
When summer's loveliness and light fall round
    me dark and cold,
I 'll bear indeed life's heaviest curse,—a heart
    that hath waxed old!
                WILLIAM MOTHERWELL.

SONG OF THE SUMMER WINDS.

Up the dale and down the bourne,
  O'er the meadow swift we fly;
Now we sing, and now we mourn,
  Now we whistle, now we sigh.

By the grassy-fringèd river,
  Through the murmuring reeds we sweep;
Mid the lily-leaves we quiver,
  To their very hearts we creep.

Now the maiden rose is blushing
  At the frolic things we say,
While aside her cheek we 're rushing,
  Like some truant bees at play.

Through the blooming graves we rustle,
  Kissing every bud we pass,—

As we did it in the bustle,
  Scarcely knowing how it was.

Down the glen, across the mountain,
  O'er the yellow heath we roam,
Whirling round about the fountain,
  Till its little breakers foam.

Bending down the weeping willows,
  While our vesper hymn we sigh;
Then unto our rosy pillows
  On our weary wings we hie.

There of idlenesses dreaming,
  Scarce from waking we refrain,
Moments long as ages deeming
  Till we 're at our play again.

                          GEORGE DARLEY.

————

A DROP OF DEW.

SEE how the orient dew,
Shed from the bosom of the morn
    Into the blowing roses,
  (Yet careless of its mansion new
For the clear region where 't was born)
    Round in itself encloses,
  And in its little globe's extent
Frames, as it can, its native element.
    How it the purple flower does slight,
      Scarce touching where it lies;
    But gazing back upon the skies,
      Shines with a mournful light,
        Like its own tear,

Because so long divided from the sphere;
    Restless it rolls, and unsecure,
      Trembling, lest it grow impure,
    Till the warm sun pities its pain,
  And to the skies exhales it back again.
    So the soul, that drop, that ray
Of the clear fountain of eternal day,
Could it within the human flower be seen,
  Remembering still its former height,
  Shuns the sweet leaves and blossoms green,
  And, recollecting its own light,
Does, in its pure and circling thoughts, express
The greater heaven in a heaven less.
      In how coy a figure wound,
      Every way it turns away;
      So the world excluding round,
      Yet receiving in the day.
      Dark beneath, but bright above;
      Here disdaining, there in love.
    How loose and easy hence to go!
    How girt and ready to ascend!
    Moving but on a point below,
    It all about does upwards bend.
Such did the manna's sacred dew distil,
White and entire, although congealed and chill,—
Congealed on earth, but does, dissolving, run
Into the glories of the Almighty sun.

               ANDREW MARVELL.

JUNE.

I GAZED upon the glorious sky,
  And the green mountains round,
And thought that when I came to lie
  At rest within the ground,
'T were pleasant that in flowery June,
When brooks send up a cheerful tune,
  And groves a cheerful sound,
The sexton's hand, my grave to make,
The rich, green mountain turf should break.

A cell within the frozen mould,
  A coffin borne through sleet,
And icy clods above it rolled,
  While fierce the tempests beat—
Away! I will not think of these—
Blue be the sky and soft the breeze,
  Earth green beneath the feet,
And be the damp mould gently pressed
Into my narrow place of rest.

There, through the long, long, summer hours
  The golden light should lie,
And thick young herbs and groups of flowers
  Stand in their beauty by.
The oriole should build and tell
His love-tale close beside my cell;
  The idle butterfly
Should rest him there, and there be heard
The housewife bee and humming-bird.

And what if cheerful shouts at noon
  Come, from the village sent,
  Or song of maids beneath the moon
  With fairy laughter blent?
And what if, in the evening light,
Betrothèd lovers walk in sight
  Of my low monument?
I would the lovely scene around
Might know no sadder sight nor sound.

I know that I no more should see
  The season's glorious show,
Nor would its brightness shine for me,
  Nor its wild music flow;
But if, around my place of sleep,
The friends I love should come to weep,
  They might not haste to go.
Soft airs, and song, and light and bloom
Should keep them lingering by my tomb.

These to their softened hearts should bear
  The thought of what has been,
And speak of one who cannot share
  The gladness of the scene;
Whose part, in all the pomp that fills
The circuit of the summer hills,
  Is that his grave is green;
And deeply would their hearts rejoice
To hear again his living voice.

WILLIAM CULLEN BRYANT.

THE STORY OF A SUMMER DAY.

O PERFECT Light, which shaid away
    The darkness from the light,
And set a ruler o'er the day,
    Another o'er the night—

Thy glory, when the day forth flies,
    More vively doth appear,
Than at mid day unto our eyes
    The shining sun is clear.

The shadow of the earth anon
    Removes and drawis by,
While in the East, when it is gone,
    Appears a clearer sky.

Which soon perceive the little larks,
    The lapwing and the snipe,
And tune their songs, like Nature's clerks,
    O'er meadow, muir, and stripe.

Our hemisphere is polisht clean,
    And lightened more and more;
While everything is clearly seen,
    Which seemit dim before;

Except the glistering astres bright,
    Which all the night were clear,
Offuskit with a greater light
    No longer do appear.

The golden globe incontinent
  Sets up his shining head,
And o'er the earth and firmament
  Displays his beams abroad.

For joy the birds with boulden throats
  Against his visage sheen
Take up their kindly musick notes
  In woods and gardens green.

The dew upon the tender crops,
  Like pearlis white and round,
Or like to melted silver drops,
  Refreshis all the ground.

The misty reek, the clouds of rain
  From tops of mountains skails,
Clear are the highest hills and plain,
  The vapours take the vales.

The ample heaven, of fabrick sure,
  In cleanness does surpass
The crystal and the silver pure,
  Or clearest polisht glass.

The time so tranquil is and still,
  That nowhere shall ye find,
Save on a high and barren hill,
  An air of peeping wind.

All trees and simples, great and small,
  That balmy leaf do bear,
Than they were painted on a wall,
  No more they move or steir.

Calm is the deep and purple sea,
    Yea, smoother than the sand;
The waves, that weltering wont to be,
    Are stable like the land.

So silent is the cessile air,
    That every cry and call
The hills and dales and forest fair
    Again repeats them all.

The flourishes and fragrant flowers,
    Through Phœbus' fostering heat,
Refreshed with dew and silver showers,
    Cast up an odour sweet.

The cloggit, busy humming bees,
    That never think to drone,
On flowers and flourishes of trees,
    Collect their liquor brown.

The Sun, most like a speedy post,
    With ardent course ascends;
The beauty of the heavenly host
    Up to our zenith tends.

Not guided by a Phaëton,
    Not trainèd in a chair,
But by the high and holy One,
    Who does allwhere empire.

The burning beams down from his face
    So fervently can beat,
That man and beast now seek a place
    To save them from the heat.

The herds beneath some leafy tree,
   Amidst the flowers they lie;
The stable ships upon the sea
   Tend up their sails to dry.

With gilded eyes and open wings,
   The cock his courage shows;
With claps of joy his breast he dings,
   And twenty times he crows.

The dove with whistling wings so blue,
   The winds can fast collect,
Her purple pens turn many a hue
   Against the sun direct.

Now noon is went; gone is midday,
   The heat does slake at last;
The sun descends down West away,
   For three of clock is past.

The rayons of the sun we see
   Diminish in their strength;
The shade of every tower and tree
   Extended is in length.

Great is the calm, for everywhere
   The wind is setting down,
The reek throws right up in the air
   From every tower and town.

The gloaming comes; the day is spent;
   The sun goes out of sight;
And painted is the occident
   With purple sanguine bright.

The scarlet nor the golden thread,
   Who would their beauty try,
Are nothing like the color red
   And beauty of the sky.

Our west horizon circular,
   From time the sun be set,
Is all with rubies, as it were,
   Or roses red o'erfret.

What pleasure were to walk and see,
   Endlong a river clear,
The perfect form of every tree
   Within the deep appear.

O, then it were a seemly thing
   While all is still and calm,
The praise of God to play and sing
   With cornet and with shalm!

All labourers draw home at even,
   And can to other say,
Thanks to the gracious God of heaven,
   Which sent this summer day!
               ALEXANDER HUME.

KNEE–DEEP IN JUNE.

I.

TELL you what I like the best—
   'Long about knee-deep in June,
   'Bout the time strawberries melts
   On the vines—some afternoon

Like to jes' git out and rest,
        And not work at nothin' else!

II.

Orchard's where I' ruther be—
Needn't fence it in for me!
    Jes' the whole sky overhead
        And the whole airth underneath—
        Sorto' so 's a man kin breath
    Like he ort, and kindo' has
Elbow-room to keerlessly
    Sprawl out len'thways on the grass,
        Where the shadows thick and soft
As the kivvers on the bed
    Mother fixes in the loft
Allus, when they's company!

III.

Jes' a sort o' lazein' there—
    S' lazy, 'at you peek and peer
        Through the wa·in' leaves above,
        Like a feller 'ats in love
    And don't know it, ner don't keer!
    Ever'thing you hear and see
        Got some sort o' interest—
        Maybe find a bluebird's nest
    Tucked up there conveenently
    Fer the boys 'ats apt to be
    Up some other apple-tree!
Watch the swallers skootin' past
'Bout as peert as you could ast;
        Er the Bobwhite raise and whiz
        Where some other's whistle is.

IV.

Ketch a shadder down below,
And look up to find the crow;
Er a hawk away up there,
'Pearantly froze in the air!—
　　Hear the old hen squawk, and squat
　　Over every chick she 's got,
Sudden-like!—And she knows where
That-air hawk is, well as you!—
You jes' bet yer life she do!—
　　Eyes a-glittering like glass,
　　Waitin' till he makes a pass!

V.

Pee-wees' singin', to express
　　My opinion's second class,
Yit you 'll hear 'em more er less;
　　Sapsucks gittin' down to biz,
Weedin' out the lonesomeness;
　　Mr. Bluejay, full o' sass,
　　　　In them base-ball clothes o' his,
Sportin' 'round the orchard jes'
Like he owned the premises!
　　Sun out in the fields kin sizz,
But flat on your back, I guess,
　　In the shade 's where glory is!
　　　　That 's jes' what I 'd like to do
　　　　Stiddy for a year or two!

VI.

Plague! if they ain't sompin' in
Work 'at kindo' goes agin

My convictions!—'long about
  Here in June especially!—
  Under some old apple tree,
    Jes' a-restin' through and through,
I could git along without
    Nothin' else at all to do
    Only jes' a-wishin' you
Was a-gittin' there like me,
And June was eternity!

VII.

Lay out there and try to see
  Jes' how lazy you kin be!—
Tumble round and souse yer head
In the clover-bloom, er pull
    Yer straw hat acrost yer eyes,
    And peek through it at the skies,
    Thinkin' of old chums 'ats dead,
      Maybe, smilin' back at you
In betwixt the beautiful
    Clouds o' gold and white and blue!—
Month a man kin railly love—
June, you know, I 'm talkin' of!

VIII.

March ain't never nothin' new!—
Aprile 's altogether too
  Brash fer me! and May—I jes'
  'Bominate its promises,—
    Little hints o' sunshine and
Green around the timber-land—
A few blossoms, and a few
Chip-birds, and a sprout er two—

Drap asleep, and it turns in
'Fore daylight and snows agin!—
But when June comes—Clear my throat
    With wild honey! Rench my hair
In the dew! and hold my coat!
    Whoop out loud! and throw my hat!—
June wants me, and I'm to spare!
Spread them shadders anywhere,
I'll git down and waller there,
    And obleeged to you at that!
                    JAMES WHITCOMB RILEY.

BALLADE OF MIDSUMMER DAYS AND NIGHTS.

WITH a ripple of leaves and a tinkle of streams
    The full world rolls in a rhythm of praise,
And the winds are one with the clouds and
        beams—
    Midsummer days! midsummer days!
    The dusk grows vast; in a purple haze,
While the west from a rapture of sunset rights,
    Faint stars their exquisite lamps upraise—
    Midsummer nights! O midsummer nights!

The wood's green heart is a nest of dreams,
    The lush grass thickens and springs and sways,
The rathe wheat rustles, the landscape gleams—
    Midsummer days! midsummer days!
    In the stilly fields, in the stilly ways,
All secret shadows and mystic lights,
    Late lovers murmurous linger and gaze—
    Midsummer nights! O midsummer nights!

There 's a music of bells from the trampling teams,
  Wild skylarks hover, the gorses blaze,
The rich ripe rose as with incense steams—
    Midsummer days! midsummer days!
A soul from the honeysuckle strays,
And the nightingale as from prophet heights
  Sings to the earth of her million Mays—
    Midsummer nights! O midsummer nights!

ENVOY.

And it 's oh! for my dear, and the charm that
    stays—
  Midsummer days! midsummer days!
It 's oh! for my love, and the dark that plights—
  Midsummer nights! O midsummer nights!
WILLIAM ERNEST HENLEY.

INVOCATION TO RAIN IN SUMMER.

  O GENTLE, gentle summer rain,
    Let not the silver lily pine,
  The drooping lily pine in vain
    To feel that dewy touch of thine,—
  To drink thy freshness once again,
  O gentle, gentle summer rain!

  In heat the landscape quivering lies;
    The cattle pant beneath the tree;
  Through parching air and purple skies
    The earth looks up, in vain, for thee;
  For thee—for thee, it looks in vain,
  O gentle, gentle summer rain.

8

Come thou, and brim the meadow streams,
  And soften all the hills with mist,
O falling dew! from burning dreams
  By thee shall herb and flower be kissed,
And Earth shall bless thee yet again,
O gentle, gentle summer rain.
                    WILLIAM COX BENNETT.

RAIN IN SUMMER.

How beautiful is the rain!
After the dust and heat,
In the broad and fiery street,
In the narrow lane,
How beautiful is the rain!

How it clatters along the roofs,
Like the tramp of hoofs!
How it gushes and struggles out
From the throat of the overflowing spout!

Across the window-pane
It pours and pours;
And swift and wide,
With a muddy tide,
Like a river down the gutter roars
The rain, the welcome rain!

The sick man from his chamber looks
At the twisted brooks;
He can feel the cool
Breath of each little pool;

His fevered brain
Grows calm again,
And he breathes a blessing on the rain.

From the neighboring school
Come the boys,
With more than their wonted noise
And commotion;
And down the wet streets
Sail their mimic fleets,
Till the treacherous pool
Ingulfs them in its whirling
And turbulent ocean.

In the country, on every side,
Where far and wide,
Like a leopard's tawny and spotted hide,
Stretches the plain,
To the dry grass and the drier grain
How welcome is the rain!

In the furrowed land
The toilsome and patient oxen stand;
Lifting the yoke-encumbered head,
With their dilated nostrils spread,
They silently inhale
The clover-scented gale,
And the vapors that arise
From the well-watered and smoking soil.
For this rest in the furrow after toil
Their large and lustrous eyes
Seem to thank the Lord,
More than man's spoken word.

Near at hand,
From under the sheltering trees,
The farmer sees
His pastures, and his fields of grain,
As they bend their tops
To the numberless beating drops
Of the incessant rain.
He counts it as no sin
That he sees therein
Only his own thrift and gain.

These, and far more than these,
The Poet sees!
He can behold
Aquarius old
Walking the fenceless fields of air;
And from each ample fold
Of the clouds about him rolled
Scattering everywhere
The showery rain,
As the farmer scatters his grain.

He can behold
Things manifold
That have not yet been wholly told,—
Have not been wholly sung nor said.
For his thought, that never stops,
Follows the water-drops
Down to the graves of the dead,
Down through chasms and gulfs profound,
To the dreary fountain-head
Of lakes and rivers underground;
And sees them, when the rain is done,

On the bridge of colors seven
Climbing up once more to heaven,
Opposite the setting sun.

Thus the Seer
With vision clear,
Sees forms appear and disappear,
In the perpetual round of strange,
Mysterious change
From birth to death, from death to birth,
From earth to heaven, from heaven to earth;
Till glimpses more sublime
Of things, unseen before,
Unto his wandering eyes reveal
The Universe, as an immeasurable wheel
Turning forevermore
In the rapid and rushing river of Time.

HENRY WADSWORTH LONGFELLOW.

BEFORE THE RAIN.

WE knew it would rain, for all the morn
  A spirit on slender ropes of mist
Was lowering its golden buckets down
  Into the vapory amethyst

Of marshes and swamps and dismal fens—
  Scooping the dew that lay in the flowers,
Dipping the jewels out of the sea,
  To scatter them over the land in showers.

We knew it would rain, for the poplars showed
  The white of their leaves, the amber grain

Shrunk in the wind—and the lightning now
Is tangled in tremulous skeins of rain.

THOMAS BAILEY ALDRICH.

SIGNS OF RAIN.*

FORTY REASONS FOR NOT ACCEPTING AN INVITA-
TION OF A FRIEND TO MAKE AN EXCURSION WITH
HIM.

1 THE hollow winds begin to blow;
2 The clouds look black, the glass is low,
3 The soot falls down, the spaniels sleep,
4 And spiders from their cobwebs peep.
5 Last night the sun went pale to bed,
6 The moon in halos hid her head;
7 The boding shepherd heaves a sigh,
8 For see, a rainbow spans the sky!
9 The walls are damp, the ditches smell,
10 Closed is the pink-eyed pimpernel.
11 Hark how the chairs and tables crack!
12 Old Betty's nerves are on the rack;
13 Loud quacks the duck, the peacocks cry,
14 The distant hills are seeming nigh.
15 How restless are the snorting swine!
16 The busy flies disturb the kine,
17 Low o'er the grass the swallow wings,
18 The cricket, too, how sharp he sings!
19 Puss on the hearth, with velvet paws,
20 Sits wiping o'er her whiskered jaws;

* "Verified by Darwin," says C. C. Bombaugh in his
"Gleanings from the Harvest Fields of Literature,"
though his version of the lines varies somewhat from this.

21 Through the clear streams the fishes rise,
22 And nimbly catch the incautious flies.
23 The glow-worms, numerous and light,
24 Illumed the dewy dell last night;
25 At dusk the squalid toad was seen,
26 Hopping and crawling o'er the green;
27 The whirling dust the wind obeys,
28 And in the rapid eddy plays;
29 The frog has changed his yellow vest,
30 And in a russet coat is dressed.
31 Though June, the air is cold and still,
32 The mellow blackbird's voice is shrill;
33 My dog, so altered in his taste,
34 Quits mutton-bones on grass to feast;
35 And see yon rooks, how odd their flight!
36 They imitate the gliding kite,
37 And seem precipitate to fall,
38 As if they felt the piercing ball.
39 'T will surely rain; I see with sorrow,
40 Our jaunt must be put off to-morrow.

DR. EDWARD JENNER.

SUMMER STORM.

UNTREMULOUS in the river clear,
Toward the sky's image, hangs the imaged bridge;
So still the air that I can hear
The slender clarion of the unseen midge;
Out of the stillness, with a gathering creep,
Like rising wind in leaves, which now decreases,
Now lulls, now swells, and all the while increases,
The huddling trample of a drove of sheep

Tilts the loose planks, and then as gradually
    ceases
  In dust on the other side; life's emblem deep,
A confused noise between two silences,
Finding at last in dust precarious peace.
On the wide marsh the purple-blossomed grasses
  Soak up the sunshine; sleeps the brimming tide,
Save when the wedge-shaped wake in silence
    passes
  Of some slow water-rat, whose sinuous glide
  Wavers the long green sedge's shade from side
    to side;
But up the west, like a rock-shivered surge,
  Climbs a great cloud edged with sun-whitened
    spray;
Huge whirls of foam boil toppling o'er its verge,
  And falling still it seems, and yet it climbs
    alway.

    Suddenly all the sky is hid
    As with the shutting of a lid,
  One by one great drops are falling
      Doubtful and slow;
  Down the pane they are crookedly crawling,
      And the wind breathes low;
  Slowly the circles widen on the river,
    Widen and mingle, one and all;
  Here and there the slenderer flowers shiver,
    Struck by an icy rain-drop's fall.

Now on the hills I hear the thunder mutter,
  The wind is gathering in the west;
The upturned leaves first whiten and flutter,
  Then droop to a fitful rest;

Up from the stream with sluggish flap
  Struggles the gull and floats away;
Nearer and nearer rolls the thunder-clap,—
  We shall not see the sun go down to-day:
Now leaps the wind on the sleepy marsh,
  And tramples the grass with terrified feet,
The startled river turns leaden and harsh,
    You can hear the quick heart of the tempest
      beat.

    Look! look! that livid flash!
And instantly follows the rattling thunder,
As if some cloud-crag, split asunder,
    Fell, splintering with a ruinous crash,
On the Earth, which crouches in silence under;
  And now a solid gray wall of rain
Shuts off the landscape, mile by mile;
  For a breath's space I see the blue wood again,
And, ere the next heart-beat, the wind-hurled pile,
    That seemed but now a league aloof,
    Bursts crackling o'er the sun-parched roof;
Against the windows the storm comes dashing,
Through tattered foliage the hail tears crashing,
        The blue lightning flashes,
        The rapid hail clashes,
      The white waves are tumbling,
        And, in one baffled roar,
      Like the toothless sea mumbling
        A rock-bristled shore,
      The thunder is rumbling
      And crashing and crumbling,—
Will silence return nevermore?

Hush! Still as death,
The tempest holds his breath
As from a sudden will;
The rain stops short, but from the eaves
You see it drop, and hear it from the leaves,
All is so bodingly still;
Again, now, now, again
Plashes the rain in heavy gouts,
The crinkled lightning
Seems ever brightening,
And loud and long
Again the thunder shouts
His battle-song,—
One quivering flash,
One wildering crash,
Followed by silence dead and dull,
As if the cloud, let go,
Leapt bodily below
To whelm the earth in one mad overthrow,
And then a total lull.

Gone, gone, so soon!
No more my half-crazed fancy there
Can shape a giant in the air,
No more I see his streaming hair,
The writhing portent of his form;—
The pale and quiet moon
Makes her calm forehead bare,
And the last fragments of the storm,
Like shattered rigging from a fight at sea,
Silent and few, are drifting over me.

JAMES RUSSELL LOWELL.

AFTER THE RAIN.

The rain has ceased, and in my room
The sunshine pours an airy flood;
And on the church's dizzy vane
The ancient Cross is bathed in blood.

From out the dripping ivy-leaves,
Antiquely carven, gray and high,
A dormer, facing westward, looks
Upon the village like an eye.

And now it glimmers in the sun,
A square of gold, a disc, a speck:
And in the belfry sits a Dove
With purple ripples on her neck.

THOMAS BAILEY ALDRICH.

A STORM IN THE DISTANCE.

I see the cloud-born squadrons of the gale,
  Their lines of rain like glittering spears deprest,
While all the affrighted land grows darkly pale
  In flashing charge on earth's half-shielded
    breast.

Sounds like the rush of trampling columns float
  From that fierce conflict; volleyed thunders
      peal,
Blent with the maddened wind's wild bugle-note;
  The lightnings flash, the solid woodlands reel!

Ha! many a foliaged guardian of the height,
  Majestic pine or chestnut, riven and bare,
Falls in the rage of that aerial fight,
  Led by the Prince of all the Powers of air!

Vast boughs like shattered banners hurtling fly
  Down the thick tumult: while, like emerald
    snow,
Millions of orphaned leaves make wild the sky,
  Or drift in shuddering helplessness below.

Still, still, the levelled lances of the rain
  At earth's half-shielded breast take glittering
    aim;
All space is rife with fury, racked with pain,
  Earth bathed in vapor, and heaven rent by
    flame!

At last the cloud-battalions through long rifts
  Of luminous mists retire:—the strife is done,
And earth once more her wounded beauty lifts,
  To meet the healing kisses of the sun.

                    PAUL HAMILTON HAYNE.

RAIN.

More than the wind, more than the snow,
  More than the sunshine, I love rain:
Whether it droppeth soft and low,
  Whether it rusheth amain.

Dark as the night it spreadeth its wings,
  Slow and silently, up on the hills;

Then sweeps o'er the vale, like a steed that springs
  From the grasp of a thousand wills.

Swift sweeps under heaven the raven's flight;
  And the land and the lakes and the main
Lie belted beneath with steel-bright light,
  The light of the swift-rushing rain.

On evenings of summer, when sunlight is low,
  Soft the rain falls from opal-hued skies:
And the flowers the most delicate summer can
    show
  Are not stirred by its gentle surprise.

It falls on the pools, and no wrinkling it makes,
  But touching melts in, like the smile
That sinks in the face of a dreamer, but breaks
  Not the calm of his dream's happy wile.

The grass rises up as it falls on the meads,
  The bird softlier sings in his bower,
And the circles of gnats circle on like winged
    seeds
  Through the soft sunny lines of the shower.
                    EBENEZER JONES.

THE DANCING OF THE AIR.

AND now behold your tender nurse, the air,
  And common neighbor that aye runs around,
How many pictures and impressions fair
  Within her empty regions are there found,
  Which to your senses dancing do propound!

For what are breath, speech, echoes, music, winds,
But dancings of the air in sundry kinds?

For when you breathe, the air in order moves,
  Now in, now out, in time and measure true;
And when you speak, so well she dancing loves,
  That doubling oft, and oft redoubling new,
    With thousand forms she doth herself endue:
For all the words that from your lips repair,
Are naught but tricks and turnings of the air.

Hence is her prattling daughter, Echo, born,
  That dances to all voices she can hear:
There is no sound so harsh that she doth scorn,
  Nor any time wherein she will forbear
    The airy pavement with her feet to wear:
And yet her hearing sense is nothing quick,
For after time she endeth every trick.

And thou, sweet Music, dancing's only life,
  The ear's sole happiness, the air's best speech,
Loadstone of fellowship, charming-rod of strife,
  The soft mind's paradise, the sick mind's leech—
    With thine own tongue thou trees and stones
      canst teach,
That, when the air doth dance her finest measure,
Then art thou born, the gods' and men's sweet
    pleasure.

Lastly, where keep the winds their revelry,
  Their violent turnings, and wild whirling hays,
But in the air's translucent gallery,

Where she herself is turned a hundred ways,
　While with these maskers wantonly she plays?
Yet in this misrule, they such rule embrace,
As two at once encumber not the place.

SIR JOHN DAVIES.

WICKLOW WINDS.

FROM " WICKLOW."

YES, this is Wicklow; round our feet
　And o'er our heads its woodlands smile;
Behold it, love—the garden sweet
　And playground of our stormy isle.

　　.　　.　　.　　.　　.　　.

Is it not fair—the leafy land?
　Not boasting Nature's sterner pride,
Voluptuous beauty, scenes that stand
　By minds immortal deified.

　　.　　.　　.　　.　　.　　.

Fair when the woodland strains and creaks
　As loud the gathering whirlwinds blow,
And through the smoke-like mists the Peaks
　In warm autumnal purples glow;

When madly toss the bracken's plumes
　Storm-swept upon the seaward steep,
As far below them foams and fumes
　On beach and cliff the wrathful deep,

Till cloud and tempest, creeping lower,
  Old Djouce's ridges swathe in night,
And down through all his hollows pour
  The foaming torrents swoln and white;

Or when o'er Powerscourt's leafless woods,
  With crests that down the tempest lean,
Bend, braving winter's fiercest moods,
  The pines in all their wealth of green.

GEORGE FRANCIS SAVAGE-ARMSTRONG.

ODE TO THE WEST WIND.

I.

O WILD West Wind, thou breath of Autumn's
    being,
Thou, from whose unseen presence the leaves dead
Are driven, like ghosts from an enchanter fleeing,

Yellow, and black, and pale, and hectic red,
Pestilence-stricken multitudes! O thou,
Who chariotest to their dark, wintry bed

The wingèd seeds, where they lie cold and low,
Each like a corpse within its grave, until
Thine azure sister of the Spring shall blow

Her clarion o'er the dreaming earth, and fill
(Driving sweet buds, like flocks, to feed in air)
With living hues and odors, plain and hill:

Wild spirit, which art moving everywhere;
Destroyer and preserver; hear, O hear!

II.

Thou on whose stream, 'mid the steep sky's com-
    motion,
Loose clouds like earth's decaying leaves are shed,
Shook from the tangled boughs of heaven and
    ocean,

Angels of rain and lightning: there are spread
On the blue surface of thine airy surge,
Like the bright hair uplifted from the head

Of some fierce Mænad, even from the dim verge
Of the horizon to the zenith's height,
The locks of the approaching storm.   Thou dirge

Of the dying year, to which this closing night
Will be the dome of a vast sepulchre
Vaulted with all thy congregated might

Of vapors; from whose solid atmosphere
Black rain, and fire, and hail, will burst: O hear!

III.

Thou who didst waken from his summer dreams
The blue Mediterranean, where he lay,
Lulled by the coil of his crystalline streams,

Beside a pumice isle in Baiæ's bay,
And saw in sleep old palaces and towers,
Quivering within the waves' intenser day,

All overgrown with azure moss and flowers
So sweet the sense faints picturing them! Thou
For whose path the Atlantic's level powers
  9

Cleave themselves into chasms, while, far below,
The sea-blooms, and the oozy woods which wear
The sapless foliage of the ocean, know

Thy voice, and suddenly grow gray with fear,
And tremble and despoil themselves: O hear!

IV.

If I were a dead leaf thou mightest bear;
If I were a swift cloud to fly with thee;
A wave to pant beneath thy power and share

The impulse of thy strength—only less free
Than thou, O uncontrollable! If even
I were as in my boyhood, and could be

The comrade of thy wanderings over heaven
As then, when to outstrip thy skyey speed
Scarce seemed a vision, I would ne'er have striven

As thus with thee in prayer in my sore need.
Oh! lift me as a wave, a leaf, a cloud!
I fall upon the thorns of life! I bleed!

A heavy weight of hours has chained and bowed
One too like thee—tameless, and swift, and proud.

V.

Make me thy lyre, even as the forest is.
What if my leaves are falling like its own!
The tumult of thy mighty harmonies

Will take from both a deep autumnal tone—
Sweet though in sadness. Be thou, spirit fierce,
My spirit! Be thou me, impetuous one!

Drive my dead thoughts over the universe,
Like withered leaves, to quicken a new birth;
And, by the incantation of this verse,

Scatter, as from an unextinguished hearth
Ashes and sparks, my words among mankind!
Be through my lips to unawakened earth

The trumpet of a prophecy! O wind,
If winter comes, can spring be far behind?

PERCY BYSSHE SHELLEY.

THE CLOUD CHORUS.

FROM "THE CLOUDS."

SOCRATES SPEAKS.

HITHER, come hither, ye Clouds renowned, and
　　unveil yourselves here;
　Come, though ye dwell on the sacred crests of
　　Olympian snow,
Or whether ye dance with the Nereid Choir in the
　　gardens clear,
　Or whether your golden urns are dipped in
　　Nile's overflow,
　　Or whether you dwell by Mæotis mere
　　Or the snows of Mimas, arise! appear!
　And hearken to us, and accept our gifts ere ye
　　rise and go.

THE CLOUDS SING.

Immortal Clouds from the echoing shore
  Of the father of streams from the sounding sea,
Dewy and fleet, let us rise and soar;
  Dewy and gleaming and fleet are we!
Let us look on the tree-clad mountain-crest,
  On the sacred earth where the fruits rejoice,
On the waters that murmur east and west,
  On the tumbling sea with his moaning voice.
For unwearied glitters the Eye of the Air,
        And the bright rays gleam;
Then cast we our shadows of mist, and fare
In our deathless shapes to glance everywhere
From the height of the heaven, on the land and
        air,
        And the Ocean Stream.
Let us on, ye Maidens that bring the Rain,
  Let us gaze on Pallas's citadel,
In the country of Cecrops fair and dear,
  The mystic land of the holy cell,
  Where the Rites unspoken securely dwell,
And the gifts of the gods that know not stain,
  And a people of mortals that know not fear.
For the temples tall and the statues fair,
And the feasts of the gods are holiest there;
The feasts of Immortals, the chaplets of flowers,
  And the Bromian mirth at the coming of spring,
And the musical voices that fill the hours,
  And the dancing feet of the maids that sing!

From the Greek of ARISTOPHANES.

Translation of ANDREW LANG.

THE CLOUD.

I ʙʀɪɴɢ fresh showers for the thirsting flowers,
　　From the seas and the streams;
I bear light shade for the leaves when laid
　　In their noonday dreams.
From my wings are shaken the dews that waken
　　The sweet buds every one,
When rocked to rest on their mother's breast,
　　As she dances about the sun.
I wield the flail of the lashing hail,
　　And whiten the green plains under;
And then again I dissolve it in rain,
　　And laugh as I pass in thunder.

I sift the snow on the mountains below,
　　And their great pines groan aghast;
And all the night 't is my pillow white,
　　While I sleep in the arms of the blast.
Sublime on the towers of my skyey bowers
　　Lightning, my pilot, sits:
In a cavern under is fettered the thunder;
　　It struggles and howls by fits.

Over earth and ocean, with gentle motion,
　　This pilot is guiding me,
Lured by the love of the genii that move
　　In the depths of the purple sea;
Over the rills and the crags and the hills,
　　Over the lakes and plains,
Wherever he dream, under mountain or stream,
　　The spirit he loves remains;

And I all the while bask in heaven's blue smile,
    Whilst he is dissolving in rains.

The sanguine sunrise, with his meteor eyes,
    And his burning plumes outspread,
Leaps on the back of my sailing rack,
    When the morning star shines dead.
As, on the jag of a mountain crag
    Which an earthquake rocks and swings,
An eagle, alit, one moment may sit
    In the light of its golden wings;
And when sunset may breathe, from the lit sea
      beneath,
    Its ardors of rest and of love,
And the crimson pall of eve may fall
    From the depth of heaven above,
With wings folded I rest on mine airy nest,
    As still as a brooding dove.

That orbèd maiden with white fire laden,
    Whom mortals call the moon,
Glides glimmering o'er my fleece-like floor
    By the midnight breezes strewn;
And wherever the beat of her unseen feet,
    Which only the angels hear,
May have broken the woof of my tent's thin roof,
    The stars peep behind her and peer;
And I laugh to see them whirl and flee,
    Like a swarm of golden bees,
When I widen the rent in my wind-built tent,
    Till the calm rivers, lakes, and seas,
Like strips of the sky fallen through me on high,
    Are each paved with the moon and these.

I bind the sun's throne with a burning zone,
    And the moon's with a girdle of pearl;
The volcanoes are dim, and the stars reel and
    swim,
    When the whirlwinds my banner unfurl.
From cape to cape, with a bridge-like shape,
    Over a torrent sea,
Sunbeam-proof, I hang like a roof,
    The mountains its columns be.
The triumphal arch through which I march
    With hurricane, fire, and snow,
When the powers of the air are chained to my
    chair,
    Is the million-colored bow;
The sphere-fire above its soft colors wove,
    While the moist earth was laughing below.

I am the daughter of the earth and water;
    And the nursling of the sky;
I pass through the pores of the ocean and shores;
    I change, but I cannot die.
For after the rain, when, with never a stain,
    The pavilion of heaven is bare,
And the winds and sunbeams, with their convex
    gleams,
    Build up the blue dome of air,—
I silently laugh at my own cenotaph,
    And out of the caverns of rain,
Like a child from the womb, like a ghost from the
    tomb,
    I rise and upbuild it again.

                    PERCY BYSSHE SHELLEY.

SUMMER MOODS.

I love at eventide to walk alone,
Down narrow glens, o'erhung with dewy thorn,
Where from the long grass underneath, the snail,
Jet black, creeps out, and sprouts his timid horn.
I love to muse o'er meadows newly mown,
Where withering grass perfumes the sultry air;
Where bees search round, with sad and weary
        drone,
In vain, for flowers that bloomed but newly
        there;
While in the juicy corn the hidden quail
Cries, "Wet my foot;" and, hid as thoughts un-
        born,
The fairy-like and seldom-seen land-rail
Utters "Craik, craik," like voices underground,
Right glad to meet the evening's dewy veil,
And see the light fade into gloom around.

                              JOHN CLARE.

IN PRAISE OF ANGLING.

Quivering fears, heart-tearing cares,
Anxious sighs, untimely tears,
        Fly, fly to courts,
        Fly to fond worldlings' sports,
Where strained sardonic smiles are glozing still,
And grief is forced to laugh against her will,
        Where mirth 's but mummery,
        And sorrows only real be.

Fly from our country pastimes, fly,
Sad troops of human misery;
 Come, serene looks,
 Clear as the crystal brooks,
Or the pure azured heaven that smiles to see
The rich attendance on our poverty;
 Peace and a secure mind,
 Which all men seek, we only find.

Abusèd mortals! did you know
Where joy, heart's ease, and comforts grow,
 You 'd scorn proud towers
 And seek them in these bowers,
Where winds, sometimes, our woods perhaps may
  shake,
But blustering care could never tempest make;
 Nor murmurs e'er come nigh us,
 Saving of fountains that glide by us.

Here 's no fantastic mask or dance,
But of our kids that frisk and prance;
 Nor wars are seen,
 Unless upon the green
Two harmless lambs are butting one the other,
Which done, both bleating run, each to his mother,
 And wounds are never found,
 Save what the ploughshare gives the
  ground.

Here are no entrapping baits
To hasten to too hasty fates;
 Unless it be
 The fond credulity

Of silly fish, which (worldling like) still look
Upon the bait, but never on the hook;
> Nor envy, 'less among
> The birds, for price of their sweet song.

Go, let the diving negro seek
For gems, hid in some forlorn creek:
> We all pearls scorn
> Save what the dewy morn
Congeals upon each little spire of grass,
Which careless shepherds beat down as they pass;
> And gold ne'er here appears,
> Save what the yellow Ceres bears.

Blest silent groves, O, may you be,
Forever, mirth's best nursery!
> May pure contents
> Forever pitch their tents
Upon these downs, these meads, these rocks, these
> mountains!
And peace still slumber by these purling foun-
> tains,
> Which we may every year
> Meet, when we come a-fishing here.

SIR HENRY WOTTON.

THE ANGLER'S WISH.

I in these flowery meads would be,
These crystal streams should solace me;
To whose harmonious bubbling noise
I, with my angle, would rejoice,
> Sit here, and see the turtle-dove
> Court his chaste mate to acts of love;

Or, on that bank, feel the west-wind
Breathe health and plenty; please my mind,
To see sweet dew-drops kiss these flowers,
And then washed off by April showers;
 Here, hear my Kenna * sing a song:
 There, see a blackbird feed her young,

Or a laverock build her nest;
Here, give my weary spirits rest,
And raise my low-pitched thoughts above
Earth, or what poor mortals love.
 Thus, free from lawsuits, and the noise
 Of princes' courts, I would rejoice;

Or, with my Bryan and a book,
Loiter long days near Shawford brook;
There sit by him, and eat my meat;
There see the sun both rise and set;
There bid good morning to next day;
There meditate my time away;
 And angle on; and beg to have
 A quiet passage to a welcome grave.

      IZAAK WALTON.

THE ANGLER.

 O THE gallant fisher's life,
  It is the best of any!
 'T is full of pleasure, void of strife,
  And 't is beloved by many;
   Other joys
   Are but toys;

---

* "Kenna." the name of his supposed mistress, seems to have been formed from the name of his wife, which was Ken.

Only this
Lawful is;
For our skill
Breeds no ill,
But content and pleasure.

.   .   .   .   .

When we please to walk abroad
  For our recreation,
In the fields is our abode,
  Full of delectation,
    Where, in a brook,
    With a hook,—
    Or a lake,—
    Fish we take;
    There we sit,
    For a bit,
  Till we fish entangle.

We have gentles in a horn,
  We have paste and worms too;
We can watch both night and morn,
  Suffer rain and storms too;
    None do here
    Use to swear:
    Oaths do fray
    Fish away;
    We sit still,
    Watch our quill:
  Fishers must not wrangle.

If the sun's excessive heat
  Make our bodies swelter,

To an osier hedge we get,
  For a friendly shelter;
      Where, in a dike,
      Perch or pike,
      Roach or dace,
      We do chase,
      Bleak or gudgeon,
      Without grudging;
  We are still contented.

Or we sometimes pass an hour
  Under a green willow,
That defends us from a shower,
  Making earth our pillow;
      Where we may
      Think and pray,
      Before death
      Stops our breath;
      Other joys
      Are but toys,
  And to be lamented.

                JOHN CHALKHILL.

SWIMMING.

FROM " THE TWO FOSCARI."

          How many a time have I
Cloven, with arm still lustier, breast more daring,
The wave all roughened; with a swimmer's stroke
Flinging the billows back from my drenched hair,
And laughing from my lips the audacious brine,
Which kissed it like a wine-cup, rising o'er
The waves as they arose, and prouder still

The loftier they uplifted me; and oft,
In wantonness of spirit, plunging down
Into their green and glassy gulfs, and making
My way to shells and sea-weed, all unseen
By those above, till they waxed fearful; then
Returning with my grasp full of such tokens
As showed that I had searched the deep; exulting,
With a far-dashing stroke, and drawing deep
The long-suspended breath, again I spurned
The foam which broke around me, and pursued
My track like a sea-bird.—I was a boy then.

LORD BYRON.

THE PLEASURE-BOAT.

COME, hoist the sail, the fast let go!
  They're seated side by side;
Wave chases wave in pleasant flow;
  The bay is fair and wide.

The ripples lightly tap the boat;
  Loose! Give her to the wind!
She shoots ahead; they're all afloat;
  The strand is far behind.

No danger reach so fair a crew!
  Thou goddess of the foam,
I 'll ever pay thee worship due,
  If thou wilt bring them home.

Fair ladies, fairer than the spray
  The prow is dashing wide,

Soft breezes take you on your way,
   Soft flow the blessèd tide.

O, might I like those breezes be,
   And touch that arching brow,
I 'd dwell forever on the sea
   Where ye are floating now.

The boat goes tilting on the waves;
   The waves go tilting by;
There dips the duck,—her back she laves;
   O'erhead the sea-gulls fly.

Now, like the gulls that dart for prey,
   The little vessel stoops;
Now, rising, shooting along her way,
   Like them, in easy swoops.

The sunlight falling on her sheet,
   It glitters like the drift,
Sparkling, in scorn of summer's heat
   High up some mountain rift.

The winds are fresh; she 's driving fast
   Upon the bending tide;
The crinkling sail, and crinkling mast,
   Go with her side by side.

Why dies the breeze away so soon?
   Why hangs the pennant down?
The sea is glass; the sun at noon.—
   Nay, lady, do not frown;

For, see, the wingèd fisher's plume
  Is painted on the sea;
Below, a cheek of lovely bloom.
  Whose eyes look up to thee?

She smiles; thou need'st must smile on her.
  And see, beside her face,
A rich, white cloud that doth not stir:
  What beauty, and what grace!

And pictured beach of yellow sand,
  And peakèd rock and hill,
Change the smooth sea to fairy-land;
  How lovely and how still!

From that far isle the thresher's flail
  Strikes close upon the ear;
The leaping fish, the swinging sail
  Of yonder sloop, sound near.

The parting sun sends out a glow
  Across the placid bay,
Touching with glory all the show.—
  A breeze! Up helm! Away!

Careening to the wind, they reach,
  With laugh and call, the shore.
They 've left their footprints on the beach,
  But them I hear no more.

                    RICHARD HENRY DANA.

THE SOLITARY WOODSMAN.

When the gray lake-water rushes
Past the dripping alder-bushes,
    And the bodeful autumn wind
In the fir-tree weeps and hushes,—

When the air is sharply damp
Round the solitary camp,
    And the moose-bush in the thicket
Glimmers like a scarlet lamp,—

When the birches twinkle yellow,
And the cornel bunches mellow,
    And the owl across the twilight
Trumpets to his downy fellow,—

When the nut-fed chipmunks romp
Through the maples' crimson pomp,
    And the slim viburnum flashes
In the darkness of the swamp,—

When the blueberries are dead,
When the rowan clusters red,
    And the shy bear, summer-sleekened,
In the bracken makes his bed,—

On a day there comes once more
To the latched and lonely door,
    Down the wood-road striding silent,
One who has been here before.

10

Green spruce branches for his head,
Here he makes his simple bed,
 Crouching with the sun, and rising
When the dawn is frosty red.

All day long he wanders wide
With the gray moss for his guide,
 And his lonely axe-stroke startles
The expectant forest-side.

Toward the quiet close of day
Back to camp he takes his way,
 And about his sober footsteps
Unafraid the squirrels play.

On his roof the red leaf falls,
At his door the blue jay calls,
 And he hears the wood-mice hurry
Up and down his rough log walls;

Hears the laughter of the loon
Thrill the dying afternoon,—
 Hears the calling of the moose
Echo to the early moon.

And he hears the partridge drumming,
The belated hornet humming,—
 All the faint, prophetic sounds
That foretell the winter 's coming.

And the wind about his eaves
Through the chilly night-wet grieves,
 And the earth's dumb patience fills him,
Fellow to the falling leaves.

CHARLES G. D. ROBERTS.

SEPTEMBER.

SWEET is the voice that calls
From the babbling waterfalls
In meadows where the downy seeds are flying;
And soft the breezes blow,
And eddying come and go
In faded gardens where the rose is dying.

Among the stubbled corn
The blithe quail pipes at morn,
The merry partridge drums in hidden places,
And glittering insects gleam
Above the reedy stream,
Where busy spiders spin their filmy laces.

At eve, cool shadows fall
Across the garden wall,
And on the clustered grapes to purple turning;
And pearly vapors lie
Along the eastern sky,
Where the broad harvest-moon is redly burning.

Ah, soon on field and hill
The wind shall whistle chill,
And patriarch swallows call their flocks together,
To fly from frost and snow,
And seek for lands where blow
The fairer blossoms of a balmier weather.

The cricket chirps all day,
"O fairest summer, stay!"
The squirrel eyes askance the chestnuts brown-
ing;

The wild fowl fly afar
Above the foamy bar,
And hasten southward ere the skies are frowning.

Now comes a fragrant breeze
Through the dark cedar-trees,
And round about my temples fondly lingers,
In gentle playfulness,
Like to the soft caress
Bestowed in happier days by loving fingers.

Yet, though a sense of grief
Comes with the falling leaf,
And memory makes the summer doubly pleasant,
In all my autumn dreams
A future summer gleams,
Passing the fairest glories of the present!

GEORGE ARNOLD.

THE LATTER RAIN.

THE latter rain,—it falls in anxious haste
Upon the sun-dried fields and branches bare,
Loosening with searching drops the rigid waste
As if it would each root's lost strength repair;
But not a blade grows green as in the spring;
No swelling twig puts forth its thickening leaves;
The robins only mid the harvests sing,
Pecking the grain that scatters from the sheaves;
The rain falls still,—the fruit all ripened drops,
It pierces chestnut-bur and walnut-shell;
The furrowed fields disclose the yellow crops;

Each bursting pod of talents used can tell;
And all that once received the early rain
Declare to man it was not sent in vain.

JONES VERY.

TO AUTUMN.

SEASON of mists and mellow fruitfulness!
  Close bosom-friend of the maturing sun!
Conspiring with him how to load and bless
  With fruit the vines that round the thatch-eaves
      run—
To bend with apples the mossed cottage trees,
  And fill all fruit with ripeness to the core—
    To swell the gourd, and plump the hazel
      shells
With a sweet kernel—to set budding, more
And still more, later flowers for the bees,
Until they think warm days will never cease,
    For summer has o'er-brimmed their clammy
      cells.

Who hath not seen thee oft amid thy store?
  Sometimes whoever seeks abroad may find
Thee sitting careless on a granary floor,
  Thy hair soft-lifted by the winnowing wind;
Or on a half-reaped furrow sound asleep,
  Drowsed with the fume of poppies, while thy
      hook
    Spares the next swath and all its twinèd
      flowers;
And sometime like a gleaner thou dost keep
  Steady thy laden head across a brook;

Or by a cider-press, with patient look,
   Thou watchest the last oozings, hours by
     hours.

Where are the songs of Spring? Ay, where are
     they?
  Think not of them—thou hast thy music too:
While barred clouds bloom the soft-dying day,
  And touch the stubble-plains with rosy hue:
Then in a wailful choir the small gnats mourn
  Among the river sallows, borne aloft
    Or sinking, as the light wind lives or dies;
And full-grown lambs loud bleat from hilly bourn;
  Hedge-crickets sing; and now with treble soft
  The redbreast whistles from a garden-croft,
    And gathering swallows twitter in the skies.
                 JOHN KEATS.

HARVEST SONG.

    SICKLES sound;
     On the ground
   Fast the ripe ears fall;
  Every maiden's bonnet
  Has blue blossoms on it:
   Joy is over all.

    Sickles ring,
    Maidens sing
   To the sickle's sound;
  Till the moon is beaming,
  And the stubble gleaming,
   Harvest songs go round.

All are springing,
All are singing,
Every lisping thing,
Man and master meet,
From one dish they eat;
Each is now a king.

Hans and Michael
Whet the sickle,
Piping merrily.
Now they mow; each maiden
Soon with sheaves is laden,
Busy as a bee.

Now the blisses,
And the kisses!
Now the wit doth flow
Till the beer is out;
Then, with song and shout,
Home they go, yo ho!

From the German of LUDWIG H. C. HÖLTY.
Translation of CHARLES TIMOTHY BROOKS.

LIFE IN THE AUTUMN WOODS.

[VIRGINIA.]

SUMMER has gone,
And fruitful Autumn has advanced so far
That there is warmth, not heat, in the broad sun,
And you may look, with naked eye, upon
The ardors of his car;
The stealthy frosts, whom his spent looks embolden,
Are making the green leaves golden.

What a brave splendor
Is in the October air! how rich, and clear,
And bracing, and all-joyous! We must render
Love to the Spring-time, with its sproutings
          tender,
          As to a child quite dear;
But Autumn is a thing of perfect glory,
          A manhood not yet hoary.

I love the woods,
In this good season of the liberal year;
I love to seek their leafy solitudes,
And give myself to melancholy moods,
          With no intruder near,
And find strange lessons, as I sit and ponder,
          In every natural wonder.

But not alone,
As Shakespeare's melancholy courtier loved
          Ardennes,
Love I the browning forest; and I own
I would not oft have mused, as he, but flown
          To hunt with Amiens—
And little thought, as up the bold deer bounded,
          Of the sad creature wounded.

A brave and good,
But world-worn knight—soul-wearied with his
          part
In this vexed life—gave man for solitude,
And built a lodge, and lived in Wantley wood,
          To hear the belling hart.
It was a gentle taste, but its sweet sadness
          Yields to the hunter's madness.

What passionate
And keen delight is in the proud swift chase!
Go out what time the lark at heaven's red gate
Soars joyously singing—quite infuriate
    With the high pride of his place;
What time the unrisen sun arrays the morning
    In its first bright adorning.

    Hark! the quick horn—
As sweet to hear as any clarion—
Piercing with silver call the ear of morn;
And mark the steeds, stout Curtal and Topthorne,
    And Greysteil and the Don—
Each one of them his fiery mood displaying
    With pawing and with neighing.

    Urge your swift horse
After the crying hounds in this fresh hour;
Vanquish high hills, stem perilous streams per-
      force,
On the free plain give free wings to your course,
    And you will know the power
Of the brave chase,—and how of griefs the sorest
    A cure is in the forest.

    Or stalk the deer;
The same red lip of dawn has kissed the hills,
The gladdest sounds are crowding on your ear,
There is a life in all the atmosphere:—
    Your very nature fills
With the fresh hour, as up the hills aspiring
    You climb with limbs untiring.

It is a fair
And goodly sight to see the antlered stag
With the long sweep of his swift walk repair
To join his brothers; or the plethoric bear
    Lying in some high crag,
With pinky eyes half closed, but broad head
      shaking,
    As gadflies keep him waking.

    And these you see,
And, seeing them, you travel to their death
With a slow, stealthy step, from tree to tree,
Noting the wind, however faint it be.
    The hunter draws a breath
In times like these, which, he will say, repays him
    For all care that waylays him.

    A strong joy fills
(A joy beyond the tongue's expressive power)
My heart in Autumn weather—fills and thrills!
And I would rather stalk the breezy hills
    Descending to my bower
Nightly, by the sweet spirit of Peace attended,
    Than pine where life is splendid.
              PHILIP PENDLETON COOKE.

HUNTING SONG.

WAKEN, lords and ladies gay,
On the mountain dawns the day;
    All the jolly chase is here,
    With hawk and horse and hunting-spear!

Hounds are in their couples yelling,
Hawks are whistling, horns are knelling,
  Merrily, merrily mingle they,
  " Waken, lords and ladies gay."

Waken, lords and ladies gay,
The mist has left the mountain gray,
  Springlets in the dawn are steaming,
  Diamonds on the brake are gleaming,
And foresters have busy been
To track the buck in thicket green;
  Now we come to chant our lay,
  " Waken, lords and ladies gay."

Waken, lords and ladies gay,
To the greenwood haste away;
  We can show you where he lies,
  Fleet of foot and tall of size;
We can show the marks he made
When 'gainst the oak his antlers frayed;
  You shall see him brought to bay;
  Waken, lords and ladies gay.

Louder, louder chant the lay,
Waken, lords and ladies gay!
  Tell them, youth and mirth and glee
  Run a course as well as we;
Time, stern huntsman, who can balk,
Stanch as hound and fleet as hawk?
  Think of this, and rise with day,
  Gentle lords and ladies gay!

SIR WALTER SCOTT.

THE HUNTER'S SONG.

Rise! Sleep no more! 'T is a noble morn.
The dews hang. thick on the fringèd thorn,
And the frost shrinks back like a beaten hound,
Under the steaming, steaming ground.
Behold, where the billowy clouds flow by,
And leave us alone in the clear gray sky!
Our horses are ready and steady.—So, ho!
I 'm gone, like a dart from the Tartar's bow.
Hark, hark!—Who calleth the maiden Morn
From her sleep in the woods and the stubble
*   corn?*
          The horn,—the horn!
The merry, sweet ring of the hunter's horn.

Now, through the copse where the fox is found,
And over the stream at a mighty bound,
And over the high lands and over the low,
O'er furrows, o'er meadows, the hunters go!
Away!—as a hawk flies full at his prey,
So flieth the hunter, away, away!
From the burst at the cover till set of sun,
When the red fox dies, and—the day is done.
Hark, hark!—What sound on the wind is borne?
'T is the conquering voice of the hunter's horn:
          The horn,—the horn!
The merry, bold voice of the hunter's horn.

Sound! Sound the horn! To the hunter good
What 's the gully deep or the roaring flood?

Right over he bounds, as the wild stag bounds,
At the heels of his swift, sure, silent hounds.
Oh, what delight can a mortal lack,
When he once is firm on his horse's back,
With his stirrups short, and his snaffle strong,
And the blast of the horn for his morning song?
Hark, hark!—Now home! and dream till morn
Of the bold, sweet sound of the hunter's horn!
　　　　The horn,—the horn!
Oh, the sound of all sounds is the hunter's horn!
　　　　　BRYAN WALLER PROCTER (*Barry Cornwall*).

THE HUNTED SQUIRREL.

FROM " BRITANNIA'S PASTORALS," BK. I. SONG 5.

THEN as a nimble squirrel from the wood,
Ranging the hedges for his filbert-food,
Sits pertly on a bough his brown nuts cracking,
And from the shell the sweet white kernel taking,
Till with their crooks and bags a sort of boys,
To share with him, come with so great a noise
That he is forced to leave a nut nigh broke,
And for his life leap to a neighbor oak,
Thence to a beech, thence to a row of ashes;
Whilst through the quagmires and red water
　　　plashes
The boys run dabbling thorough thick and thin,
One tears his hose, another breaks his shin,
This, torn and tattered, hath with much ado
Got by the briars; and that hath lost his shoe:
This drops his band; that headlong falls for haste;
Another cries behind for being last:

With sticks and stones, and many a sounding hol-
　　low,
The little fool with no small sport they follow,
Whilst he from tree to tree, from spray to spray,
Gets to the wood, and hides him in his dray.

WILLIAM BROWNE.

A HUNTING WE WILL GO.

THE dusky night rides down the sky,
　　And ushers in the morn:
The hounds all join in glorious cry,
　　The huntsman winds his horn,
　　　　　And a hunting we will go.

The wife around her husband throws
　　Her arms to make him stay;
" My dear, it rains, it hails, it blows;
　　You cannot hunt to-day."
　　　　　Yet a hunting we will go.

Away they fly to 'scape the rout,
　　Their steeds they soundly switch;
Some are thrown in, and some thrown out,
　　And some thrown in the ditch.
　　　　　Yet a hunting we will go.

Sly Reynard now like lightning flies,
　　And sweeps across the vale;
And when the hounds too near he spies,
　　He drops his bushy tail.
　　　　　Then a hunting we will go.

Fond Echo seems to like the sport,
　　And join the jovial cry;

The woods, the hills, the sound retort,
  And music fills the sky,
        When a hunting we do go.

At last his strength to faintness worn,
  Poor Reynard ceases flight;
Then hungry, homeward we return,
  To feast away the night,
        And a drinking we do go.

Ye jovial hunters,. in the morn
  Prepare then for the chase;
Rise at the sounding of the horn
  And health with sport embrace,
        When a hunting we do go.
            HENRY FIELDING.

THE STAG HUNT.

FROM "THE LADY OF THE LAKE," CANTO I.

THE stag at eve had drunk his fill,
Where danced the moon on Monan's rill,
And deep his midnight lair had made
In lone Glenartney's hazel shade;
But, when the sun his beacon red
Had kindled on Benvoirlich's head,
The deep-mouthed bloodhound's heavy bay
Resounded up the rocky way,
And faint, from farther distance borne,
Were heard the clanging hoof and horn.

As Chief who hears his warder call,
"To arms! the foemen storm the wall,"

The antlered monarch of the waste
Sprung from his heathery couch in haste.
But, ere his fleet career he took,
The dew-drops from his flanks he shook;
Like crested leader proud and high
Tossed his beamed frontlet to the sky;
A moment gazed adown the dale,
A moment snuffed the tainted gale,
A moment listened to the cry,
That thickened as the chase drew nigh;
Then, as the headmost foes appeared,
With one brave bound the copse he cleared,
And, stretching forward free and far,
Sought the wild heaths of Uam-Var.

Yelled on the view the opening pack;
Rock, glen, and cavern paid them back;
To many a mingled sound at once
The awakened mountain gave response.
A hundred dogs bayed deep and strong,
Clattered a hundred steeds along,
Their peal the merry horns rung out,
A hundred voices joined the shout;
With hark and whoop and wild halloo,
No rest Benvoirlich's echoes knew.
Far from the tumult fled the roe;
Close in her covert cowered the doe;
The falcon, from her cairn on high,
Cast on the rout a wondering eye,
Till far beyond her piercing ken
The hurricane had swept the glen.
Faint, and more faint, its failing din
Returned from cavern, cliff, and linn,

And silence settled, wide and still,
On the lone wood and mighty hill.

.   .   .   .   .   .

'T were long to tell what steeds gave o'er,
As swept the hunt through Cambus-more;
What reins were tightened in despair,
When rose Benledi's ridge in air;
Who flagged upon Bochastle's heath,
Who shunned to stem the flooded Teith,—
For twice that day, from shore to shore,
The gallant stag swam stoutly o'er.
Few were the stragglers, following far,
That reached the lake of Vennachar;
And when the Brigg of Turk was won,
The headmost horseman rode alone.
Alone, but with unbated zeal,
That horseman plied the scourge and steel;
For, jaded now, and spent with toil,
Embossed with foam, and dark with soil,
While every gasp with sobs he drew,
The laboring stag strained full in view.
Two dogs of black Saint Hubert's breed,
Unmatched for courage, breath, and speed,
Fast on his flying traces came,
And all but won that desperate game;
For, scarce a spear's length from his haunch,
Vindictive toiled the bloodhounds staunch;
Nor nearer might the dogs attain,
Nor farther might the quarry strain.
Thus up the margin of the lake,
Between the precipice and brake,
O'er stock and rock their race they take.

11

The hunter marked that mountain high,
The lone lake's western boundary,
And deemed the stag must turn to bay,
Where that huge rampart barred the way;
Already glorying in the prize,
Measured his antlers with his eyes;
For the death-wound and death-halloo
Mustered his breath, his whinyard drew;
But thundering as he came prepared,
With ready arm and weapon bared,
The wily quarry shunned the shock,
And turned him from the opposing rock;
Then, dashing down a darksome glen,
Soon lost to hound and hunter's ken,
In the deep Trosachs' wildest nook
His solitary refuge took.
There while, close couched, the thicket shed
Cold dews and wild-flowers on his head,
He heard the baffled dogs in vain
Rave through the hollow pass amain,
Chiding the rocks that yelled again.

Close on the hounds the hunter came,
To cheer them on the vanished game;
But, stumbling in the rugged dell,
The gallant horse exhausted fell.
The impatient rider strove in vain
To rouse him with the spur and rein,
For the good steed, his labors o'er,
Stretched his stiff limbs, to rise no more;
Then, touched with pity and remorse,
He sorrowed o'er the expiring horse:
" I little thought, when first thy rein

I slacked upon the banks of Seine,
That Highland eagle e'er should feed
On thy fleet limbs, my matchless steed!
Woe worth the chase, woe worth the day,
That costs thy life, my gallant gray!"

Then through the dell his horn resounds,
From vain pursuit to call the hounds.
Back limped, with slow and crippled pace,
The sulky leaders of the chase;
Close to their master's side they pressed,
With drooping tail and humbled crest;
But still the dingle's hollow throat
Prolonged the swelling bugle-note.
The owlets started from their dream,
The eagles answered with their scream,
Round and around the sounds were cast,
Till echo seemed an answering blast;
And on the hunter hied his way,
To join some comrades of the day;
Yet often paused, so strange the road,
So wondrous were the scenes it showed.

SIR WALTER SCOTT.

THE STAG HUNT.

FROM " THE SEASONS: AUTUMN."

THE stag too, singled from the herd where long
He ranged, the branching monarch of the shades,
Before the tempest drives. At first, in speed
He, sprightly, puts his faith; and, roused by
      fear,
Gives all his swift aerial soul to flight.

Against the breeze he darts, that way the more
To leave the lessening murderous cry behind:
Deception short! though fleeter than the winds
Blown o'er the keen-aired mountain by the north,
He bursts the thickets, glances through the
    glades,
And plunges deep into the wildest wood,—
If slow, yet sure, adhesive to the track
Hot-steaming, up behind him come again
The inhuman rout, and from the shady depth
Expel him, circling through his every shift.
He sweeps the forest oft; and sobbing sees
The glades, mild opening to the golden day,
Where, in kind contest, with his butting friends
He wont to struggle, or his loves enjoy.
Oft in the full-descending flood he tries
To lose the scent, and lave his burning sides;
—Oft seeks the herd; the watchful herd, alarmed,
With selfish care avoid a brother's woe.
What shall he do?   His once so vivid nerves,
So full of buoyant spirit, now no more
Inspire the course; but fainting breathless toil,
Sick, seizes on his heart: he stands at bay;
And puts his last weak refuge in despair.
The big round tears run down his dappled face;
He groans in anguish; while the growling pack,
Blood-happy, hang at his fair jutting chest,
And mark his beauteous checkered sides with
    gore.

                         JAMES THOMSON.

THE OLD SQUIRE.

I LIKE the hunting of the hare
  Better than that of the fox;
I like the joyous morning air,
  And the crowing of the cocks.

I like the calm of the early fields,
  The ducks asleep by the lake,
The quiet hour which Nature yields
  Before mankind is awake.
I like the pheasants and feeding things

  Of the unsuspicious morn;
I like the flap of the wood-pigeon's wings
  As she rises from the corn.

I like the blackbird's shriek, and his rush
  From the turnips as I pass by,
And the partridge hiding her head in a bush,
  For her young ones cannot fly.

I like these things, and I like to ride,
  When all the world is in bed,
To the top of the hill where the sky grows wide,
  And where the sun grows red.

The beagles at my horse-heels trot
  In silence after me;
There's Ruby, Roger, Diamond, Dot,
  Old Slut and Margery,—

A score of names well used, and dear,
  The names my childhood knew;
The horn, with which I rouse their cheer,
  Is the horn my father blew.

I like the hunting of the hare
  Better than that of the fox;
The new world still is all less fair
  Than the old world it mocks.

I covet not a wider range
  Than these dear manors give;
I take my pleasures without change,
  And as I lived I live.

I leave my neighbors to their thought;
  My choice it is, and pride,
On my own lands to find my sport,
  In my own fields to ride.

The hare herself no better loves
  The field where she was bred,
Than I the habit of these groves,
  My own inherited.

I know my quarries every one,
  The meuse where she sits low;
The road she chose to-day was run
  A hundred years ago.

The lags, the gills, the forest ways,
  The hedgerows one and all,
These are the kingdoms of my chase,
  And bounded by my wall;

Nor has the world a better thing,
  Though one should search it round,
Than thus to live one's own sole king,
  Upon one's own sole ground.

I like the hunting of the hare;
  It brings me, day by day,
The memory of old days as fair,
  With dead men passed away.

To these, as homeward still I ply
  And pass the churchyard gate,
Where all are laid as I must lie,
  I stop and raise my hat.

I like the hunting of the hare;
  New sports I hold in scorn.
I like to be as my fathers were,
  In the days ere I was born.

WILFRED SCAWEN BLUNT.

INDIAN SUMMER.

No more the battle or the chase
  The phantom tribes pursue,
But each in its accustomed place
  The Autumn hails anew:
And still from solemn councils set
  On every hill and plain,
The smoke of many a calumet
  Ascends to heaven again.

JOHN BANISTER TABB.

NO !

No sun—no moon!
No morn—no noon—
No dawn—no dust—no proper time of day—

No sky—no earthly view—
No distance looking blue—
No road—no street—no " t' other side the way "—
No end to any Row—
No indications where the Crescents go—
No top to any steeple—
No recognitions of familiar people—
No courtesies for showing 'em—
No knowing 'em!
No travelling at all—no locomotion,
No inkling of the way—no notion—
" No go "—by land or ocean—
No mail—no post—
No news from any foreign coast—
No park—no ring—no afternoon gentility—
No company—no nobility—
No warmth, no cheerfulness, no healthful ease,
No comfortable feel in any member—
No shade, no shine, no butterflies, no bees,
No fruits, no flowers, no leaves, no birds,
November!

THOMAS HOOD.

WHEN THE FROST IS ON THE PUNKIN.

WHEN the frost is on the punkin and the fodder 's
in the shock,
And you hear the kyouck and gobble of the strut-
tin' turkey-cock,
And the clackin' of the guineys, and the cluckin'
of the hens,
And the rooster's hallylooyer as he tiptoes on the
fence;

O it 's then 's the times a feller is a-feelin' at his
    best,
With the risin' sun to greet him from a night of
    peaceful rest,
As he leaves the house, bare-headed, and goes out
    to feed the stock,
When the frost is on the punkin and the fodder 's
    in the shock.

They 's something kindo' harty-like about the at-
    musfere
When the heat of summer 's over and the coolin'
    fall is here—
Of course we miss the flowers, and the blossums on
    the trees,
And the mumble of the hummin'-birds and buzzin'
    of the bees;
But the air 's so appetizin' ; and the landscape
    through the haze
Of a crisp and sunny morning of the airly autumn
    days
Is a pictur' that no painter has the colorin' to
    mock—
When the frost is on the punkin and the fodder 's
    in the shock.

The husky, rusty russel of the tossels of the corn,
And the raspin' of the tangled leaves, as golden
    as the morn;
The stubble in the furries—kindo' lonesome-like,
    but still
A-preachin' sermuns to us of the barns they
    growed to fill;

The strawstack in the medder, and the reaper in
  the shed;
The hosses in theyr stalls below—the clover overhead!—
O, it sets my hart a-clickin' like the tickin' of a
  clock,
When the frost is on the punkin and the fodder 's
  in the shock.

JAMES WHITCOMB RILEY.

———

AUTUMN: A DIRGE.

THE warm sun is failing, the bleak wind is wail-
  ing,
The bare boughs are sighing, the pale flowers are
  dying,
        And the year
On the earth her deathbed, in a shroud of leaves
  dead,
        Is lying.
  Come, months, come away,
  From November to May,
  In your saddest array;
  Follow the bier
  Of the dead cold year,
And like dim shadows watch by her sepulchre.

The chill rain is falling, the nipt worm is crawling,
The rivers are swelling, the thunder is knelling
        For the year;

The blithe swallows are flown, and the lizards each
    gone
        To his dwelling;
Come, months, come away,
Put on white, black, and gray;
Let your light sisters play—
Ye, follow the bier
Of the dead cold year,
And make her grave green with tear on tear.
                PERCY BYSSHE SHELLEY.

WHEN ICICLES HANG BY THE WALL.

FROM "LOVE'S LABOR 'S LOST," ACT V. SC. 2.

WHEN icicles hang by the wall,
    And Dick the shepherd blows his nail,
And Tom bears logs into the hall,
    And milk comes frozen home in pail,
When blood is nipped, and ways be foul,
Then nightly sings the staring owl,
        To-whoo;
To-whit, to-whoo, a merry note,
While greasy Joan doth keel the pot.

When all aloud the wind doth blow,
    And coughing drowns the parson's saw,
And birds sit brooding in the snow,
    And Marian's nose looks red and raw,
When roasted crabs hiss in the bowl,

Then nightly sings the staring owl,
    To-whoo;
To-whit, to-whoo, a merry note,
While greasy Joan doth keel the pot.
SHAKESPEARE.

WINTER.

A SONG TO BE SUNG BEHIND THE STOVE.

OLD Winter is the man for me—
    Stout-hearted, sound, and steady;
Steel nerves and bones of brass hath he:
    Come snow, come blow, he 's ready!

If ever man was well, 't is he;
    He keeps no fire in his chamber,
And yet from cold and cough is free
    In bitterest December.

He dresses him out-doors at morn,
    Nor needs he first to warm him;
Toothache and rheumatis' he 'll scorn,
    And colic don't alarm him.

In summer when the woodland rings,
    He asks " What mean these noises? "
Warm sounds he hates and all warm things
    Most heartily despises.

But when the fox's bark is loud;
    When the bright hearth is snapping;

When children round the chimney crowd,
 All shivering and clapping;—

When stone and bone with frost do break,
 And pond and lake are cracking,—
Then you may see his old sides shake,
 Such glee his frame is racking.

Near the North Pole, upon the strand,
 He has an icy tower;
Likewise in lovely Switzerland
 He keeps a summer bower.

So up and down—now here—now there—
 His regiments manœuvre;
When he goes by, we stand and stare,
 And cannot choose but shiver.

From the German of MATTHIAS CLAUDIUS.
Translation of CHARLES TIMOTHY BROOKS.

FROST.

How small a tooth hath mined the season's
 heart!
How cold a touch hath set the wood on fire,
Until it blazes like a costly pyre
Built for some Ganges emperor, old and swart,
Soul-sped on clouds of incense! Whose the art
That webs the streams, each morn, with silver
 wire,
Delicate as the tension of a lyre,—

Whose falchion pries the chestnut-bur apart?
It is the Frost, a rude and Gothic sprite,
Who doth unbuild the Summer's palaced wealth,
And puts her dear loves all to sword or flight;
Yet in the hushed, unmindful winter's night
The spoiler builds again with jealous stealth,
And sets a mimic garden, cold and bright.

                              EDITH MATILDA THOMAS.

SNOW–FLAKES.

OUT of the bosom of the Air,
  Out of the cloud-folds of her garments shaken,
Over the woodlands brown and bare,
  Over the harvest fields forsaken,
    Silent and soft and slow
    Descends the snow.

Even as our cloudy fancies take
  Suddenly shape in·some divine expression,
Even as the troubled heart doth make
  In the white countenance confession,
    The troubled sky reveals
    The grief it feels.

This is the poem of the air,
  Slowly in silent syllables recorded;
This is the secret of despair,
  Long in its cloudy bosom hoarded,
    Now whispered and revealed
    To wood and field.

                    HENRY WADSWORTH LONGFELLOW.

DECEMBER.

WHEN the feud of hot and cold
　　Leaves the autumn woodlands bare;
When the year is getting old,
　　And flowers are dead, and keen the air;

When the crow has new concern,
　　And early sounds his raucous note;
And—where the late witch-hazels burn—
　　The squirrel from a chuckling throat

Tells that one larder's space is filled,
　　And tilts upon a towering tree;
And, valiant, quick, and keenly thrilled,
　　Upstarts the tiny chickadee;

When the sun's still shortening arc
　　Too soon night's shadows dun and gray
Brings on, and fields are drear and dark,
　　And summer birds have flown away,—

I feel the year's slow-beating heart,
　　The sky's chill prophecy I know;
And welcome the consummate art
　　Which weaves this spotless shroud of
　　　snow!

                              JOEL BENTON.

SNOW–FLAKES.

WHENEVER a snow-flake leaves the sky,
It turns and turns to say " Good-bye!
Good-bye, dear clouds, so cool and gray!"
Then lightly travels on its way.

And when a snow-flake finds a tree,
" Good-day!" it says—" Good-day to thee!
Thou art so bare, and lonely, dear,
I 'll rest and call my comrades here."

But when a snow-flake, brave and meek,
Lights on a rosy maiden's cheek,
It starts—" How warm and soft the day!
'T is summer!"—and it melts away.

MARY MAPES DODGE.

THE SNOW–STORM.

ANNOUNCED by all the trumpets of the sky,
Arrives the snow; and, driving o'er the fields,
Seems nowhere to alight; the whited air
Hides hills and woods, the river, and the heaven,
And veils the farmhouse at the garden's end.
The sled and traveller stopped, the courier's feet
Delayed, all friends shut out, the housemates sit
Around the radiant fireplace, enclosed
In a tumultuous privacy of storm.
Come see the north-wind's masonry!
Out of an unseen quarry, evermore

Furnished with tile, the fierce artificer
Curves his white bastions with projected roof
Round every windward stake or tree or door;
Speeding, the myriad-handed, his wild work
So fanciful, so savage; naught cares he
For number or proportion. Mockingly,
On coop or kennel he hangs Parian wreaths;
A swan-like form invests the hidden thorn;
Fills up the farmer's lane from wall to wall,
Maugre the farmer's sighs; and at the gate
A tapering turret overtops the work.
And when his hours are numbered, and the world
Is all his own, retiring as he were not,
Leaves, when the sun appears, astonished Art
To mimic in slow structures, stone by stone,
Built in an age, the mad wind's night-work,
The frolic architecture of the snow.

RALPH WALDO EMERSON.

THE SNOW-STORM.

THE great soft downy snow-storm like a cloak
Descends to wrap the lean world head to feet;
It gives the dead another winding-sheet,
It buries all the roofs until the smoke
Seems like a soul that from its clay has broke.
It broods moon-like upon the Autumn wheat,
And visits all the trees in their retreat
To hood and mantle that poor shivering folk.
With wintry bloom it fills the harshest grooves
In jagged pine-stump fences. Every sound
It hushes to the footstep of a nun.
Sweet Charity! that brightens where it moves

12

Inducing darkest bits of churlish ground
To give a radiant answer to the sun.

ETHELWYN WETHERALD.

THE SNOW-SHOWER.

STAND here by my side and turn, I pray,
　On the lake below thy gentle eyes;
The clouds hang over it, heavy and gray,
　And dark and silent the water lies;
And out of that frozen mist the snow
In wavering flakes begins to flow;
　　　　　　　Flake after flake
They sink in the dark and silent lake.

See how in a living swarm they come
　From the chambers beyond that misty veil;
Some hover awhile in air, and some
　Rush prone from the sky like summer hail.
All, dropping swiftly or settling slow,
Meet, and are still in the depths below;
　　　　　　　Flake after flake
Dissolved in the dark and silent lake.

Here delicate snow-stars, out of the cloud,
　Come floating downward in airy play,
Like spangles dropped from the glistening crowd
　That whiten by night the Milky Way;
There broader and burlier masses fall;
The sullen water buries them all,—
　　　　　　　Flake after flake,—
All drowned in the dark and silent lake.

And some, as on tender wings they glide
   From their chilly birth-cloud, dim and gray,
Are joined in their fall, and, side by side,
   Come clinging along their unsteady way;
As friend with friend, or husband with wife,
Makes hand in hand the passage of life;
                  Each mated flake
Soon sinks in the dark and silent lake.

Lo! while we are gazing, in swifter haste
   Stream down the snows, till the air is white,
As, myriads by myriads madly chased,
   They fling themselves from their shadowy
      height.
The fair, frail creatures of middle sky,
What speed they make, with their grave so nigh;
                  Flake after flake
To lie in the dark and silent lake!

I see in thy gentle eyes a tear;
   They turn to me in sorrowful thought;
Thou thinkest of friends, the good and dear,
   Who were for a time, and now are not;
Like these fair children of cloud and frost,
That glisten a moment and then are lost,—
                  Flake after flake,—
All lost in the dark and silent lake.

Yet look again, for the clouds divide;
   A gleam of blue on the water lies;
And far away, on the mountain-side,
   A sunbeam falls from the opening skies.
But the hurrying host that flew between

The cloud and the water no more is seen;
> Flake after flake
At rest in the dark and silent lake.

WILLIAM CULLEN BRYANT.

"THE SNOWING OF THE PINES."

SOFTER than silence, stiller than still air
Float down from high pine-boughs the slender
    leaves.
The forest floor its annual boon receives
That comes like snowfall, tireless, tranquil, fair.
Gently they glide, gently they clothe the bare
Old rocks with grace. Their fall a mantle weaves
Of paler yellow than autumnal sheaves
Or those strange blossoms the witch-hazels wear.
Athwart long aisles the sunbeams pierce their
    way;
High up, the crows are gathering for the night;
The delicate needles fill the air; the jay
Takes through their golden mist his radiant
    flight;
They fall and fall, till at November's close
The snow-flakes drop as lightly—snows on snows.

THOMAS WENTWORTH HIGGINSON.

A SNOW-STORM.

SCENE IN A VERMONT WINTER.

'T IS a fearful night in the winter time,
    As cold as it ever can be;
The roar of the blast is heard like the chimes
    Of the waves on an angry sea.

The moon is full; but her silver light
The storm dashes out with its wings to-night;
And over the sky from south to north
Not a star is seen, as the wind comes forth
　　In the strength of a mighty glee.

All day had the snow come down,—all day
　　As it never came down before;
And over the hills, at sunset, lay
　　Some two or three feet, or more;
The fence was lost, and the wall of stone;
The windows blocked and the well-curbs gone;
The haystack had grown to a mountain lift,
And the wood-pile looked like a monster drift,
　　As it lay by the farmer's door.

The night sets in on a world of snow,
　　While the air grows sharp and chill,
And the warning roar of a fearful blow
　　Is heard on the distant hill;
And the norther, see! on the mountain peak
In his breath how the old trees writhe and shriek!
He shouts on the plain, ho-ho! ho-ho!
He drives from his nostrils the blinding snow,
　　And growls with a savage will.

Such a night as this to be found abroad,
　　In the drifts and the freezing air,
Sits a shivering dog, in the field, by the road,
　　With the snow in his shaggy hair.
He shuts his eyes to the wind and growls;
He lifts his head and moans and howls;
Then crouching low, from the cutting sleet,

His nose is pressed on his quivering feet,—
   Pray, what does the dog do there?

A farmer came from the village plain,—
   But he lost the travelled way;
And for hours he trod with might and main
   A path for his horse and sleigh;
But colder still the cold winds blew,
And deeper still the deep drifts grew,
And his mare, a beautiful Morgan brown,
At last in her struggles floundered down,
   Where a log in a hollow lay.

In vain, with a neigh and a frenzied snort,
   She plunged in the drifting snow,
While her master urged, till his breath grew short,
   With a word and a gentle blow;
But the snow was deep, and the tugs were tight;
His hands were numb and had lost their might;
So he wallowed back to his half-filled sleigh,
And strove to shelter himself till day,
   With his coat and the buffalo.

He has given the last faint jerk of the rein,
   To rouse up his dying steed;
And the poor dog howls to the blast in vain,
   For help in his master's need.
For awhile he strives with a wistful cry
To catch a glance from his drowsy eye,
And wags his tail if the rude winds flap
The skirt of the buffalo over his lap,
   And whines when he takes no heed.

The wind goes down and the storm is o'er,—
  'T is the hour of midnight, past;
The old trees writhe and bend no more
  In the whirl of the rushing blast.
The silent moon with her peaceful light
Looks down on the hills with snow all white,
And the giant shadow of Camel's Hump,
The blasted pine and the ghostly stump,
  Afar on the plain are cast.

But cold and dead by the hidden log
  Are they who came from the town,—
The man in his sleigh, and his faithful dog,
  And his beautiful Morgan brown,—
In the wide snow-desert, far and grand,
With his cap on his head and the reins in his
    hand,—
The dog with his nose on his master's feet,
And the mare half seen from the crusted sleet,
  Where she lay when she floundered down.

CHARLES GAMAGE EASTMAN.

WINTER.

THE day had been a calm and sunny day.
  And tinged with amber was the sky at even;
The fleecy clouds at length had rolled away,
  And lay in furrows on the eastern heaven;—
The moon arose and shed a glimmering ray,
And round her orb a misty circle lay.

The hoar-frost glittered on the naked heath,
  The roar of distant winds was loud and deep,

The dry leaves rustled in each passing breath,
   And the gay world was lost in quiet sleep.
Such was the time when, on the landscape brown,
Through a December air the snow came down.

The morning came, the dreary morn, at last,
   And showed the whitened waste. The shiver-
      ing herd
Lowed on the hoary meadow-ground, and fast
   Fell the light flakes upon the earth unstirred;
The forest firs with glittering snows o'erlaid
Stood like hoar priests in robes of white arrayed.
             JOHN HOWARD BRYANT.

WINTER SCENES.

FROM " THE SEASONS: WINTER."

THE keener tempests rise; and fuming dun
From all the livid east, or piercing north,
Thick clouds ascend; in whose capacious womb
A vapory deluge lies, to snow congealed.
Heavy they roll their fleecy world along;
And the sky saddens with the gathered storm.
Through the hushed air the whitening shower de-
   scends
At first thin wavering; till at last the flakes
Fall broad and wide and fast, dimming the day
With a continual flow. The cherished fields
Put on their winter robe of purest white.
'T is brightness all; save where the new snow
   melts
Along the mazy current. Low the woods

Bow their hoar head; and, ere the languid sun
Faint from the west emits his evening ray,
Earth's universal face, deep hid and chill,
Is one wide dazzling waste, that buries wide
The works of man. Drooping, the laborer-ox
Stands covered o'er with snow, and then demands
The fruit of all his toil. The fowls of heaven,
Tamed by the cruel season, crowd around
The winnowing store, and claim the little boon
Which Providence assigns them. One alone,
The redbreast, sacred to the household gods,
Wisely regardful of the embroiling sky,
In joyless fields and thorny thickets leaves
His shivering mates, and pays to trusted man
His annual visit. Half afraid, he first
Against the window beats; then, brisk, alights
On the warm hearth; then, hopping o'er the floor,
Eyes all the smiling family askance,
And pecks, and starts, and wonders where he is:
Till, more familiar grown, the table-crumbs
Attract his slender feet. The foodless wilds
Pour forth their brown inhabitants. The hare,
Though timorous of heart, and hard beset
By death in various forms, dark snares, and dogs,
And more unpitying man, the garden seeks,
Urged on by fearless want. The bleating kind
Eye the bleak heaven, and next the glistening
      earth,
With looks of dumb despair; then, sad dispersed,
Dig for the withered herb through heaps of snow.

                              JAMES THOMSON.

WINTER SONG.

Summer joys are o'er;
Flowerets bloom no more,
Wintry winds are sweeping;
Through the snow-drifts peeping,
  Cheerful evergreen
  Rarely now is seen.

Now no plumèd throng
Charms the wood with song;
Ice-bound trees are glittering;
Merry snow-birds, twittering,
  Fondly strive to cheer
  Scenes so cold and drear.

Winter, still I see
Many charms in thee,—
Love thy chilly greeting,
Snow-storms fiercely beating,
  And the dear delights
  Of the long, long nights.

From the German of LUDWIG H. C. HÖLTY.
Translation of CHARLES TIMOTHY BROOKS.

WINTER MORNING.

FROM "THE WINTER MORNING WALK:"
"THE TASK," BK. V.

'T is the morning, and the sun with ruddy orb
Ascending fires the horizon; while the clouds,
That crowd away before the driving wind,
More ardent as the disc emerges more,

Resembles most some city in a blaze,
Seen through the leafless wood. His slanting ray
Slides ineffectual down the snowy vale,
And, tingeing all with his own rosy hue,
From every herb and every spiry blade
Stretches a length of shadow o'er the field.

 . . . . . .

The verdure of the plain lies buried deep
Beneath the dazzling deluge; and the bents,
And coarser grass, upspearing o'er the rest,
Of late unsightly and unseen, now shine
Conspicuous, and in bright apparel clad,
And, fledged with icy feathers, nod superb.
The cattle mourn in corners, where the fence
Screens them, and seem half petrified to sleep
In unrecumbent sadness. There they wait
Their wonted fodder; not, like hungering man,
Fretful if unsupplied; but silent, meek,
And patient of the slow-paced swain's delay.

 . . . . . .

Forth goes the woodman, leaving unconcerned
The cheerful haunts of men,—to wield the axe
And drive the wedge in yonder forest drear,
From morn to eve his solitary task.
Shaggy and lean and shrewd with pointed ears,
And tail cropped short, half lurcher and half cur,
His dog attends him. Close behind his heel
Now creeps he slow; and now, with many a frisk
Wide-scampering, snatches up the drifted snow
With ivory teeth, or ploughs it with his snout;
Then shakes his powdered coat, and barks for joy.

 . . . . . .

Now from the roost, or from the neighboring pale,

Where, diligent to catch the first faint gleam
Of smiling day, they gossiped side by side,
Come trooping at the housewife's well-known call
The feathered tribes domestic. Half on wing,
And half on foot, they brush the fleecy flood,
Conscious and fearful of too deep a plunge.
The sparrows peep, and quit the sheltering eaves
To seize the fair occasion. Well they eye
The scattered grain, and, thievishly resolved
To escape the impending famine, often scared
As oft return, a pert voracious kind.
Clean riddance quickly made, one only care
Remains to each, the search of sunny nook,
Or shed impervious to the blast. Resigned
To sad necessity, the cock foregoes
His wonted strut, and, wading at their head
With well-considered steps, seems to resent
His altered gait and stateliness retrenched.
How find the myriads, that in summer cheer
The hills and valleys with their ceaseless songs,
Due sustenance, or where subsist they now?
Earth yields them naught; the imprisoned worm
    is safe
Beneath the frozen clod; all seeds of herbs
Lie covered close; and berry-bearing thorns,
That feed the thrush (whatever some suppose),
Afford the smaller minstrels no supply.
The long protracted vigor of the year
Thins all their numerous flocks. In chinks and
    holes
Ten thousand seek an unmolested end,
As instinct prompts; self-buried ere they die.

WILLIAM COWPER.

SLEIGH SONG.

Jingle, jingle, clear the way,
'T is the merry, merry sleigh!
As it swiftly scuds along,
Hear the burst of happy song;
See the gleam of glances bright,
Flashing o'er the pathway white!
Jingle, jingle, past it flies,
Sending shafts from hooded eyes,—
Roguish archers, I 'll be bound,
Little heeding whom they wound;
See them, with capricious pranks,
Ploughing now the drifted banks;
Jingle, jingle, mid the glee
Who among them cares for me?
Jingle, jingle, on they go,
Capes and bonnets white with snow,
Not a single robe they fold
To protect them from the cold;
Jingle, jingle, mid the storm,
Fun and frolic keep them warm;
Jingle, jingle, down the hills,
O'er the meadows, past the mills,
Now 't is slow, and now 't is fast;
Winter will not always last.
Jingle, jingle, clear the way!
'T is the merry, merry sleigh.

G. W. PETTEE.

OUR SKATER BELLE.

ALONG the frozen lake she comes
  In linking crescents, light and fleet;
The ice-imprisoned Undine hums
  A welcome to her little feet.

I see the jaunty hat, the plume
  Swerve birdlike in the joyous gale,—
The cheeks lit up to burning bloom,
  The young eyes sparkling through the veil.

The quick breath parts her laughing lips,
  The white neck shines through tossing curls;
Her vesture gently sways and dips,
  As on she speeds in shell-like whirls.

Men stop and smile to see her go;
  They gaze, they smile in pleased surprise;
They ask her name; they long to show
  Some silent friendship in their eyes.

She glances not; she passes on;
  Her steely footfall quicker rings;
She guesses not the benison
  Which follows her on noiseless wings.

Smooth be her ways, secure her tread
  Along the devious lines of life,
From grace to grace successive led,—
  A noble maiden, nobler wife!

ANONYMOUS.

O WINTER! WILT THOU NEVER GO?

O WINTER! wilt thou never, never go?
O summer! but I weary for thy coming,
Longing once more to hear the Luggie flow,
And frugal bees, laboriously humming.
Now the east-wind diseases the infirm,
And they must crouch in corners from rough
    weather;
Sometimes a winter sunset is a charm,—
When the fired clouds, compacted, blaze together,
And the large sun dips red behind the hills.
I, from my window, can behold this pleasure;
And the eternal moon, what time she fills
Her orb with argent, treading a soft measure,
With queenly motions of a bridal mood,
Through the white spaces of infinitude.

DAVID GRAY.

A SONG OF SEASONS.

SING a song of Spring-time!
    Catkins by the brook,
Adders-tongues uncounted,
    Ferns in every nook;
The cataract on the hillside
    Leaping like a fawn;
Sing a song of Spring-time,—
    Ah, but Spring-time's gone!

Sing a song of Summer!
    Flowers among the grass,

Clouds like fairy frigates,
　　Pools like looking-glass,
Moonlight through the branches,
　　Voices on the lawn;
Sing a song of Summer,—
　　Ah, but Summer 's gone!

Sing a song of Autumn!
　　Grain in golden sheaves,
Woodbine's crimson clusters
　　Round the cottage eaves,
Days of crystal clearness,
　　Frosted fields at dawn;
Sing a song of Autumn,—
　　Ah, but Autumn 's gone!

Sing a song of Winter!
　　North-wind's bitter chill,
Home and ruddy firelight,
　　Kindness and good-will,
Hemlock in the churches,
　　Daytime soon withdrawn;
Sing a song of Winter,—
　　Ah, but Winter 's gone!

Sing a song of loving!
　　Let the seasons go;
Hearts can make their gardens
　　Under sun or snow;
Fear no fading blossom,
　　Nor the dying day;
Sing a song of loving,—
　　That will last for aye!

ELIZABETH ROBERTS MACDONALD.

IV.

INLAND WATERS: HIGHLANDS.

THE VALLEY BROOK.

FRESH from the fountains of the wood
  A rivulet of the valley came,
And glided on for many a rood,
  Flushed with the morning's ruddy flame.

The air was fresh and soft and sweet;
  The slopes in spring's new verdure lay,
And wet with dew-drops at my feet
  Bloomed the young violets of May.

No sound of busy life was heard
  Amid those pastures lone and still,
Save the faint chirp of early bird,
  Or bleat of flocks along the hill.

I traced that rivulet's winding way;
  New scenes of beauty opened round,
Where meads of brighter verdure lay,
  And lovelier blossoms tinged the ground.

"Ah, happy valley stream!" I said,
  "Calm glides thy wave amid the flowers,
Whose fragrance round thy path is shed
  Through all the joyous summer hours.

"O, could my years, like thine, be passed
  In some remote and silent glen,
Where I could dwell and sleep at last,
  Far from the bustling haunts of men!"

But what new echoes greet my ear?
  The village school-boy's merry call;
And mid the village hum I hear
  The murmur of the waterfall.

I looked; the widening veil betrayed
  A pool that shone like burnished steel,
Where that bright valley stream was stayed
  To turn the miller's ponderous wheel.

Ah! why should I, I thought with shame,
  Sigh for a life of solitude,
When even this stream without a name
  Is laboring for the common good.

No longer let me shun my part
  Amid the busy scenes of life,
But with a warm and generous heart
  Press onward in the glorious strife.

JOHN HOWARD BRYANT.

SONG OF THE BROOK.

FROM "THE BROOK: AN IDYL."

I COME from haunts of coot and hern:
  I make a sudden sally
And sparkle out among the fern,
  To bicker down a valley.

By thirty hills I hurry down,
　Or slip between the ridges,
By twenty thorps, a little town,
　And half a hundred bridges.

Till last by Philip's farm I flow
　To join the brimming river,
For men may come and men may go,
　But I go on forever.

I chatter over stony ways,
　In little sharps and trebles,
I bubble into eddying bays,
　I babble on the pebbles.

With many a curve my banks I fret
　By many a field and fallow,
And many a fairy foreland set
　With willow-weed and mallow.

I chatter, chatter, as I flow
　To join the brimming river;
For men may come and men may go,
　But I go on forever.

I wind about, and in and out,
　With here a blossom sailing,
And here and there a lusty trout,
　And here and there a grayling,

And here and there a foamy flake
　Upon me, as I travel
With many a silvery waterbreak
　Above the golden gravel,

And draw them all along, and flow
　　To join the brimming river;
For men may come and men may go,
　　But I go on forever.

I steal by lawns and grassy plots:
　　I slide by hazel covers;
I move the sweet forget-me-nots
　　That grow for happy lovers.

I slip, I slide, I gloom, I glance,
　　Among my skimming swallows;
I make the netted sunbeam dance
　　Against my sandy shallows;

I murmur under moon and stars
　　In brambly wildernesses;
I linger by my shingly bars;
　　I loiter round my cresses;

And out again I curve and flow
　　To join the brimming river;
For men may come and men may go,
　　But I go on forever.

　　　　　　　　ALFRED, LORD TENNYSON.

———

THE SHADED WATER.

WHEN that my mood is sad, and in the noise
　　And bustle of the crowd I feel rebuke,
I turn my footsteps from its hollow joys
　　And sit me down beside this little brook;

The waters have a music to mine ear
    It glads me much to hear.

It is a quiet glen, as you may see,
    Shut in from all intrusion by the trees,
That spread their giant branches, broad and free,
    The silent growth of many centuries;
And make a hallowed time for hapless moods,
    A sabbath of the woods.

Few know its quiet shelter,—none, like me,
    Do seek it out with such a fond desire,
Poring in idlesse mood on flower and tree,
    And listening as the voiceless leaves respire,—
When the far-travelling breeze, done wandering,
    Rests here his weary wing.

And all the day, with fancies ever new,
    And sweet companions from their boundless
        store,
Of merry elves bespangled all with dew,
    Fantastic creatures of the old-time lore,
Watching their wild but unobtrusive play,
    I fling the hours away.

A gracious couch—the root of an old oak
    Whose branches yield it moss and canopy—
Is mine, and, so it be from woodman's stroke
    Secure, shall never be resigned by me;
It hangs above the stream that idly flies,
    Heedless of any eyes.

There, with eye sometimes shut, but upward bent,
    Sweetly I muse through many a quiet hour,

While every sense on earnest mission sent,
Returns, thought-laden, back with bloom and
      flower;
Pursuing, though rebuked by those who moil,
    A profitable toil.

And still the waters, trickling at my feet,
    Wind on their way with gentlest melody,
Yielding sweet music, which the leaves repeat,
    Above them, to the gay breeze gliding by,—
Yet not so rudely as to send one sound
    Through the thick copse around.

Sometimes a brighter cloud than all the rest
    Hangs o'er the archway opening through the
      trees,
Breaking the spell that, like a slumber, pressed
    On my worn spirit its sweet luxuries,—
And with awakened vision upward bent,
    I watch the firmament.

How like its sure and undisturbed retreat—
    Life's sanctuary at last, secure from storm—
To the pure waters trickling at my feet,
    The bending trees that overshade my form!
So far as sweetest things of earth may seem
    Like those of which we dream.

Such, to my mind, is the philosophy
    The young bird teaches, who, with sudden flight,
Sails far into the blue that spreads on high,
    Until I lose him from my straining sight,—
With a most lofty discontent to fly
    Upward, from earth to sky.

                 WILLIAM GILMORE SIMMS.

A FAREWELL.

FLOW down, cold rivulet, to the sea
    Thy tribute wave deliver:
No more by thee my steps shall be,
    For ever and for ever.

Flow, softly flow, by lawn and lea,
    A rivulet then a river:
No where by thee my steps shall be,
    For ever and for ever.

But here will sigh thine alder tree,
    And here thine aspen shiver;
And here by thee will hum the bee,
    For ever and for ever.

A thousand suns will stream on thee,
    A thousand moons will quiver;
But not by thee my steps shall be,
    For ever and for ever.
                ALFRED, LORD TENNYSON.

THE BIRCH STREAM.

AT noon, within the dusty town,
Where the wild river rushes down,
    And thunders hoarsely all day long,
I think of thee, my hermit stream,
Low singing in thy summer dream
    Thine idle, sweet, old, tranquil song.

Northward, Katahdin's chasmed pile
Looms through thy low, long, leafy aisle;
   Eastward, Olamon's summit shines;
And I upon thy grassy shore,
The dreamful, happy child of yore,
   Worship before mine olden shrines.

Again the sultry noontide hush
Is sweetly broken by the thrush,
   Whose clear bell rings and dies away
Beside thy banks, in coverts deep,
Where nodding buds of orchis sleep
   In dusk, and dream not it is day.

Again the wild cow-lily floats
Her golden-freighted, tented boats
   In thy cool coves of softened gloom,
O'ershadowed by the whispering reed,
And purple plumes of pickerel-weed,
   And meadow-sweet in tangled bloom.

The startled minnows dart in flocks
Beneath thy glimmering amber rocks,
   If but a zephyr stirs the brake;
The silent swallow swoops, a flash
Of light, and leaves, with dainty plash,
   A ring of ripples in her wake.

Without, the land is hot and dim;
The level fields in languor swim,
   Their stubble-grasses brown as dust;
And all along the upland lanes,
Where shadeless noon oppressive reigns,
   Dead roses wear their crowns of rust.

Within, is neither blight nor death;
The fierce sun wooes with ardent breath,
 But cannot win thy sylvan heart.
Only the child who loves thee long,
With faithful worship pure and strong,
 Can know how dear and sweet thou art.

So loved I thee in days gone by,
So love I yet, though leagues may lie
 Between us, and the years divide;
A breath of coolness, dawn, and dew,
A joy forever fresh and true,
 Thy memory doth with me abide.

ANNA BOYNTON AVERILL.

SONG OF THE RIVER.

CLEAR and cool, clear and cool,
By laughing shallow and dreaming pool;
Cool and clear, cool and clear,
By shining shingle and foaming weir;
Under the crag where the ouzel sings,
And the ivied wall where the church-bell rings,
Undefiled for the undefiled;
Play by me, bathe in me, mother and child!

Dank and foul, dank and foul,
By the smoky town in its murky cowl;
Foul and dank, foul and dank,
By wharf, and sewer, and slimy bank;
Darker and darker the further I go,
Baser and baser the richer I grow;

Who dare sport with the sin-defiled?
Shrink from me, turn from me, mother and child!

Strong and free, strong and free,
The flood-gates are open, away to the sea:
Free and strong, free and strong,
Cleansing my streams as I hurry along
To the golden sands and the leaping bar,
And the taintless tide that awaits me afar,
As I lose myself in the infinite main,
Like a soul that has sinned and is pardoned again,
Undefiled for the undefiled;
Play by me, bathe in me, mother and child!

CHARLES KINGSLEY.

AFTON WATER.

FLOW gently, sweet Afton, among thy green braes;
Flow gently, I 'll sing thee a song in thy praise;
My Mary 's asleep by thy murmuring stream,
Flow gently, sweet Afton, disturb not her dream.

Thou stock-dove whose echo resounds through the
     glen,
Ye wild whistling blackbirds in yon thorny den,
Thou green-crested lapwing, thy screaming for-
     bear;
I charge you disturb not my slumbering fair.

How lofty, sweet Afton, thy neighboring hills,
Far marked with the courses of clear-winding
     rills!
There daily I wander as noon rises high,
My flocks and my Mary's sweet cot in my eye.

How pleasant thy banks and green valleys below,
Where wild in the woodlands the primroses blow!
There oft as mild evening weeps over the lea,
The sweet-scented birk shades my Mary and me.

Thy crystal stream, Afton, how lovely it glides,
And winds by the cot where my Mary resides;
How wanton thy waters her snowy feet lave,
As, gathering sweet flowerets, she stems thy clear
    wave!

Flow gently, sweet Afton, among thy green braes;
Flow gently, sweet river, the theme of my lays;
My Mary 's asleep by thy murmuring stream,
Flow gently, sweet Afton, disturb not her dream.
ROBERT BURNS.

THE SNOWS.*

OVER the Snows
Buoyantly goes
The lumberers' bark canoe:
Lightly they sweep,
Wilder each leap,
Rending the white-caps through.
Away! Away!
With the speed of a startled deer,
While the steersman true
And his laughing crew
Sing of their wild career:

" Mariners glide
Far o'er the tide

---

* The name given to a foaming rapid on the Upper
Ottawa River, in Canada.

In ships that are stanch and strong:
　　Safely as they
　　Speed we away,
Waking the woods with song."
　　Away! Away!
With the speed of a startled deer,
　　While the laughing crew
　　Of the swift canoe
Sing of the raftsmen's cheer:

　　" Through forest and brake,
　　O'er rapid and lake,
We 're sport for the sun and rain;
　　Free as the child
　　Of the Arab wild,
Hardened to toil and pain.
　　Away! Away!
With the speed of a startled deer,
　　While our buoyant flight
　　And the rapid's might
Heighten our swift career."

　　Over the Snows
　　Buoyantly goes
The lumberers' bark canoe:
　　Lightly they sweep,
　　Wilder each leap,
Tearing the white-caps through.
　　Away! Away!
With the speed of a startled deer,
　　There 's a fearless crew
　　In each light canoe
To sing of the raftsmen's cheer.

CHARLES SANGSTER.

MY RIVER.

River! my river in the young sunshine!
  Oh, clasp afresh in thine embrace
This longing, burning frame of mine,
  And kiss my breast, and kiss my face!
So—there!—Ha, ha!—already in thine arms!
  I feel thy love—I shout—I shiver;
But thou outlaughest loud a flouting song, proud
      river,
    And now again my bosom warms!

The droplets of the golden sunlight glide
  Over and off me, sparkling, as I swim
Hither and thither down thy mellow tide,
    Or loll amid its crypts with outstretched
      limb;
I fling abroad my arms, and lo!
  Thy wanton waves curl slyly round me;
  But ere their loose chains have well bound
      me,
Again they burst away and let me go!

O sun-loved river! wherefore dost thou hum,
  Hum, hum alway, thy strange, deep, mystic
      song
Unto the rocks and strands?—for they are
      dumb,
  And answer nothing as thou flowest along.
Why singest so all hours of night and day?
Ah, river! my best river! thou, I guess, art seeking
Some land where souls have still the gift of speak-
      ing
  With nature in her own old wondrous way!

Lo! highest heaven looms far below me here;
  I see it in thy waters, as they roll,
    So beautiful, so blue, so clear,
'T would seem, O river mine, to be thy very soul!
Oh, could I hence dive down to such a sky,
  Might I but bathe my spirit in that glory,
  So far outshining all in ancient fairy story,
    I would indeed have joy to die!

What on cold earth is deep as thou? Is aught?
  Love is as deep, love only is as deep:
Love lavisheth all, yet loseth, lacketh naught;
    Like thee, too, love can neither pause nor
      sleep.
Roll on, thou loving river, thou! Lift up
Thy waves, those eyes bright with a riotous laugh-
    ing!
Thou makest me immortal! I am quaffing
  The wine of rapture from no earthly cup!

At last thou bearest me, with soothing tone,
  Back to thy bank of rosy flowers:
Thanks, then, and fare thee well! Enjoy thy bliss
    alone!
    And through the year's melodious hours
Echo forever from thy bosom broad
All glorious tales that sun and moon be telling:
And woo down to their soundless fountain dwell-
    ing
      The holy stars of God!

From the German of EDUARD MÖRIKE.

ON THE RHINE.

'T was morn, and beautiful the mountain's brow—
Hung with the clusters of the bending vine—
Shone in the early light, when on the Rhine
We sailed and heard the waters round the prow
In murmurs parting; varying as we go,
Rocks after rocks come forward and retire,
As some gray convent wall or sunlit spire
Starts up along the banks, unfolding slow.
Here castles, like the prisons of despair,
Frown as we pass;—there, on the vineyard's side,
The bursting sunshine pours its streaming tide;
While Grief, forgetful amid scenes so fair,
Counts not the hours of a long summer's day,
Nor heeds how fast the prospect winds away.

WILLIAM LISLE BOWLES.

OXUS.

FROM " SOHRAB AND RUSTUM."

But the majestic river floated on,
Out of the mist and hum of that low land,
Into the frosty starlight, and there moved,
Rejoicing, through the hushed Chorasmian waste,
Under the solitary moon;—he flowed
Right for the polar star, past Orgunjè,
Brimming, and bright, and large; then sands begin
 begin
To hem his watery march, and dam his streams,
And split his currents; that for many a league

The shorn and parcelled Oxus strains along
Through beds of sand and matted rushy isles—
Oxus, forgetting the bright speed he had
In his high mountain-cradle in Pamere,
A foiled circuitous wanderer—till at last
The longed-for dash of waves is heard, and wide
His luminous home of waters opens, bright
And tranquil, from whose floor the new-bathed
      stars
Emerge, and shine upon the Aral Sea.

                                    MATTHEW ARNOLD.

THE FALL OF NIAGARA.

THE thoughts are strange that crowd into my
      brain,
While I look upward to thee. It would seem
As if God poured thee from his hollow hand,
And hung his bow upon thine awful front,
And spoke in that loud voice which seemed to him
Who dwelt in Patmos for his Saviour's sake
The sound of many waters; and had bade
Thy flood to chronicle the ages back,
And notch his centuries in the eternal rocks.

    Deep calleth unto deep. And what are we,
That hear the question of that voice sublime?
O, what are all the notes that ever rung
From war's vain trumpet, by thy thundering side?
Yea, what is all the riot man can make
In his short life, to thy unceasing roar?
And yet, bold babbler, what art thou to Him

Who drowned a world, and heaped the waters far
Above its loftiest mountains?—a light wave,
That breaks, and whispers of its Maker's might.

JOHN GARDINER CALKINS BRAINARD.

TO SENECA LAKE.

On thy fair bosom, silver lake,
    The wild swan spreads his snowy sail,
And round his breast the ripples break,
    As down he bears before the gale.

On thy fair bosom, waveless stream,
    The dipping paddle echoes far,
And flashes in the moonlight gleam,
    And bright reflects the polar star.

The waves along thy pebbly shore,
    As blows the north-wind, heave their foam,
And curl around the dashing oar,
    As late the boatman hies him home.

How sweet, at set of sun, to view
    Thy golden mirror spreading wide,
And see the mist of mantling blue
    Float round the distant mountain's side.

At midnight hour, as shines the moon,
    A sheet of silver spreads below,
And swift she cuts, at highest noon,
    Light clouds, like wreaths of purest snow.

14

On thy fair bosom, silver lake,
  O, I could ever sweep the oar,
When early birds at morning wake,
  And evening tells us toil is o'er!

JAMES GATES PERCIVAL.

THE BUGLE.

FROM " THE PRINCESS."

THE splendor falls on castle walls
  And snowy summits old in story:
The long light shakes across the lakes,
  And the wild cataract leaps in glory.
Blow, bugle, blow, set the wild echoes flying,
Blow, bugle; answer, echoes, dying, dying, dying.

O hark! O hear! how thin and clear,
  And thinner, clearer, farther going!
O sweet and far, from cliff and scar,
  The horns of Elfland faintly blowing!
Blow, let us hear the purple glens replying:
Blow, bugle; answer, echoes, dying, dying, dying.

O love, they die in yon rich sky,
  They faint on hill or field or river;
Our echoes roll from soul to soul,
  And grow forever and forever.
Blow, bugle, blow, set the wild echoes flying,
And answer, echoes, answer, dying, dying, dying.

ALFRED, LORD TENNYSON.

THE LAKE ISLE OF INNISFREE.

I WILL arise and go now, and go to Innisfree,
And a small cabin build there, of clay and wattles
    made;
Nine bean rows will I have there, a hive for the
    honey bee,
And live alone in the bee-loud glade.

And I shall have some peace there, for peace comes
    dropping slow,
Dropping from the veils of the morning to where
    the cricket sings;
There 's midnight all a-glimmer, and noon a purple
    glow,
And evening full of the linnet's wings.

I will arise and go now, for always night and day
I hear lake water lapping with low sounds by the
    shore;
While I stand on the roadway, or on the pave-
    ments gray,
I hear it in the deep heart's core.

WILLIAM BUTLER YEATS.

CALM ON LAKE LEMAN.

FROM "CHILDE HAROLD," CANTO III.

CLEAR, placid Leman! thy contrasted lake,
With the wild world I dwelt in, is a thing
Which warns me, with its stillness, to forsake
Earth's troubled waters for a purer spring.

This quiet sail is as a noiseless wing
To waft me from distraction; once I loved
Torn ocean's roar, but thy soft murmuring
Sounds sweet as if a sister's voice reproved,
That I with stern delights should e'er have been
  so moved.

It is the hush of night, and all between
Thy margin and the mountains, dusk, yet clear,
Mellowed and mingling, yet distinctly seen,
Save darkened Jura, whose capt heights appear
Precipitously steep; and drawing near,
There breathes a living fragrance from the
  shore,
Of flowers yet fresh with childhood; on the ear
Drops the light drip of the suspended oar,
Or chirps the grasshopper one good-night carol
  more:

He is an evening reveller, who makes
His life an infancy, and sings his fill;
At intervals, some bird from out the brakes
Starts into voice a moment, then is still.
There seems a floating whisper on the hill,
But that is fancy; for the starlight dews
All silently their tears of love instil,
Weeping themselves away, till they infuse
Deep into Nature's breast the spirit of her hues.
                                        LORD BYRON.

THE SILENCE OF THE HILLS.

THE windy forest, rousing from its sleep,
Voices its heart in hoarse Titanic roar;
The ocean bellows from its rocky shore;
The cataract, that haunts the rugged steep,
Makes mighty music in its headlong leap;
The clouds have voices, and the rivers pour
Their floods in thunder down to ocean's floor;—
The hills alone mysterious silence keep.
They cannot rend the ancient chain that bars
Their iron lips, nor answer back the sea
That calls to them far off in vain; the stars
They cannot hail, nor their wild brooks. Ah me!
What cries from out their stony hearts will break,
In God's great day, when all that sleep shall wake!

WILLIAM PRESCOTT FOSTER.

STORM IN THE ALPS.

FROM "CHILDE HAROLD," CANTO III.

THE sky is changed!—and such a change! O
    night,
And storm, and darkness, ye are wondrous
    strong,
Yet lovely in your strength, as is the light
Of a dark eye in woman! Far along,
From peak to peak, the rattling crags among
Leaps the live thunder! Not from one lone
    cloud,
But every mountain now hath found a tongue,

And Jura answers, through her misty shroud,
Back to the joyous Alps, who call to her aloud!

And this is in the night:—most glorious night!
Thou wert not sent for slumber! let me be
A sharer in thy fierce and far delight,—
A portion of the tempest and of thee!
How the lit lake shines, a phosphoric sea,
And the big rain comes dancing to the earth!
And now again 't is black,—and now, the glee
Of the loud hills shakes with its mountain-
    mirth,
As if they did rejoice o'er a young earthquake's
    birth.

LORD BYRON.

DOVER CLIFF.

FROM " KING LEAR," ACT IV. SC. 6.

COME on, sir; here 's the place: stand still!
    How fearful
And dizzy 't is, to cast one's eyes so low!
The crows and choughs that wing the midway air
Show scarce so gross as beetles: half-way down
Hangs one that gathers samphire,—dreadful
    trade!
Methinks he seems no bigger than his head:
The fishermen, that walk upon the beach,
Appear like mice; and yon tall anchoring bark,
Diminished to her cock; her cock, a buoy
Almost too small for sight: the murmuring surge,
That on the unnumbered idle pebbles chafes,

Cannot be heard so high.—I 'll look no more;
Lest my brain turn, and the deficient sight
Topple down headlong.

SHAKESPEARE.

CHORAL SONG.

FROM "THE BACCHÆ."

On the mountains wild 't is sweet,
When faint with rapid dance our feet,
Our limbs on earth all careless thrown
With the sacred fawn-skins strown,
To quaff the goat's delicious blood,
A strange, a rich, a savage food.
    Then off again the revel goes
O'er Phrygian, Lydian mountain brows;
    Evoë! Evoë! leads the road,
    Bacchus's self the maddening god!
And flows with milk the plain, and flows with
    wine,
Flows with the wild bees' nectar-dews divine;
And soars, like smoke, the Syrian incense
    pale—
    The while the frantic Bacchanal
The beaconing pine torch on her wand
    Whirls around with rapid hand,
And drives the wandering dance about,
    Beating time with joyous shout,
    And casts upon the breezy air
    All her rich luxuriant hair;
    Ever the burthen of her song:—
    " Raging, maddening, haste along,

Bacchus's daughters, ye the pride
Of golden Tmolus's fabled side;
While your heavy cymbals ring,
Still your ' Evoë! Evoë!' sing!"
Evoë! the Evian god rejoices
In Phrygian tones and Phrygian voices,
When the soft holy pipe is breathing sweet,
In notes harmonious to her feet,
Who to the mountain, to the mountain
speeds;
Like some young colt that by its mother
feeds,
Gladsome with many a frisking bound,
The Bacchanal goes forth and treads the echoing
ground.

From the Greek of EURIPIDES.
Translation of H. H. MILMAN.

AN ALPINE DESCENT.

My mule refreshed, his bells
Jingled once more, the signal to depart,
And we set out in the gray light of dawn,
Descending rapidly,—by waterfalls
Fast frozen, and among huge blocks of ice
That in their long career had stopt midway;
At length, unchecked, unbidden, he stood still,
And all his bells were muffled. Then my guide,
Lowering his voice, addressed me:—" Through this
chasm
On, and say nothing,—for a word, a breath,
Stirring the air, may loosen and bring down

A winter's snow,—enough to overwhelm
The horse and foot that, night and day, defiled
Along this path to conquer at Marengo."

SAMUEL ROGERS.

FROM MONT BLANC.

MONT BLANC yet gleams on high:—the power is
    there,
The still and solemn power of many sights,
And many sounds, and much of life and death.
In the calm darkness of the moonless nights,
In the lone glare of day, the snows descend
Upon that Mountain; none beholds them there,
Nor when the flakes burn in the sinking sun,
Or the star-beams dart thro' them:—Winds con-
    tend
Silently there, and heap the snow with breath
Rapid and strong, but silently! Its home
The voiceless lightning in these solitudes
Keeps innocently, and like vapor broods
Over the snow. The secret strength of things
Which governs thought, and to the infinite dome
Of heaven is as a law, inhabits thee!
And what were thou, and earth, and stars, and
    sea,
If to the human mind's imaginings
Silence and solitude were vacancy?

PERCY BYSSHE SHELLEY.

V.

TREES: FLOWERS: PLANTS.

THE PRIMEVAL FOREST.

FROM "EVANGELINE," INTRODUCTION.

THIS is the forest primeval. The murmuring
    pines and the hemlocks,
Bearded with moss, and in garments green, in-
    distinct in the twilight,
Stand like Druids of eld, with voices sad and
    prophetic,
Stand like harpers hoar, with beards that rest on
    their bosoms.
Loud from its rocky caverns, the deep-voiced
    neighboring ocean
Speaks, and in accents disconsolate answers the
    wail of the forest.
This is the forest primeval; but where are the
    hearts that beneath it
Leaped like the roe, when he hears in the woodland
    the voice of the huntsman?

                HENRY WADSWORTH LONGFELLOW.

THE GREENWOOD TREE.

FROM "AS YOU LIKE IT," ACT II. SC. 5.

UNDER the greenwood tree
Who loves to lie with me,
And tune his merry note
Unto the sweet bird's throat,
Come hither, come hither, come hither;
Here shall he see
No enemy
But Winter and rough weather.

Who doth ambition shun
And loves to live i' the sun,
Seeking the food he eats,
And pleased with what he gets,
Come hither, come hither, come hither;
Here shall he see
No enemy
But Winter and rough weather.

SHAKESPEARE.

THE WIND AND THE PINE-TREE.

FROM "EDWIN THE FAIR."

THE tale was this:
The wind, when first he rose and went abroad
Through the waste region, felt himself at fault,
Wanting a voice; and suddenly to earth
Descended with a wafture and a swoop,

Where, wandering volatile from kind to kind,
He wooed the several trees to give him one.
First he besought the ash; the voice she lent
Fitfully with a free and lasting change
Flung here and there its sad uncertainties:
The aspen next; a fluttered frivolous twitter
Was her sole tribute: from the willow came,
So long as dainty summer dressed her out,
A whispering sweetness, but her winter note
Was hissing, dry, and reedy: lastly the pine
Did he solicit, and from her he drew
A voice so constant, soft, and lowly deep,
That there he rested, welcoming in her
A mild memorial of the ocean-cave
Where he was born.

SIR HENRY TAYLOR.

THE BRAVE OLD OAK.

A SONG to the oak, the brave old oak,
  Who hath ruled in the greenwood long;
Here's health and renown to his broad green
      crown,
  And his fifty arms so strong.
There's fear in his frown when the sun goes down,
  And the fire in the west fades out;
And he showeth his might on a wild midnight,
  When the storm through his branches shout.

  Then here's to the oak, the brave old oak,
    Who stands in his pride alone;
  And still flourish he, a hale green tree,
    When a hundred years are gone!

In the days of old, when the spring with cold
  Had brightened his branches gray,
Through the grass at his feet crept maidens sweet,
  To gather the dew of May.
And on that day to the rebeck gay
  They frolicked with lovesome swains;
They are gone, they are dead, in the churchyard
      laid,
  But the tree it still remains.

    Then here's, etc.

He saw the rare times when the Christmas chimes
  Were a merry sound to hear,
When the squire's wide hall and the cottage small
  Were filled with good English cheer.
Now gold hath the sway we all obey,
  And a ruthless king is he;
But he never shall send our ancient friend
  To be tossed on the stormy sea.

      Then here's to the oak, the brave old oak,
        Who stands in his pride alone;
      And still flourish he, a hale green tree,
        When a hundred years are gone!
                HENRY FOTHERGILL CHORLEY.

THE HOLLY-TREE.

O READER! hast thou ever stood to see
      The holly-tree?
The eye that contemplates it well perceives
      Its glossy leaves

Ordered by an intelligence so wise
As might confound the atheist's sophistries.

Below, a circling fence, its leaves are seen
    Wrinkled and keen;
No grazing cattle, through their prickly round,
    Can reach to wound;
But as they grow where nothing is to fear,
Smooth and unarmed the pointless leaves appear.

I love to view these things with curious eyes,
    And moralize;
And in this wisdom of the holly-tree
    Can emblems see
Wherewith, perchance, to make a pleasant rhyme,
One which may profit in the after-time.

Thus, though abroad, perchance, I might appear
    Harsh and austere;
To those who on my leisure would intrude,
    Reserved and rude;
Gentle at home amid my friends I 'd be,
Like the high leaves upon the holly-tree.

And should my youth—as youth is apt, I know—
    Some harshness show,
All vain asperities I, day by day,
    Would wear away,
Till the smooth temper of my age should be
Like the high leaves upon the holly-tree.

And as, when all the summer trees are seen
    So bright and green,

The holly-leaves their fadeless hues display
      Less bright than they;
But when the bare and wintry woods we see,
What then so cheerful as the holly-tree?

So, serious should my youth appear among
      The thoughtless throng;
So would I seem, amid the young and gay,
      More grave than they;
That in my age as cheerful I might be
As the green winter of the holly-tree.

                    ROBERT SOUTHEY.

A FOREST HYMN.

THE groves were God's first temples. Ere man
    learned
To hew the shaft, and lay the architrave,
And spread the roof above them,—ere he framed
The lofty vault, to gather and roll back
The sound of anthems; in the darkling wood,
Amidst the cool and silence, he knelt down,
And offered to the Mightiest solemn thanks
And supplication. For his simple heart
Might not resist the sacred influences
Which, from the stilly twilight of the place,
And from the gray old trunks that high in heaven
Mingled their mossy boughs, and from the sound
Of the invisible breath that swayed at once
All their green tops, stole over him, and bowed
His spirit with the thought of boundless power
And inaccessible majesty. Ah, why
Should we, in the world's riper years, neglect
God's ancient sanctuaries, and adore

Only among the crowd, and under roofs
That our frail hands have raised? Let me, at
    least,
Here, in the shadow of this agèd wood,
Offer one hymn,—thrice happy if it find
Acceptance in his ear.

                Father, thy hand
Hath reared these venerable columns, thou
Didst weave this verdant roof. Thou didst look
    down
Upon the naked earth, and forthwith rose
All these fair ranks of trees. They in thy sun
Budded, and shook their green leaves in thy
    breeze,
And shot towards heaven. The century-living
    crow,
Whose birth was in their tops, grew old and died
Among their branches, till at last they stood,
As now they stand, massy and tall and dark,
Fit shrine for humble worshipper to hold
Communion with his Maker. These dim vaults,
These winding aisles, of human pomp or pride
Report not. No fantastic carvings show
The boast of our vain race to change the form
Of thy fair works. But thou art here,—thou
    fill'st
The solitude. Thou art in the soft winds
That run along the summit of these trees
In music; thou art in the cooler breath
That from the inmost darkness of the place
Comes, scarcely felt; the barky trunks, the ground,
The fresh moist ground, are all instinct with thee.

Here is continual worship;—nature, here,
In the tranquillity that thou dost love,
Enjoys thy presence. Noiselessly around,
From perch to perch, the solitary bird
Passes; and yon clear spring, that, midst its herbs,
Wells softly forth and wandering steeps the roots
Of half the mighty forest, tells no tale
Of all the good it does. Thou hast not left
Thyself without a witness, in these shades,
Of thy perfections. Grandeur, strength, and grace
Are here to speak of thee. This mighty oak,—
By whose immovable stem I stand and seem
Almost annihilated,—not a prince,
In all that proud old world beyond the deep,
E'er wore his crown as loftily as he
Wears the green coronal of leaves with which
Thy hand has graced him. Nestled at his root
Is beauty, such as blooms not in the glare
Of the broad sun. That delicate forest flower
With scented breath, and look so like a smile,
Seems, as it issues from the shapeless mould,
An emanation of the indwelling Life,
A visible token of the upholding Love,
That are the soul of this wide universe.

My heart is awed within me when I think
Of the great miracle that still goes on,
In silence, round me,—the perpetual work
Of thy creation, finished, yet renewed
Forever. Written on thy works I read
The lesson of thy own eternity.
Lo! all grow old and die; but see again,
How on the faltering footsteps of decay
15

Youth presses,—ever gay and beautiful youth
In all its beautiful forms. These lofty trees
Wave not less proudly that their ancestors
Moulder beneath them. O, there is not lost
One of Earth's charms! upon her bosom yet,
After the flight of untold centuries,
The freshness of her far beginning lies,
And yet shall lie. Life mocks the idle hate
Of his arch-enemy Death,—yea, seats himself
Upon the tyrant's throne, the sepulchre,
And of the triumphs of his ghastly foe
Makes his own nourishment. For he came forth
From thine own bosom, and shall have no end.

    There have been holy men who hid themselves
Deep in the woody wilderness, and gave
Their lives to thought and prayer, till they out-
      lived
The generation born with them, nor seemed
Less aged than the hoary trees and rocks
Around them;—and there have been holy men
Who deemed it were not well to pass life thus.
But let me often to these solitudes
Retire, and in thy presence reassure
My feeble virtue. Here its enemies,
The passions, at thy plainer footsteps shrink
And tremble, and are still. O God! when thou
Dost scare the world with tempests, set on fire
The heavens with falling thunderbolts, or fill,
With all the waters of the firmament,
The swift dark whirlwind that uproots the woods
And drowns the villages; when, at thy call,
Uprises the great deep, and throws himself

Upon the continent, and overwhelms
Its cities,—who forgets not, at the sight
Of these tremendous tokens of thy power,
His pride, and lays his strifes and follies by?
O, from these sterner aspects of thy face
Spare me and mine, nor let us need the wrath
Of the mad unchainèd elements to teach
Who rules them. Be it ours to meditate,
In these calm shades, thy milder majesty,
And to the beautiful order of thy works
Learn to conform the order of our lives.

WILLIAM CULLEN BRYANT.

THE ARAB TO THE PALM.

NEXT to thee, O fair gazelle,
O Beddowee girl, beloved so well;

Next to the fearless Nedjidee,
Whose fleetness shall bear me again to thee;

Next to ye both, I love the palm,
With his leaves of beauty, his fruit of balm;

Next to ye both, I love the tree
Whose fluttering shadow wraps us three
With love and silence and mystery!

Our tribe is many, our poets vie
With any under the Arab sky;
Yet none can sing of the palm but I.

The marble minarets that begem
Cairo's citadel-diadem
Are not so light as his slender stem.

He lifts his leaves in the sunbeam's glance,
As the Almehs lift their arms in dance,—

A slumberous motion, a passionate sign,
That works in the cells of the blood like wine.

Full of passion and sorrow is he,
Dreaming where the beloved may be;

And when the warm south-winds arise,
He breathes his longing in fervid sighs,

Quickening odors, kisses of balm,
That drop in the lap of his chosen palm.

The sun may flame, and the sands may stir,
But the breath of his passion reaches her.

O tree of love, by that love of thine,
Teach me how I shall soften mine!

Give me the secret of the sun,
Whereby the wooed is ever won!

If I were a king, O stately tree,
A likeness, glorious as might be,
In the court of my palace I 'd build for thee;

With a shaft of silver, burnished bright,
And leaves of beryl and malachite;

With spikes of golden bloom ablaze,
And fruits of topaz and chrysoprase;

And there the poets, in thy praise,
Should night and morning frame new lays,—

New measures, sung to tunes divine;
But none, O palm, should equal mine!

BAYARD TAYLOR.

THE PALM–TREE.

Is it the palm, the cocoa-palm,
On the Indian Sea, by the isles of balm?
Or is it a ship in the breezeless calm?

A ship whose keel is of palm beneath,
Whose ribs of palm have a palm-bark sheath,
And a rudder of palm it steereth with.

Branches of palm are its spars and rails,
Fibres of palm are its woven sails,
And the rope is of palm that idly trails!

What does the good ship bear so well?
The cocoa-nut with its stony shell,
And the milky sap of its inner cell.

What are its jars, so smooth and fine,
But hollowed nuts, filled with oil and wine,
And the cabbage that ripens under the Line?

Who smokes his nargileh, cool and calm?
The master, whose cunning and skill could charm
Cargo and ship from the bounteous palm.

In the cabin he sits on a palm-mat soft,
From a beaker of palm his drink is quaffed,
And a palm thatch shields from the sun aloft!

His dress is woven of palmy strands,
And he holds a palm-leaf scroll in his hands,
Traced with the Prophet's wise commands!

The turban folded about his head
Was daintily wrought of the palm-leaf braid,
And the fan that cools him of palm was made.

Of threads of palm was the carpet spun
Whereon he kneels when the day is done,
And the foreheads of Islam are bowed as one!

To him the palm is a gift divine,
Wherein all uses of man combine,—
House and raiment and food and wine!

And, in the hour of his great release,
His need of the palm shall only cease
With the shroud wherein he lieth in peace.

" Allah il Allah!" he sings his psalm
On the Indian Sea, by the isles of balm;
" Thanks to Allah, who gives the palm!"

JOHN GREENLEAF WHITTIER.

THE GRAPE--VINE SWING.

LITHE and long as the serpent train,
  Springing and clinging from tree to tree,
Now darting upward, now down again,
  With a twist and a twirl that are strange to see;
Never took serpent a deadlier hold,
  Never the cougar a wilder spring,
Strangling the oak with the boa's fold,
  Spanning the beach with the condor's wing.

Yet no foe that we fear to seek,—
  The boy leaps wild to thy rude embrace;
Thy bulging arms bear as soft a cheek
  As ever on lover's breast found place;
On thy waving train is a playful hold
  Thou shalt never to lighter grasp persuade,
While a maiden sits in thy drooping fold,
  And swings and sings in the noonday shade!

O giant strange of our Southern woods!
  I dream of thee still in the well-known spot,
Though our vessel strains o'er the ocean floods,
  And the northern forest beholds thee not;
I think of thee still with a sweet regret,
  As the cordage yields to my playful grasp,—
Dost thou spring and cling in our woodlands yet?
  Does the maiden still swing in thy giant clasp?
                    WILLIAM GILMORE SIMMS.

THE PLANTING OF THE APPLE–TREE.

Come, let us plant the apple-tree.
Cleave the tough greensward with the spade;
Wide let its hollow bed be made;
There gently lay the roots, and there
Sift the dark mould with kindly care,
  And press it o'er them tenderly,
As round the sleeping infant's feet
We softly fold the cradle-sheet;
  So plant we the apple-tree.

What plant we in this apple-tree?
Buds, which the breath of summer days
Shall lengthen into leafy sprays;
Boughs where the thrush with crimson breast
Shall haunt, and sing, and hide her nest;
  We plant, upon the sunny lea,
A shadow for the noontide hour,
A shelter from the summer shower,
  When we plant the apple-tree.

What plant we in this apple-tree?
Sweets for a hundred flowery springs
To load the May-wind's restless wings,
When, from the orchard row, he pours
Its fragrance through our open doors;
  A world of blossoms for the bee,
Flowers for the sick girl's silent room,
For the glad infant sprigs of bloom,
  We plant with the apple-tree.

What plant we in this apple-tree!
Fruits that shall swell in sunny June,
And redden in the August noon,
And drop, when gentle airs come by,
That fan the blue September sky,
　While children come, with cries of glee,
And seek them where the fragrant grass
Betrays their bed to those who pass,
　At the foot of the apple-tree.

And when, above this apple-tree,
The winter stars are quivering bright,
And winds go howling through the night,
Girls, whose young eyes o'erflow with mirth,
Shall peel its fruit by cottage hearth,
　And guests in prouder homes shall see,
Heaped with the grape of Cintra's vine
　And golden orange of the Line,
　The fruit of the apple-tree.

The fruitage of this apple-tree
Winds and our flag of stripe and star
Shall bear to coasts. that lie afar,
Where men shall wonder at the view,
And ask in what fair groves they grew;
　And sojourners beyond the sea
Shall think of childhood's careless day
And long, long hours of summer play,
　In the shade of the apple-tree.

Each year shall give this apple-tree
A broader flush of roseate bloom,
A deeper maze of verdurous gloom,
And loosen, when the frost-clouds lower,

The crisp brown leaves in thicker shower,
  The years shall come and pass, but we
Shall hear no longer, where we lie,
The summer's songs, the autumn's sigh,
  In the boughs of the apple-tree.

  And time shall waste this apple-tree.
O, when its aged branches throw
Thin shadows on the ground below,
Shall fraud and force and iron will
Oppress the weak and helpless still?
  What shall the tasks of mercy be,
Amid the toils, the strifes, the tears
Of those who live when length of years
  Is wasting this apple-tree?

  " Who planted this old apple-tree? "
The children of that distant day
Thus to some agèd man shall say;
And, gazing on its mossy stem,
The gray-haired man shall answer them:
  " A poet of the land was he,
Born in the rude but good old times;
'T is said he made some quaint old rhymes
  On planting the apple-tree."

                WILLIAM CULLEN BRYANT.

AMONG THE REDWOODS.

FAREWELL to such a world! Too long I press
  The crowded pavement with unwilling feet.
Pity makes pride, and hate breeds hatefulness,
  And both are poisons. In the forest sweet

The shade, the peace! Immensity, that seems
To drown the human life of doubts and dreams.

Far off the massive portals of the wood,
   Buttressed with shadow, misty-blue, serene,
Waited my coming. Speedily I stood
   Where the dun wall rose roofed in plumy green.
Dare one go in?—Glance backward! Dusk as
      night
Each column, fringed with sprays of amber light.

Let me, along this fallen bole, at rest,
   Turn to the cool, dim roof my glowing face.
Delicious dark on weary eyelids prest!
   Enormous solitude of silent space,
But for a low and thunderous ocean sound,
Too far to hear, felt thrilling through the ground.

No stir nor call the sacred hush profanes;
   Save when from some bare tree-top, far on high,
Fierce disputations of the clamorous cranes
   Fall muffled, as from out the upper sky.
So still, one dreads to wake the dreaming air,
Breaks a twig softly, moves the foot with care.

The hollow dome is green with empty shade,
   Struck through with slanted shafts of after-
      noon;
Aloft, a little rift of blue is made,
   Where slips a ghost that last night was the
      moon.
Beside its pearl a sea-cloud stays its wing,
Beneath, a tilted hawk is balancing.

The heart feels not in every time and mood
  What is around it. Dull as any stone
I lay; then, like a darkening dream, the wood
  Grew Karnac's temple, where I breathed alone
In the awed air strange incense, and uprose
Dim, monstrous columns in their dread repose.

The mind not always sees; but if there shine
  A bit of fern-lace bending over moss,
A silky glint that rides a spider-line,
  On a trefoil two shadow spears that cross,
Three grasses that toss up their nodding heads,
With spring and curve like clustered fountain-
      threads,

Suddenly, through side windows of the eye,
  Deep solitudes, where never souls have met;
Vast spaces, forest corridors that lie
  In a mysterious world, unpeopled yet.
Because the outward eye was elsewhere caught,
The awfulness and wonder come unsought.

If death be but resolving back again
  Into the world's deep soul, this is a kind
Of quiet, happy death, untouched by pain
  Or sharp reluctance. For I feel my mind
Is interfused with all I hear and see;
As much a part of All as cloud or tree.

Listen! A deep and solemn wind on high;
  The shafts of shining dust shift to and fro;

The columned trees sway imperceptibly,
    And creak as mighty masts when trade-winds
        blow.
The cloudy sails are set; the earth ship swings
Along the sea of space to grander things.

EDWARD ROWLAND SILL.

THE VOICE OF THE GRASS.

HERE I come creeping, creeping everywhere;
        By the dusty roadside,
        On the sunny hillside,
        Close by the noisy brook,
        In every shady nook,
I come creeping, creeping everywhere.

Here I come creeping, smiling everywhere;
        All round the open door,
        Where sit the agèd poor;
        Here where the children play,
        In the bright and merry May,
I come creeping, creeping everywhere.

Here I come creeping, creeping everywhere;
        In the noisy city street
        My pleasant face you'll meet,
        Cheering the sick at heart
        Toiling his busy part,—
Silently creeping, creeping everywhere.

Here I come creeping, creeping everywhere;
        You cannot see me coming,
        Nor hear my low sweet humming;

For in the starry night,
And the glad morning light,
I come quietly creeping everywhere.

Here I come creeping, creeping everywhere;
More welcome than the flowers
In summer's pleasant hours;
The gentle cow is glad,
And the merry bird not sad,
To see me creeping, creeping everywhere.

Here I come creeping, creeping everywhere;
When you 're numbered with the dead
In your still and narrow bed,
In the happy spring I 'll come
And deck your silent home,—
Creeping, silently creeping everywhere.

Here I come creeping, creeping everywhere;
My humble song of praise
Most joyfully I raise
To Him at whose command
I beautify the land,
Creeping, silently creeping everywhere.
                              SARAH ROBERTS.

FLOWERS.

SPAKE full well, in language quaint and olden,
One who dwelleth by the castled Rhine,
When he called the flowers, so blue and golden,
Stars, that in earth's firmament do shine.

Stars they are, wherein we read our history,
  As astrologers and seers of eld;
Yet not wrapped about with awful mystery,
  Like the burning stars which they beheld.

Wondrous truths, and manifold as wondrous,
  God hath written in those stars above;
But not less in the bright flowerets under us
  Stands the revelation of his love.

Bright and glorious is that revelation,
  Writ all over this great world of ours,
Making evident our own creation,
  In these stars of earth, these golden flowers.

And the poet, faithful and far-seeing,
  Sees alike, in stars and flowers, a part
Of the self-same, universal being
  Which is throbbing in his brain and heart.

Gorgeous flowerets in the sunlight shining,
  Blossoms flaunting in the eye of day,
Tremulous leaves, with soft and silver lining,
  Buds that open only to decay;

Brilliant hopes, all woven in gorgeous tissues,
  Flaunting gayly in the golden light;
Large desires, with most uncertain issues,
  Tender wishes, blossoming at night;

These in flowers and men are more than seeming;
  Workings are they of the self-same powers
Which the poet, in no idle dreaming,
  Seeth in himself and in the flowers.

Everywhere about us are they glowing—
  Some, like stars, to tell us Spring is born;
Others, their blue eyes with tears o'erflowing,
  Stand, like Ruth, amid the golden corn;

Not alone in Spring's armorial bearing,
  And in Summer's green emblazoned field,
But in arms of brave old Autumn's wearing,
  In the centre of his brazen shield;

Not alone in meadows and green alleys,
  On the mountain-top, and by the brink
Of sequestered pools in woodland valleys,
  Where the slaves of Nature stoop to drink;

Not alone in her vast dome of glory,
  Not on graves of bird and beast alone,
But in old cathedrals, high and hoary,
  On the tombs of heroes, carved in stone;

In the cottage of the rudest peasant;
  In ancestral homes, whose crumbling towers,
Speaking of the Past unto the Present,
  Tell us of the ancient Games of Flowers.

In all places, then, and in all seasons,
  Flowers expand their light and soul-like wings,
Teaching us, by most persuasive reasons,
  How akin they are to human things.

And with childlike, credulous affection,
  We behold their tender buds expand—
Emblems of our own great resurrection,
  Emblems of the bright and better land.

                    HENRY WADSWORTH LONGFELLOW.

THE USE OF FLOWERS.

God might have bade the earth bring forth
  Enough for great and small,
The oak-tree and the cedar-tree,
  Without a flower at all.
We might have had enough, enough
  For every want of ours,
For luxury, medicine, and toil,
  And yet have had no flowers.

Then wherefore, wherefore were they made,
  All dyed with rainbow light,
All fashioned with supremest grace,
  Upspringing day and night:—
Springing in valleys green and low,
  And on the mountains high,
And in the silent wilderness
  Where no man passes by?

Our outward life requires them not,—
  Then wherefore had they birth?—
To minister delight to man,
  To beautify the earth;
To comfort man,—to whisper hope,
  Whene'er his faith is dim,
For who so careth for the flowers
  Will care much more for him!

MARY HOWITT.

16

HYMN TO THE FLOWERS.

DAY-STARS! that ope your frownless eyes to
    twinkle
From rainbow galaxies of earth's creation,
And dew-drops on her lonely altars sprinkle
    As a libation.

Ye matin worshippers! who bending lowly
  Before the uprisen sun, God's lidless eye,
Throw from your chalices a sweet and holy
    Incense on high.

Ye bright mosaics! that with storied beauty
  The floor of Nature's temple tessellate,
What numerous emblems of instructive duty
    Your forms create!

'Neath cloistered boughs, each floral bell that
    swingeth
And tolls its perfume on the passing air,
Makes Sabbath in the fields, and ever ringeth
    A call to prayer.

Not to the domes where crumbling arch and col-
    umn
Attest the feebleness of mortal hand,
But to that fane, most catholic and solemn,
    Which God hath planned;

To that cathedral, boundless as our wonder,
  Whose quenchless lamps the sun and moon
    supply;

Its choir the wings and waves, its organ thunder,
 Its dome the sky.

There, as in solitude and shade I wander
 Through the green aisles, or stretched upon the
    sod,
Awed by the silence, reverently ponder
 The ways of God,

Your voiceless lips, O flowers! are living preach-
    ers,
 Each cup a pulpit, every leaf a book,
Supplying to my fancy numerous teachers
 From loneliest nook.

Floral apostles! that in dewy splendor
 " Weep without woe, and blush without a
    crime,"
O, may I deeply learn, and ne'er surrender
 Your lore sublime!

" Thou wert not, Solomon, in all thy glory,
 Arrayed," the lilies cry, " in robes like ours!
How vain your grandeur! ah, how transitory
 Are human flowers!"

In the sweet-scented pictures, heavenly artist,
 With which thou paintest Nature's wide-spread
    hall,
What a delightful lesson thou impartest
 Of love to all!

Not useless are ye, flowers! though made for
    pleasure;
  Blooming o'er field and wave, by day and night,
From every source your sanction bids me treasure
    Harmless delight.

Ephemeral sages! what instructors hoary
  For such a world of thought could furnish
    scope?
Each fading calyx a *memento mori,*
    Yet fount of hope.

Posthumous glories! angel-like collection!
  Upraised from seed or bulb interred in earth,
Ye are to me a type of resurrection
    And second birth.

Were I in churchless solitudes remaining,
  Far from all voice of teachers and divines,
My soul would find, in flowers of God's ordaining,
    Priests, sermons, shrines!

              HORACE SMITH.

THE LIFE OF FLOWERS.

WHEN hath wind or rain
Borne hard upon weak plant that wanted me,
And I (however they might bluster round)
Walkt off? 'T were most ungrateful; for sweet
    scents
Are the swift vehicles of still sweeter thoughts,
And nurse and pillow the dull memory
That would let drop without them her best stores.

They bring me tales of youth and tones of love,
And 't is and ever was my wish and way
To let all flowers live freely, and all die
(Whene'er their Genius bids their souls depart)
Among their kindred in their native place.
I never pluck the rose; the violet's head
Hath shaken with my breath upon its bank
And not reproacht me; the ever-sacred cup
Of the pure lily hath between my hands
Felt safe, unsoiled, nor lost one grain of gold.

WALTER SAVAGE LANDOR.

THE EARLY PRIMROSE.

MILD offspring of a dark and sullen sire,
Whose modest form, so delicately fine,
  Was nursed in whirling storms
  And cradled in the winds;

Thee, when young Spring first questioned Win-
  ter's sway,
And dared the sturdy blusterer to the fight,
  Thee on this bank he threw
  To mark his victory.

In this low vale the promise of the year,
Serene, thou openest to the nipping gale,
  Unnoticed and alone,
  Thy tender elegance.

So virtue blooms, brought forth amid the storms
Of chill adversity; in some lone walk
  Of life she rears her head,
  Obscure and unobserved;

While every bleaching breeze that on her blows
Chastens her spotless purity of breast,
    And hardens her to bear
    Serene the ills of life.

                HENRY KIRKE WHITE.

TO DAFFODILS.

    FAIRE daffadills, we weep to see
    You haste away so soone;
As yet the early-rising sun
    Has not attained his noone.
        Stay, stay,
    Until the hastening day
        Has run
    But to the even-song;
And having prayed together, we
    Will goe with you along.

We have short time to stay as you,
    We have as short a spring;
As quick a growth, to meet decay,
    As you or anything.
        We die,
    As your hours doe, and drie
        Away,
    Like to the summer's raine,
Or as the pearles of morning's dew,
    Ne'er to be found againe.

                ROBERT HERRICK.

DAFFODILS.

I WANDERED lonely as a cloud
  That floats on high o'er vales and hills,
When all at once I saw a crowd,—
  A host of golden daffodils
Beside the lake, beneath the trees,
Fluttering and dancing in the breeze.

Continuous as the stars that shine
  And twinkle on the Milky Way,
They stretched in never-ending line
  Along the margin of a bay:
Ten thousand saw I, at a glance,
Tossing their heads in sprightly dance.

The waves beside them danced, but they
  Outdid the sparkling waves in glee;
A poet could not but be gay
  In such a jocund company;
I gazed—and gazed—but little thought
What wealth the show to me had brought.

For oft, when on my couch I lie,
  In vacant or in pensive mood,
They flash upon that inward eye
  Which is the bliss of solitude;
And then my heart with pleasure fills,
And dances with the daffodils.

                    WILLIAM WORDSWORTH.

TO THE DANDELION.

Dear common flower, that grow'st beside the
            way,
Fringing the dusty road with harmless gold!
        First pledge of blithesome May,
Which children pluck, and, full of pride, uphold—
    High-hearted buccaneers, o'erjoyed that they
An Eldorado in the grass have found,
        Which not the rich earth's ample round
        May match in wealth!—thou art more dear to
            me
        Than all the prouder summer-blooms may be.

Gold such as thine ne'er drew the Spanish prow
Through the primeval hush of Indian seas;
        Nor wrinkled the lean brow
Of age to rob the lover's heart of ease.
    'T is the spring's largess, which she scatters now
To rich and poor alike, with lavish hand;
        Though most hearts never understand
        To take it at God's value, but pass by
        The offered wealth with unrewarded eye.

Thou art my tropics and mine Italy;
To look at thee unlocks a warmer clime;
        The eyes thou givest me
Are in the heart, and heed not space or time:
    Not in mid June the golden-cuirassed bee
Feels a more summer-like warm ravishment
        In the white lily's breezy tent,
        His conquered Sybaris, than I, when first
        From the dark green thy yellow circles burst.

Then think I of deep shadows on the grass;
Of meadows where in sun the cattle graze,
    Where, as the breezes pass,
The gleaming rushes lean a thousand ways;
    Of leaves that slumber in a cloudy mass,
Or whiten in the wind; of waters blue,
      That from the distance sparkle through
    Some woodland gap; and of a sky above,
    Where one white cloud like a stray lamb doth
      move.

    My childhood's earliest thoughts are linked
      with thee;
The sight of thee calls back the robin's song,
    Who, from the dark old tree
Beside the door, sang clearly all day long;
    And I, secure in childish piety,
Listened as if I heard an angel sing
      With news from heaven, which he did bring
    Fresh every day to my untainted ears,
    When birds and flowers and I were happy
      peers.

    How like a prodigal doth nature seem
When thou, for all thy gold, so common art!
    Thou teachest me to deem
More sacredly of every human heart,
    Since each reflects in joy its scanty gleam
Of heaven, and could some wondrous secret show,
      Did we but pay the love we owe,
    And with a child's undoubting wisdom look
    On all these living pages of God's book.
               JAMES RUSSELL LOWELL.

TRAILING ARBUTUS.

Darlings of the forest!
  Blossoming, alone,
When Earth's grief is sorest
  For her jewels gone—
Ere the last snow-drift melts, your tender buds
  have blown.

Tinged with color faintly,
  Like the morning sky,
Or, more pale and saintly,
  Wrapped in leaves ye lie—
Even as children sleep in faith's simplicity.

There the wild wood-robin,
  Hymns your solitude;
And the rain comes sobbing
  Through the budding wood,
While the low south wind sighs, but dare not be
  more rude.

Were your pure lips fashioned
  Out of air and dew,
Starlight unimpassioned,
  Dawn's most tender hue,
And scented by the woods that gathered sweets
  for you?

Fairest and most lonely,
  From the world apart;

Made for beauty only,
Veiled from Nature's heart
With such unconscious grace as makes the dream
of Art!

Were not mortal sorrow
An immortal shade,
Then would I to-morrow
Such a flower be made,
And live in the dear woods where my lost child-
hood played.

ROOSE TERRY COOKE.

THE WOODSPURGE.

THE wind flapped loose, the wind was still,
Shaken out dead from tree and hill:
I had walked on at the wind's will,—
I sat now, for the wind was still.

Between my knees my forehead was,—
My lips, drawn in, said not Alas!
My hair was over in the grass,
My naked ears heard the day pass.

My eyes, wide open, had the run
Of some ten weeds to fix upon;
Among those few, out of the sun,
The woodspurge flowered, three cups in one.

From perfect grief there need not be
Wisdom or even memory:
One thing then learnt remains to me,—
The woodspurge has a cup of three.

DANTE GABRIEL ROSSETTI.

THE RHODORA.

LINES ON BEING ASKED, WHENCE IS THE FLOWER?

In May, when sea-winds pierced our solitudes,
I found the fresh rhodora in the woods,
Spreading its leafless blooms in a damp nook,
To please the desert and the sluggish brook:
The purple petals fallen in the pool
 Made the black waters with their beauty gay,—
Here might the red-bird come his plumes to cool,
 And court the flower that cheapens his array.
Rhodora! if the sages ask thee why
This charm is wasted on the marsh and sky,
Dear, tell them, that if eyes were made for seeing,
Then beauty is its own excuse for being.
 Why thou wert there, O rival of the rose!
I never thought to ask; I never knew,
 But in my simple ignorance suppose
The self-same Power that brought me there
  brought you.

RALPH WALDO EMERSON.

EARLY JUNE.

FROM " THYRSIS."

So, some tempestuous morn in early June,
 When the year's primal burst of bloom is o'er,
 Before the roses and the longest day—
 When garden-walks and all the grassy floor
  With blossoms red and white of fallen May
  And chestnut-flowers are strewn—.

So have I heard the cuckoo's parting cry,
From the .wet field, through the vext garden-
trees,
Come with the volleying rain and tossing
breeze :
The bloom is gone, and with the bloom go I!

Too quick despairer, wherefore wilt thou go?
Soon will the high Midsummer pomps come on,
Soon will the musk carnations break and
swell,
Soon shall we have gold-dusted snapdragon,
Sweet-William with his homely cottage-
smell,
And stocks in fragrant blow;
Roses that down the alleys shine afar,
And open, jasmine-muffled lattices,
And groups under the dreaming garden-
trees,
And the full moon, and the white evening-star.

MATTHEW ARNOLD.

TO VIOLETS.

WELCOME, maids of honor!
You doe bring
In the Spring,
And wait upon her.

She has virgins many,
Fresh and faire;
Yet you are
More sweet than any.

Y' are the maiden Posies,
     And, so grac't,
     To be plac't
'Fore damask roses.

Yet though thus respected,
     By and by
     Ye doe lie,
Poore girles! neglected.

ROBERT HERRICK.

A SEPTEMBER VIOLET.

For days the peaks wore hoods of cloud,
   The slopes were veiled in chilly rain;
We said: It is the Summer's shroud,
And with the brooks we moaned aloud,—
   Will sunshine never come again?

At last the west wind brought us one
   Serene, warm, cloudless, crystal day,
As though September, having blown
A blast of tempest, now had thrown
   A gauntlet to the favored May.

Backward to spring our fancies flew,
   And, careless of the course of time,
The bloomy days began anew.
Then, as a happy dream comes true,
   Or, as a poet finds his rhyme—

Half wondered at, half unbelieved—
   I found thee, friendliest of the flowers.

Then Summer's joys came back, green-leaved,
And its doomed dead, awhile reprieved,
   First learned how truly they were ours.

Dear violet! Did the Autumn bring
   The vernal dreams, till thou, like me,
Didst climb to thy imagining?
Or was it that the thoughtful Spring
   Did come again, in search of thee?

ROBERT UNDERWOOD JOHNSON.

THE WREATH.

Now will I weave white violets, daffodils
   With myrtle spray,
And lily bells that trembling laughter fills,
   And the sweet crocus gay:
With these blue hyacinth, and the lover's rose
   That she may wear—
My sun-maiden—each scented flower that blows,
   Upon her scented hair.

From the Greek of MELEAGER.
Translation of WILLIAM M. HARDINGE.

THE DEATH OF THE FLOWERS.

THE melancholy days are come, the saddest of the
   year,
Of wailing winds, and naked woods, and meadows
   brown and sear.
Heaped in the hollows of the grove, the autumn
   leaves lie dead;

They rustle to the eddying gust, and to the rab-
　　bit's tread.
The robin and the wren are flown, and from the
　　shrubs the jay,
And from the wood-top calls the crow through all
　　the gloomy day.

Where are the flowers, the fair young flowers, that
　　lately sprang and stood
In brighter light and softer airs, a beauteous sis-
　　terhood?
Alas! they all are in their graves; the gentle race
　　of flowers
Are lying in their lowly beds with the fair and
　　good of ours.
The rain is falling where they lie; but the cold
　　November rain
Calls not from out the gloomy earth the lovely
　　ones again.

The wind-flower and the violet, they perished long
　　ago,
And the brier-rose and the orchis died amid the
　　summer glow;
But on the hill the golden-rod, and the aster in
　　the wood,
And the yellow sunflower by the brook in autumn
　　beauty stood,
Till fell the frost from the clear cold heaven, as
　　falls the plague on men,
And the brightness of their smile was gone from
　　upland, glade, and glen.

And now, when comes the calm mild day, as still
    such days will come,
To call the squirrel and the bee from out their
    winter home;
When the sound of dropping nuts is heard,
    though all the trees are still,
And twinkle in the smoky light the waters of the
    rill;
The south-wind searches for the flowers whose
    fragrance late he bore,
And sighs to find them in the wood and by the
    stream no more.

And then I think of one who in her youthful
    beauty died,
The fair meek blossom that grew up and faded
    by my side.
In the cold moist earth we laid her, when the
    forests cast the leaf,
And we wept that one so lovely should have a life
    so brief;
Yet not unmeet it was that one, like that young
    friend of ours,
So gentle and so beautiful, should perish with the
    flowers.

WILLIAM CULLEN BRYANT.

SUNRISE: A HYMN OF THE MARSHES.

In my sleep I was fain of their fellowship, fain
Of the live-oak, the marsh and the main.
The little green leaves would not let me alone in
    my sleep.

17

Upbreathed from the marshes, a message of range
    and of sweep.

   .   .   .   .

I have waked, I have come, my belovèd! I might
    not abide:
I have come ere the dawn, O belovèd! my live-oaks,
    to hide
    In your gospelling glooms—to be
As a lover in heaven, the marsh my marsh, and the
    sea my sea.

Tell me, sweet burly-barked man-bodied Tree
That mine arms in the dark are embracing, dost
    know
From what fount are these tears at thy feet which
    flow?
They rise not from reason, but deeper inconse-
    quent deeps.
    Reason 's not one that weeps.
    What logic of greeting lies
Betwixt dear over-beautiful trees and the rain of
    the eyes?
O cunning green leaves, little masters! like as ye
    gloss
All the dull-tissued dark with your luminous
    darks that emboss
The vague blackness of night with pattern and
    plan,

   .   .   .   .

    Friendly, sisterly, sweetheart leaves,
Oh! rain me down from your darks that contain
    me
Wisdoms ye winnow from winds that pain me:

Soft down tremors of sweet-within-sweet,
That advise me of more than they bring; repeat
Me the woods-smell that swiftly but now brought
      health
From the heaven-side bank of the river of death;
Teach me the terms of silence, preach me
The passion of patience, sift me, impeach me;
    And there, oh! there,
As ye hang with your myriad palms upturned in
      the air,
      Pray me a myriad prayer.

     My gossip, the owl, is it thou
That out of the leaves of the low hanging bough,
As I pass to the beach, art stirred?
Dumb woods, have ye uttered a bird?
Reverend Marsh, low-couched along the sea,
Old Chemist, rapt in alchemy.
     Distilling silence, lo!
That which our father-age had died to know,
The menstruum that dissolves all matter—thou
Hast found it; for this silence, filling now
The globèd clarity of receiving space,
This solves us all: man, matter, doubt, disgrace,
Death, love, sin, sanity,
Must in your silence' clear solution lie.
Too clear! that crystal nothing who'll peruse?
The blackest night could bring us brighter news.
Yet precious qualities of silence haunt
Round these vast margins, ministrant.
Oh! if thy soul's at latter gasp for space,
With trying to breathe no bigger than thy race
Just to be fellowed, when that thou hast found

No man with room or grace enough of bound
To entertain that New thou tell'st, thou art—
'T is here, 't is here thou canst unhand thy heart
And breathe it freely, and breathe it free
By rangy marsh, in lone sea-liberty.

The tide 's at full; the marsh with flooded streams
Glimmers, a limpid labyrinth of dreams.
Each winding creek in grave entrancement lies,
A rhapsody of morning stars. The skies
Shine scant with one forked galaxy—
The marsh brags ten; looped on his breast they
　　lie.

　　Oh! what if a sound should be made!
　　Oh! what if a bound should be laid
To this bow-and-string tension of beauty and
　　silence a-spring,
To the bend of beauty the bow, or the hold of
　　silence the string!
I fear me, I fear me yon dome of diaphanous
　　gleam
Will break as a bubble o'erblown in a dream,
Yon dome of too tenuous tissues of space and of
　　night,
Overweighted with stars, overfreighted with light,
Oversated with beauty and silence, will seem
But a bubble that broke in a dream,
If a bound of degree to this grace be said
　　Or a sound or a motion made.

But no: it is made; list! somewhere—mystery!
　　where?
In the leaves? in the air?

In my heart? is a motion made:
'T is a motion of dawn, like a flicker of shade on
     shade
In the leaves, 't is palpable; low multitudinous
     stirring
Upwinds through the woods; the little ones, softly
     conferring,
Have settled, my lord 's to be looked for; so; they
     are still;
But the air and my heart and the earth are a-
     thrill.
And look where the wild duck sails around the
     bend of the river;
And look where a passionate shiver
Expectant is bending the blades
Of the marsh-grass in serial shimmers and
     shades;
And invisible wings, fast fleeting, fast fleeting,
     are beating
The dark overhead as my heart beats; and steady
     and free
Is the ebb-tide flowing from marsh to sea.
    (Run home, little streams,
    With your lapful of stars and dreams),
And a sailor is hoisting a-peak,
For list! down the inshore curve of the creek
    How merrily flutters the sail,
And lo! in the East! Will the East unveil?
The East is unveiled, the East has confessed
A flush! 't is dead! 't is alive! 't is dead ere the
     West
Was aware of it! nay, 't is abiding, 't is unwith-
     drawn!
Have a care, sweet Heaven! 'T is Dawn!

Now a dream of a flame through that dream of a
    flush is uprolled:
To the zenith ascending, a dome of undazzling
    gold
Is builded, in shape as a beehive, from out of the
    sea;
The hive is of gold undazzling; but oh! the Bee,
    The star-fed Bee, the build-fire Bee,
Of dazzling gold is the great Sun-Bee
That shall flash from the hive-hole over the sea.

Yet now the dew-drop, now the morning gray
Shall live their little lucid, sober day;
Ere with the Sun their souls exhale away.
Now in each pettiest, personal sphere of dew
The summed morn shines complete as in the blue,
Big dew-drop of all Heaven. With these lit
    shrines
O'er silvered to the furtherest sea-confines,
The sacramental marsh, one pious plain
Of worship lies. Peace to the ante-reign
Of Mary Morning, blissful mother mild,
Minded of naught but peace and of a Child.

Not slower than Majesty moves, for a mean and
    a measure
Of motion, not faster than dateless Olympian
    leisure
Might pace with unblown ample garments from
    pleasure to pleasure;
The wave-serrate sea-rim sinks unjarring, unreel-
    ing,
Forever revealing, revealing, revealing,

Edgewise, bladewise, halfwise, wholewise—'t is
     done!
    Good morrow, lord Sun!
With several voice, with ascription one,
The woods and the marsh and the sea and my soul
Unto thee, whence the glittering stream of all
     morrows doth roll,
Cry good, and past good, and most heavenly mor-
     row, lord Sun!

  •   •   •   •   •   •   •

                    SIDNEY LANIER.

THE IVY GREEN.

O, A dainty plant is the ivy green,
    That creepeth o'er ruins old!
Of right choice food are his meals, I ween,
    In his cell so lone and cold.
The walls must be crumbled, the stones decayed,
    To pleasure his dainty whim;
And the mouldering dust that years have made
    Is a merry meal for him.
        Creeping where no life is seen,
        A rare old plant is the Ivy green.

Fast he stealeth on, though he wears no wings,
    And a staunch old heart has he!
How closely he twineth, how tight he clings
    To his friend, the huge oak-tree!
And slyly he traileth along the ground,
    And his leaves he gently waves,
And he joyously twines and hugs around
    The rich mould of dead men's graves.

Creeping where grim death has been,
A rare old plant is the Ivy green.

Whole ages have fled, and their works decayed,
   And nations have scattered been;
But the stout old ivy shall never fade
   From its hale and hearty green.
The brave old plant in its lonely days
   Shall fatten upon the past;
For the stateliest building man can raise
   Is the ivy's food at last.
         Creeping on where Time has been,
         A rare old plant is the Ivy green.

                              CHARLES DICKENS.

THE MOUNTAIN FERN.

OH, the fern, the fern, the Irish hill fern,
That girds our blue lakes from Lough Ine to
      Lough Erne,
That waves on our crags like the plume of a king,
And bends like a nun over clear well and spring.
The fairies' tall palm-tree, the heath-bird's fresh
      nest,
And the couch the red-deer deems the sweetest
      and best;
With the free winds to fan it, and dew-drops to
      gem,
Oh, what can ye match with its beautiful stem?
From the shrine of St. Finbar, by lone Avon-
      bwee,

To the halls of Dunluce, with its towers by the
    sea,
From the hill of Knockthu to the rath of Moyvore,
Like a chaplet that circles our green island o'er,
In the bawn of the chief, by the anchorite's cell,
On the hill-top or greenwood, by streamlet or
    well,
With a spell on each leaf which no mortal can
    learn,
Oh, there never was plant like the Irish hill fern!

Oh, the fern, the fern, the Irish hill fern,
That shelters the weary, or wild roe, or kern;
Through the glens of Kilcoe rose a shout on the
    gale,
As the Saxons rushed forth in their wrath from
    the Pale,
With bandog and blood-hound, all savage to see,
To hunt through Cluncalla the wild rapparee.
Hark! a cry from yon dell on the startled ear
    rings,
And forth from the wood the young fugitive
    springs,
Through the copse, o'er the bog, and oh, saints
    be his guide!
His fleet step now falters, there 's blood on his
    side;
Yet onward he strains, climbs the cliff, fords the
    stream,
And sinks on the hill-top, 'mid bracken leaves
    green;
And thick o'er his brow are the fresh clusters
    piled,

And they cover his form as a mother her child,
And the Saxon is baffled. They never discern
Where it shelters and saves him, the Irish hill
    fern.

Oh, the fern, the fern, the Irish hill fern,
That pours a wild keen o'er the hero's gray cairn,
Go hear it at midnight, when stars are all out,
And the wind o'er the hill-side is moaning about,
With a rustle and stir, and a low wailing tone
That thrills through the heart with its whispering
    lone;
And ponder its meaning, when haply you stray
Where the halls of the stranger in ruin decay;
With night-owls for warders, the goshawk for
    guest,
And their dais of honor by cattle-hoof pressed,
With its foss choked with rushes, and spider webs
    flung,
Over walls where the marchmen their red weapons
    hung,
With a curse on their name, and a sigh for the
    hour
That tarries so long. Look what waves on the
    tower
With an omen and sign, and an augury stern,
'T is the green flag of Time, 't is the Irish hill fern.

ARTHUR GERALD GEOGHEGAN.

THE MAIZE.

" That precious seed into the furrow cast
Earliest in spring-time crowns the harvest last."
—PHŒBE CARY.

A song for the plant of my own native West,
  Where nature and freedom reside,
By plenty still crowned, and by peace ever blest,
  To the corn! the green corn of her pride!
In climes of the East has the olive been sung,
  And the grape been the theme of their lays;
But for thee shall a harp of the backwoods be
      strung,
  Thou bright, ever beautiful maize!

Afar in the forest the rude cabins rise,
  And send up their pillars of smoke,
And the tops of their columns are lost in the
      skies,
  O'er the heads of the cloud-kissing oak;
Near the skirt of the grove, where the sturdy
      arm swings
  The axe till the old giant sways,
And echo repeats every blow as it rings,
  Shoots the green and the glorious maize!

There buds of the buckeye in spring are the first,
  And the willow's gold hair then appears,
And snowy the cups of the dogwood that burst
  By the red bud, with pink-tinted tears.
And stripèd the bolls which the poppy holds up
  For the dew, and the sun's yellow rays,

And brown is the pawpaw's shade-blossoming
    cup,
  In the wood, near the sun-loving maize!

When through the dark soil the bright steel of
    the plough
Turns the mould from its unbroken bed
The ploughman is cheered by the finch on the
    bough,
  And the blackbird doth follow his tread.
And idle, afar on the landscape descried,
  The deep-lowing kine slowly graze,
And nibbling the grass on the sunny hillside
  Are the sheep, hedged away from the maize.

With spring-time and culture, in martial array
  It waves its green broadswords on high,
And fights with the gale, in a fluttering fray,
  And the sunbeams, which fall from the sky;
It strikes its green blades at the zephyrs at noon,
  And at night at the swift-flying fays,
Who ride through the darkness the beams of the
    moon,
  Through the spears and the flags of the maize!

When the summer is fierce still its banners are
    green,
  Each warrior's long beard groweth red,
His emerald-bright sword is sharp-pointed and
    keen,
  And golden his tassel-plumed head.
As a host of armed knights set a monarch at
    naught,

That defy the day-god to his gaze,
And, revived every morn from the battle that's
      fought,
  Fresh stand the green ranks of the maize!

But brown comes the autumn, and sear grows
      the corn,
  And the woods like a rainbow are dressed,
And but for the cock and the noontide horn
  Old Time would be tempted to rest.
The humming bee fans off a shower of gold
  From the mullein's long rod as it sways,
And dry grow the leaves which protecting infold
  The ears of the well-ripened maize!

At length Indian Summer, the lovely, doth come,
  With its blue frosty nights, and days still,
When distantly clear sounds the waterfall's hum,
  And the sun smokes ablaze on the hill!
A dim veil hangs over the landscape and flood,
  And the hills are all mellowed in haze,
While Fall, creeping on like a monk 'neath his
      hood,
  Plucks the thick-rustling wealth of the maize.

And the heavy wains creak to the barns large and
      gray,
  Where the treasure securely we hold,
Housed safe from the tempest, dry-sheltered away,
  Our blessing more precious than gold!
And long for this manna that springs from the
      sod

Shall we gratefully give him the praise,
The source of all bounty, our Father and God,
Who sent us from heaven the maize!

WILLIAM W. FOSDICK.

THE PUMPKIN.

O, GREENLY and fair in the lands of the sun,
The vines of the gourd and the rich melon run,
And the rock and the tree and the cottage enfold,
With broad leaves all greenness and blossoms all
  gold,
Like that which o'er Nineveh's prophet once grew,
While he waited to know that his warning was
  true,
And longed for the storm-cloud, and listened in
  vain
For the rush of the whirlwind and red fire-rain.

On the banks of the Xenil, the dark Spanish
  maiden
Comes up with the fruit of the tangled vine laden;
And the Creole of Cuba laughs out to behold
Through orange-leaves shining the broad spheres
  of gold;
Yet with dearer delight from his home in the
  North,
On the fields of his harvest the Yankee looks forth,
Where crook-necks are coiling and yellow fruit
  shines,
And the sun of September melts down on his
  vines.

Ah! on Thanksgiving Day, when from East and
    from West,
From North and from South come the pilgrim
    and guest,
When the gray-haired New-Englander sees round
    his board
The old broken links of affection restored,
When the care-wearied man seeks his mother
    once more,
And the worn matron smiles where the girl
    smiled before,
What moistens the lip and what brightens the
    eye?
What calls back the past, like the rich pumpkin-
    pie?

O, fruit loved of boyhood! the old days recalling;
When wood-grapes were purpling and brown nuts
    were falling!
When wild, ugly faces we carved in its skin,
Glaring out through the dark with a candle
    within!
When we laughed round the corn-heap, with
    hearts all in tune,
Our chair a broad pumpkin, our lantern the moon,
Telling tales of the fairy who travelled like steam
In a pumpkin-shell coach, with two rats for her
    team!

Then thanks for thy present!—none sweeter or
    better
E'er smoked from an oven or circled a platter!

Fairer hands never wrought at a pastry more
  fine,
Brighter eyes never watched o'er its baking, than
  thine!
And the prayer, which my mouth is too full to
  express,
Swells my heart that thy shadow may never be
  less,
That the days of thy lot may be lengthened below,
And the fame of thy worth like a pumpkin-vine
  grow,
And thy life be as sweet, and its last sunset sky
Golden-tinted and fair as thy own pumpkin-pie!

                    JOHN GREENLEAF WHITTIER.

THE QUESTION.

I.

I DREAMED that, as I wandered by the way,
  Bare winter suddenly was changed to spring,
And gentle odors led my steps astray,
  Mixt with a sound of waters murmuring
Along a shelving bank of turf, which lay
  Under a copse, and hardly dared to fling
Its green arms round the bosom of the stream,
But kist it and then fled, as thou mightest in
    dream.

II.

There grew pied wind-flowers and violets,
  Daisies, those pearled Arcturi of the earth,
The constellated flower that never sets;
  Faint oxslips; tender bluebells, at whose birth

The sod scarce heaved; and that tall flower that
    wets—
Like a child, half in tenderness and mirth—
Its mother's face with heaven's collected tears,
When the low wind, its playmate's voice, it hears.

III.

And in the warm hedge grew lush eglantine,
    Green cowbind and the moonlight colored May,
And cherry-blossoms, and white cups, whose wine
    Was the bright dew, yet drained not by the
        day;
And wild roses, and ivy serpentine,
    With its dark buds and leaves, wandering
        astray;
And flowers azure, black, and streakt with gold,
Fairer than any wakened eyes behold.

IV.

And nearer to the river's trembling edge
    There grew broad flag-flowers, purple prankt
        with white,
And starry river buds among the sedge,
    And floating water-lilies, broad and bright,
Which lit the oak that overhung the hedge
    With moonlight beams of their own watery
        light;
And bulrushes, and reeds of such deep green
As soothed the dazzled eye with sober sheen.

V.

Methought that of these visionary flowers
    I made a nosegay bound in such a way
18

That the same hues, which in their natural
    bowers
Were mingled or opposed, the like array
Kept these imprisoned children of the Hours
    Within my hand,—and then, elate and gay,
I hastened to the spot whence I had come,
That I might there present it!—oh! to whom?

PERCY BYSSHE SHELLEY.

SASSAFRAS.

FRINGING cypress forests dim
    Where the owl makes weird abode,
Bending down with spicy limb
    O'er the old plantation road
Through the swamp and up the hill,
    Where the dappled byways run,
Round the gin-house, by the mill,
    Floats its incense to the sun.

Swift to catch the voice of spring,
    Soon its tasselled blooms appear;
Modest in their blossoming,
    Breathing balm and waving cheer;
Rare the greeting that they send
    To the fragrant wildwood blooms,
Bidding every blossom blend
    In a chorus of perfumes.

On it leans the blackberry vine,
    With white sprays caressingly;
Round its knees the wild peas twine,
    Beckoning to the yellow bee;

Through its boughs the red-bird flits
  Like a living flake of fire,
And with love-enlightened wits
  Weaves his nest and tunes his lyre.

Oh, where skies are summer-kissed,
  And the drowsy days are long,
'Neath the sassafras to list
  To the field-hand's mellow song!
Or, more sweet than chimes that hang
  In some old cathedral dome,
Catch the distant klingle-klang
  Of the cow-bells tinkling home!

SAMUEL MINTURN PECK.

THE DAISY.

FROM THE " LEGEND OF GOOD WOMEN."

Of all the floures in the mede,
Than love I most these floures white and rede,
Soch that men callen daisies in our town;
To hem I have so great affection,
As I said erst, when comen is the May,
That in my bedde there daweth me no day
That I nam * up and walking in the mede,
To seene this flour ayenst the Sunne sprede,
Whan it up riseth early by the morrow.
That blissful sight softeneth all my sorrow,
So glad am I, whan that I have the presence
Of it, to done it all reverence,
And ever I love it, and ever ylike newe,

* I am not.

And ever shall, till that mine herte die
All swere I not, of this I will not lie.

.   .   .   .

My busie gost, that thursteth alway newe,
To seen·this flour so yong, so fresh of hew,
Constrained me, with so greedy desire,
That in my herte I fele yet the fire,
That made me rise ere it were day,
And this was now the first morow of May,
With dreadful* herte, and glad devotion
For to been at the resurrection
Of this floure, whan that it should unclose
Againe the Sunne, that rose as redde as rose.
And doune on knees anon right I me sette,
And as I could, this fresh floure I grette,
Kneeling alway, till it unclosed was,
Upon the small, soft, swete gras,
That was with floures swete embrouded all,
Of such swetenesse, and such odour overall
That for to speke of gomme, herbe, or tree,
Comparison may not ymaked be,
For it surmounteth plainly all odoures,
And of rich beaute of floures.
And Zephirus, and Flora gentelly,
Yave to these floures soft and tenderly,
His swote† breth, and made him for to sprede,
As god and goddesse of the flourie mede,
In which me thoughte I might day by day,
Dwellen alway, the joly month of May,
Withouten slepe, withouten meat or drinke:
Adoune full softly I gan to sinke,

* Fearful.   † Sweet.

And leaning on my elbow and my side,
The long day I shope me for to abide,
For nothing els, and I shall nat lie,
But for to looke upon the daisie,
That well by reason men it call may
The daisie, or els the eye of the day,
The empress and floure of floures all,
I pray to God that faire mote she fall,
And all that loven floures for her sake.

CHAUCER.

TO A MOUNTAIN DAISY.

ON TURNING ONE DOWN WITH THE PLOUGH IN
APRIL, 1786.

Wee, modest, crimson-tippèd flower,
Thou 's met me in an evil hour,
For I maun crush amang the stoure
    Thy slender stem;
To spare thee now is past my power,
    Thou bonny gem.

Alas! it 's no thy neebor sweet,
The bonnie lark, companion meet,
Bending thee 'mang the dewy weet,
    Wi' spreckled breast,
When upward springing, blithe to greet
    The purpling east.

Cauld blew the bitter-biting north
Upon thy early, humble birth;
Yet cheerfully thou glinted forth

Amid the storm,
Scarce reared above the parent earth
Thy tender form.

The flaunting flowers our gardens yield
High sheltering woods and wa's maun shield:
But thou beneath the random bield
O' clod or stane,
Adorns the histie stibble-field,
Unseen, alane.

There, in thy scanty mantle clad,
Thy snawie bosom sunward spread,
Thou lifts thy unassuming head
In humble guise;
But now the share uptears thy bed,
And low thou lies!

Such is the fate of artless maid,
Sweet floweret of the rural shade!
By love's simplicity betrayed,
And guileless trust,
Till she, like thee, all soiled, is laid
Low i' the dust.

Such is the fate of simple bard,
On life's rough ocean luckless starred!
Unskilful he to note the card
Of prudent lore,
Till billows rage, and gales blow hard,
And whelm him o'er!

Such fate to suffering worth is given,
Who long with wants and woes has striven,

By human pride or cunning driven
    To misery's brink,
Till, wrenched of every stay but Heaven,
    He, ruined, sink!

Even thou who mourn'st the daisy's fate,
That fate is thine,—no distant date:
Stern Ruin's ploughshare drives, elate,
    Full on thy bloom,
Till crushed beneath the furrow's weight
    Shall be thy doom!

ROBERT BURNS.

TO BLOSSOMS.

FAIR pledges of a fruitful tree,
    Why do ye fall so fast?
    Your date is not so past
But you may stay yet here awhile
    To blush and gently smile,
    And go at last.

What! were ye born to be
    An hour or half's delight,
    And so to bid good-night?
'T is pity Nature brought ye forth,
    Merely to show your worth,
    And lose you quite.

But you are lovely leaves, where we
    May read how soon things have
    Their end, though ne'er so brave;
And after they have shown their pride
    Like you awhile, they glide
    Into the grave.

ROBERT HERRICK.

THE MARIPOSA LILY.

INSECT or blossom?   Fragile, fairy thing,
Poised upon slender tip, and quivering
To flight! a flower of the fields of air;
A jewelled moth; a butterfly, with rare
And tender tints upon his downy wing,
A moment resting in our happy sight;
A flower held captive by a thread so slight
Its petal-wings of broidered gossamer
Are, light as the wind, with every wind astir,—
Wafting sweet odor, faint and exquisite.
O dainty nursling of the field and sky,
What fairer thing looks up to heaven's blue
And drinks the noontide sun, the dawning's dew?
Thou wingèd bloom! thou blossom-butterfly!

                              INA DONNA COOLBRITH.

THE WATER–LILY.

WHENCE, O fragrant form of light,
Hast thou drifted through the night,
Swanlike, to a leafy nest,
On the restless waves, at rest?

Art thou from the snowy zone
Of a mountain-summit blown,
Or the blossom of a dream,
Fashioned in the foamy stream?

Nay,—methinks the maiden moon,
When the daylight came too soon,
Fleeting from her bath to hide,
Left her garment in the tide.

JOHN BANISTER TABB.

COPA DE ORO.

(CALIFORNIA POPPY.)

THY satin vesture richer is than looms
  Of Orient weave for raiment of her kings!
  Not dyes of olden Tyre, not precious things
Regathered from the long-forgotten tombs
Of buried empires, not the iris plumes
  That wave upon the tropics' myriad wings,
  Not all proud Sheba's queenly offerings,
Could match the golden marvel of thy blooms.
For thou art nurtured from the treasure-veins
  Of this fair land: thy golden rootlets sup
    Her sands of gold—of gold thy petals spun.
Her golden glory, thou! on hills and plains,
  Lifting, exultant, every kingly cup
    Brimmed with the golden vintage of the sun.

INA DONNA COOLBRITH.

THE MOSS ROSE.

THE angel of the flowers, one day,
Beneath a rose-tree sleeping lay,—
That spirit to whose charge 't is given
To bathe young buds in dews of heaven.

Awaking from his light repose,
The angel whispered to the rose:
" O fondest object of my care,
Still fairest found, where all are fair;
For the sweet shade thou giv'st to me
Ask what thou wilt, 't is granted thee."
" Then," said the rose, with deepened glow,
" On me another grace bestow."
The spirit paused, in silent thought,
What grace was there that flower had not?
'T was but a moment,—o'er the rose
A veil of moss the angel throws,
And, robed in nature's simplest weed,
Could there a flower that rose exceed?

From the German of F. W. KRUMMACHER.

FLOWERS.

I WILL not have the mad Clytie,
　　Whose head is turned by the sun;
The tulip is a courtly quean,
　　Whom, therefore, I will shun:
The cowslip is a country wench,
　　The violet is a nun;—
But I will woo the dainty rose,
　　The queen of every one.

The pea is but a wanton witch,
　　In too much haste to wed,
And clasps her rings on every hand;
　　The wolfsbane I should dread;
Nor will I dreary rosemarye,
　　That always mourns the dead;

But I will woo the dainty rose,
  With her cheeks of tender red.

The lily is all in white, like a saint,
  And so is no mate for me;
And the daisy's cheek is tipped with a blush
  She is of such low degree;
Jasmine is sweet, and has many loves,
  And the broom 's betrothed to the bee;—
But I will plight with the dainty rose,
  For fairest of all is she.

THOMAS HOOD.

'T IS THE LAST ROSE OF SUMMER.

FROM "IRISH MELODIES."

'T is the last rose of summer,
  Left blooming alone;
All her lovely companions
  Are faded and gone;
No flower of her kindred,
  No rosebud, is nigh
To reflect back her blushes,
  Or give sigh for sigh!

I 'll not leave thee, thou lone one!
  To pine on the stem;
Since the lovely are sleeping,
  Go, sleep thou with them;
Thus kindly I scatter
  Thy leaves o'er the bed
Where thy mates of the garden
  Lie scentless and dead.

So soon may *I* follow,
  When friendships decay,
And from love's shining circle
  The gems drop away!
When true hearts lie withered,
  And fond ones are flown,
O, who would inhabit
  This bleak world alone?

THOMAS MOORE.

TO THE FRINGED GENTIAN.

THOU blossom, bright with autumn dew,
And colored with the heaven's own blue,
That openest when the quiet light
Succeeds the keen and frosty night;

Thou comest not when violets lean
O'er wandering brooks and springs unseen,
Or columbines, in purple dressed,
Nod o'er the ground-bird's hidden nest.

Thou waitest late, and com'st alone,
When woods are bare and birds are flown,
And frosts and shortening days portend
The aged Year is near his end.

Then doth thy sweet and quiet eye
Look through its fringes to the sky,
Blue—blue—as if that sky let fall
A flower from its cerulean wall.

I would that thus, when I shall see
The hour of death draw near to me,
Hope, blossoming within my heart,
May look to heaven as I depart.

WILLIAM CULLEN BRYANT.

THE SEA-POPPY.

A POPPY grows upon the shore
  Bursts her twin cup in summer late:
Her leaves are glaucous green and hoar,
  Her petals yellow, delicate.

Oft to her cousins turns her thought,
  In wonder if they care that she
Is fed with spray for dew, and caught
  By every gale that sweeps the sea.

She has no lovers like the Red
  That dances with the noble Corn:
Her blossoms on the waves are shed,
  Where she sits shivering and forlorn.

ROBERT SEYMOUR BRIDGES.

GOLDENROD.

WHEN the wayside tangles blaze
  In the low September sun,
When the flowers of Summer days
  Droop and wither, one by one,
Reaching up through bush and brier,
Sumptuous brow and heart of fire,
Flaunting high its wind-rocked plume,

Brave with wealth of native bloom,—
    Goldenrod!

When the meadow, lately shorn,
  Parched and languid, swoons with pain,
When her life-blood, night and morn,
  Shrinks in every throbbing vein,
Round her fallen, tarnished urn
Leaping watch-fires brighter burn;
Royal arch o'er Autumn's gate,
Bending low with lustrous weight,—
    Goldenrod!

In the pasture's rude embrace,
  All o'errun with tangled vines,
Where the thistle claims its place,
  And the straggling hedge confines,
Bearing still the sweet impress
Of unfettered loveliness,
In the field and by the wall,
Binding, clasping, crowning all,—
    Goldenrod!

Nature lies dishevelled, pale,
  With her feverish lips apart,—
Day by day the pulses fail,
  Nearer to her bounding heart;
Yet that slackened grasp doth hold
Store of pure and genuine gold;
Quick thou comest, strong and free,
Type of all the wealth to be,—
    Goldenrod!

ELAINE GOODALE EASTMAN.

VI.

ANIMATE NATURE.

—

THE FIRST BLUE-BIRD.

JEST rain and snow! and rain again!
  And dribble! drip! and blow!
Then snow! and thaw! and slush! and then—
  Some more rain and snow!

This morning I was 'most afeard
  To *wake* up—when, I jing!
I seen the sun shine out and heerd
  The first blue-bird of Spring!—
Mother she 'd raised the winder some;—
And in acrost the orchard come,
  Soft as an angel's wing,
A breezy, treesy, beesy hum,
  Too sweet for any thing!

The winter's shroud was rent apart—
  The sun bust forth in glee,—
And when *that blue-bird* sung, my hart
  Hopped out o' bed with me!
                    JAMES WHITCOMB RILEY.

BIRDS.

FROM " THE PELICAN ISLAND."

—Birds, the free tenants of land, air, and ocean,
Their forms all symmetry, their motions grace;
In plumage, delicate and beautiful,
Thick without burden, close as fishes' scales,
Or loose as full-grown poppies to the breeze;
With wings that might have had a soul within
    them,
They bore their owners by such sweet enchant-
    ment,
—Birds, small and great, of endless shapes and
    colors,
Here flew and perched, there swam and dived at
    pleasure;
Watchful and agile, uttering voices wild
And harsh, yet in accordance with the waves
Upon the beach, the wind in caverns moaning,
Or winds and waves abroad upon the water.
Some sought their food among the finny shoals,
Swift darting from the clouds, emerging soon
With slender captives glittering in their beaks;
These in recesses of steep crags constructed
Their eyries inaccessible, and trained
Their hardy broods to forage in all weathers:
Others, more gorgeously apparelled, dwelt
Among the woods, on nature's daintiest feeding,
Herbs, seeds, and roots; or, ever on the wing,
Pursuing insects through the boundless air:
In hollow trees or thickets these concealed

Their exquisitely woven nests; where lay
Their callow offspring, quiet as the down
On their own breasts, till from her search the
    dam
With laden bill returned, and shared the meal
Among her clamorous suppliants, all agape;
Then, cowering o'er them with expanded wings,
She felt how sweet it is to be a mother.
Of these, a few, with melody untaught,
Turned all the air to music within hearing,
Themselves unseen; while bolder quiristers
On loftiest branches strained their clarion-pipes,
And made the forest echo to their screams
Discordant,—yet there was no discord there,
But tempered harmony; all tones combining,
In the rich confluence of ten thousand tongues,
To tell of joy and to inspire it. Who
Could hear such concert, and not join in chorus?
JAMES MONTGOMERY.

TO THE CUCKOO.

HAIL, beauteous stranger of the grove!
    Thou messenger of spring!
Now Heaven repairs thy rural seat,
    And woods thy welcome sing.

What time the daisy decks the green,
    Thy certain voice we hear.
Hast thou a star to guide thy path,
    Or mark the rolling year?

Delightful visitant! with thee
    I hail the time of flowers,

19

And hear the sound of music sweet
    From birds among the bowers.

The school-boy, wandering through the wood
    To pull the primrose gay,
Starts, the new voice of Spring to hear,
    And imitates thy lay.

What time the pea puts on the bloom,
    Thou fliest thy vocal vale,
An annual guest in other lands,
    Another spring to hail.

Sweet bird! thy bower is ever green,
    Thy sky is ever clear;
Thou hast no sorrow in thy song,
    No winter in thy year!

O, could I fly, I 'd fly with thee!
    We 'd make, with joyful wing,
Our annual visit o'er the globe,
    Companions of the Spring.

JOHN LOGAN.

TO THE CUCKOO.

O BLITHE new-comer! I have heard,
    I hear thee and rejoice.
A cuckoo! shall I call thee bird,
    Or but a wandering voice?

While I am lying on the grass
    Thy twofold shout I hear;

From hill to hill it seems to pass,
    At once far off and near.

Though babbling only to the vale
    Of sunshine and of flowers,
Thou bringest unto me a tale
    Of visionary hours.

Thrice welcome, darling of the spring!
    Even yet thou art to me
No bird, but an invisible thing,
    A voice, a mystery;

The same whom in my school-boy days
    I listened to; that cry
Which made me look a thousand ways,
    In bush and tree and sky.

To seek thee did I often rove
    Through woods and on the green;
And thou wert still a hope, a love;
    Still longed for, never seen.

And I can listen to thee yet;
    Can lie upon the plain
And listen, till I do beget
    That golden time again.

O blessèd bird! the earth we pace
    Again appears to be
An unsubstantial, fairy place;
    That is fit home for thee!

WILLIAM WORDSWORTH.

HARK, HARK! THE LARK.

FROM "CYMBELINE," ACT II, SC. 3.

HARK, hark! the lark at heaven's gate sings,
    And Phœbus 'gins arise,
His steeds to water at those springs
    On chaliced flowers that lies;
And winking Mary-buds begin
    To ope their golden eyes;
With everything that pretty bin,
    My lady sweet, arise;
        Arise, arise!

SHAKESPEARE.

THE LARK ASCENDING.

HE rises and begins to round,
He drops the silver chain of sound
Of many links without a break,
In chirrup, whistle, slur and shake,
All intervolved and spreading wide,
Like water-dimples down a tide
Where ripple ripple overcurls
And eddy into eddy whirls;
A press of hurried notes that run
So fleet they scarce are more than one,
Yet changingly the trills repeat
And linger ringing while they fleet,
Sweet to the quick o' the ear, and dear
To her beyond the handmaid ear,
Who sits beside our inner springs,

Too often dry for this he brings,
Which seems the very jet of earth
At sight of sun, her music's mirth,
As up he wings the spiral stair,
A song of light, and pierces air
With fountain ardor, fountain play,
To reach the shining tops of day,
And drink in everything discerned,
An ecstasy to music turned,
Impelled by what his happy bill
Disperses; drinking, showering still,
Unthinking save that he may give
His voice the outlet, there to live
Renewed in endless notes of glee,
So thirsty of his voice is he,
For all to hear and all to know
That he is joy, awake, aglow,
The tumult of the heart to hear
Through pureness filtered crystal-clear,
And know the pleasure sprinkled bright
By simple singing of delight,
Shrill, irreflective, unrestrained,
Rapt, ringing, on the jet sustained
Without a break, without a fall,
Sweet-silvery, sheer lyrical,
Perennial, quavering up the chord
Like myriad dews of sunny sward
That trembling into fulness shine,
And sparkle dropping argentine;
Such wooing as the ear receives
From zephyr caught in choric leaves
Of aspens when their chattering net
Is flushed to white with shivers wet;

And such the water-spirit's chime
On mountain heights in morning's prime,
Too freshly sweet to seem excess,
Too animate to need a stress;
But wider over many heads
The starry voice ascending spreads,
Awakening, as it waxes thin,
The best in us to him akin;
And every face to watch him raised,
Puts on the light of children praised,
So rich our human pleasure ripes
When sweetness on sincereness pipes,
Though nought be promised from the seas,
But only a soft-ruffling breeze
Sweep glittering on a still content,
Serenity in ravishment.

For singing till his heaven fills,
'T is love of earth that he instils,
And ever winging up and up,
Our valley is his golden cup,
And he the wine which overflows
To lift us with him as he goes:
The woods and brooks, the sheep and kine
He is, the hills, the human line,
The meadows green, the fallows brown,
The dreams of labor in the town;
He sings the sap, the quickened veins;
The wedding song of sun and rains
He is, the dance of children, thanks
Of sowers, shout of primrose-banks,
And eye of violets while they breathe;
All these the circling song will wreathe,

And you shall hear the herb and tree,
The better heart of men shall see,
Shall feel celestially, as long
As you crave nothing save the song.
Was never voice of ours could say
Our inmost in the sweetest way,
Like yonder voice aloft, and link
All hearers in the song they drink:
Our wisdom speaks from failing blood
Our passion is too full in flood,
We want the key of his wild note
Of truthful in a tuneful throat,
The song seraphically free
Of taint of personality,
So pure that it salutes the suns
The voice of one for millions,
In whom the millions rejoice,
For giving their one spirit voice.

Yet men have we, whom we revere,
Now names, and men still housing here,
Whose lives, by many a battle-dint
Defaced, and grinding wheels on flint,
Yield substance, though they sing not, sweet
For song our highest heaven to greet:
Whom heavenly singing gives us new,
Enspheres them brilliant in our blue,
From firmest base to farthest leap,
Because their love of Earth is deep,
And they are warriors in accord
With life to serve and pass reward,
So touching purest and so heard
In the brain's reflex of yon bird;

Wherefore their soul in me, or mine,
Through self-forgetfulness divine,
In them, that song aloft maintains,
To fill the sky and thrill the plains
With showerings drawn from human stores,
As he to silence nearer soars,
Extends the world at wings and dome,
More spacious making, more our home,
Till lost on his aerial rings
In light, and then the fancy sings.

GEORGE MEREDITH.

TO THE SKYLARK.

ETHEREAL minstrel! pilgrim of the sky!
  Dost thou despise the earth where cares abound
Or, while the wings aspire, are heart and eye
  Both with thy nest upon the dewy ground?
Thy nest, which thou canst drop into at will,
Those quivering wings composed, that music still!

To the last point of vision, and beyond,
    Mount, daring warbler!—that love-prompted
        strain,
'Twixt thee and thine a never-failing bond,
  Thrills not the less the bosom of the plain;
Yet mightst thou seem, proud privilege! to sing
All independent of the leafy spring.

Leave to the nightingale her shady wood;
  A privacy of glorious light is thine,
Whence thou dost pour upon the world a flood
  Of harmony, with instinct more divine;

Type of the wise, who soar, but never roam,—
True to the kindred points of Heaven and Home!

WILLIAM WORDSWORTH.

TO THE SKYLARK.

Hail to thee, blithe spirit!
　　Bird thou never wert,
That from heaven, or near it,
　　Pourest thy full heart
In profuse strains of unpremeditated art.

　　Higher still and higher
　　From the earth thou springest,
Like a cloud of fire;
　　The blue deep thou wingest,
And　singing　still　dost　soar, and　soaring　ever
　　　　singest.

　　In the golden lightning
　　Of the setting sun,
O'er which clouds are brightening,
　　Thou dost float and run;
Like an unbodied joy whose race is just begun.

　　The pale purple even
　　Melts around thy flight;
Like a star of heaven,
　　In the broad daylight
Thou art unseen, but yet I hear thy shrill delight.

　　Keen as are the arrows
　　Of that silver sphere,

Whose intense lamp narrows
In the white dawn clear,
Until we hardly see, we feel that it is there.

All the earth and air
With thy voice is loud,
As, when night is bare,
From one lonely cloud
The moon rains out her beams, and heaven is over-
flowed.

What thou art we know not;
What is most like thee?
From rainbow clouds there flow not
Drops so bright to see,
As from thy presence showers a rain of melody.

Like a poet hidden
In the light of thought,
Singing hymns unbidden,
Till the world is wrought
To sympathy with hopes and fears it heeded not;

Like a high-born maiden
In a palace tower,
Soothing her love-laden
Soul in secret hour
With music sweet as love, which overflows her
bower;

Like a glow-worm golden,
In a dell of dew,
Scattering unbeholden
Its aerial hue
Among the flowers and grass which screen it from
the view;

Like a rose embowered
  In its own green leaves,
By warm winds deflowered,
  Till the scent it gives
Makes faint with too much sweet these heavy-
    wingèd thieves.

Sound of vernal showers
  On the twinkling grass,
Rain-awakened flowers,
  All that ever was
Joyous and fresh and clear thy music doth sur-
    pass.

Teach us, sprite or bird,
  What sweet thoughts are thine;
I have never heard
  Praise of love or wine
That panted forth a flood of rapture so divine.

Chorus hymeneal,
  Or triumphant chant,
Matched with thine, would be all
  But an empty vaunt,—
A thing wherein we feel there is some hidden
    want.

What objects are the fountains
  Of thy happy strain?
What fields, or waves, or mountains?
  What shapes of sky or plain?
What love of thine own kind? What ignorance
    of pain?

With thy clear, keen joyance
Languor cannot be:
Shadow of annoyance
Never come near thee:
Thou lovest; but ne'er knew love's sad satiety.

Waking or asleep,
Thou of death must deem
Things more true and deep
Than we mortals dream,
Or how could thy notes flow in such a crystal
stream?

We look before and after,
And pine for what is not;
Our sincerest laughter
With some pain is fraught;
Our sweetest songs are those that tell of saddest
thought.

Yet if we could scorn
Hate and pride and fear,
If we were things born
Not to shed a tear,
I know not how thy joy we ever should come near.

Better than all measures
Of delightful sound,
Better than all treasures
That in books are found,
Thy skill to poet were, thou scorner of the ground!

Teach me half the gladness
That thy brain must know,

Such harmonious madness
From my lips would flow,
The world should listen then, as I am listening
    now.

PERCY BYSSHE SHELLEY.

THE SKYLARK.

Bɪʀᴅ of the wilderness,
Blithesome and cumberless,
Sweet be thy matin o'er moorland and lea!
    Emblem of happiness,
    Blest is thy dwelling-place,—
O, to abide in the desert with thee!
    Wild is thy lay and loud
    Far in the downy cloud,
Love gives it energy, love gave it birth.
    Where, on thy dewy wing,
    Where art thou journeying?
Thy lay is in heaven, thy love is on earth.
    O'er fell and fountain sheen,
    O'er moor and mountain green,
O'er the red streamer that heralds the day.
    Over the cloudlet dim,
    Over the rainbow's rim,
Musical cherub, soar, singing, away!
    Then, when the gloaming comes,
    Low in the heather blooms
Sweet will thy welcome and bed of love be!
    Emblem of happiness,
    Blest is thy dwelling-place,—
O, to abide in the desert with thee!

JAMES HOGG.

THE LITTLE BEACH BIRD.

THOU little bird, thou dweller by the sea,
  Why takest thou its melancholy voice?
    Why with that brooding cry
    O'er the waves dost thou fly?
O, rather, bird, with me
  Through the fair land rejoice!

Thy flitting form comes ghostly dim and pale,
  As driven by a beating storm at sea;
    Thy cry is weak and scared,
    As if thy mates had shared
The doom of us. Thy wail—
  What does it bring to me?

Thou call'st along the sand, and haunt'st the
        surge,
  Restless and sad; as if, in strange accord
    With motion and with roar
    Of waves that drive to shore,
One spirit did ye urge—
  The Mystery—the Word.

Of thousands thou both sepulchre and pall,
  Old ocean, art! A requiem o'er the dead,
    From out thy gloomy cells,
    A tale of mourning tells,—
Tells of man's woe and fall,
  His sinless glory fled.

Then turn thee, little bird, and take thy flight
  Where the complaining sea shall sadness bring
    Thy spirit nevermore.
    Come, quit with me the shore,
For gladness and the light,
  Where birds of summer sing.

RICHARD HENRY DANA.

THE SANDPIPER.

Across the narrow beach we flit,
  One little sandpiper and I;
And fast I gather, bit by bit,
  The scattered driftwood bleached and dry.
The wild waves reach their hands for it,
  The wild wind raves, the tide runs high,
As up and down the beach we flit,—
  One little sandpiper and I.

Above our heads the sullen clouds
  Scud black and swift across the sky:
Like silent ghosts in misty shrouds
  Stand out the white light-houses high.
Almost as far as eye can reach
  I see the close-reefed vessels fly,
As fast we flit along the beach,—
  One little sandpiper and I.

I watch him as he skims along,
  Uttering his sweet and mournful cry;
He starts not at my fitful song,
  Or flash of fluttering drapery;

He has no thought of any wrong,
  He scans me with a fearless eye.
Stanch friends are we, well tried and strong,
  The little sandpiper and I.

Comrade, where wilt thou be to-night
  When the loosed storm breaks furiously?
My driftwood-fire will burn so bright!
  To what warm shelter canst thou fly?
I do not fear for thee, though wroth
  The tempest rushes through the sky:
For are we not God's children both,
  Thou, little sandpiper, and I?

CELIA THAXTER.

TO A WATERFOWL.

Whither, midst falling dew,
While glow the heavens with the last steps of
    day,
Far, through their rosy depths, dost thou pursue
  Thy solitary way?

  Vainly the fowler's eye
Might mark thy distant flight to do thee wrong,
As, darkly painted on the crimson sky,
  Thy figure floats along.

  Seek'st thou the plashy brink
Of weedy lake, or marge of river wide,
Or where the rocking billows rise and sink
    On the chafed ocean-side?

There is a Power whose care
Teaches thy way along that pathless coast,—
The desert and illimitable air,—
    Lone wandering, but not lost.

All day thy wings have fanned,
At that far height, the cold, thin atmosphere,
Yet stoop not, weary, to the welcome land,
    Though the dark night is near.

And soon that toil shall end;
Soon shalt thou find a summer home, and rest,
And scream among thy fellows; reeds shall bend,
    Soon, o'er thy sheltered nest.

Thou 'rt gone, the abyss of heaven
Hath swallowed up thy form; yet, on my heart
Deeply hath sunk the lesson thou hast given,
    And shall not soon depart:

He who, from zone to zone,
Guides through the boundless sky thy certain
      flight,
In the long way that I must tread alone,
    Will lead my steps aright.

WILLIAM CULLEN BRYANT.

TO THE NIGHTINGALE.

O NIGHTINGALE, that on yon bloomy spray
    Warblest at eve, when all the woods are still,
    Thou with fresh hopes the lover's heart dost fill,
  20

While the jolly hours lead on propitious May.
Thy liquid notes, that close the eye of day,
   First heard before the shallow cuckoo's bill,
   Portend success in love. Oh, if Jove's will
Have linked that amorous power to thy soft lay,
Now timely sing, ere the rude bird of hate
   Foretell my hopeless doom in some grove nigh;
As thou from year to year hast sung too late
   For my relief, yet hadst no reason why.
Whether the Muse or Love call thee his mate,
   Both them I serve, and of their train am I.

JOHN MILTON.

THE NIGHTINGALE'S SONG.

FROM " MUSIC'S DUEL."

Now westward Sol had spent the richest beams
Of noon's high glory, when, hard by the streams
Of Tiber, on the scene of a green plat,
Under protection of an oak, there sat
A sweet lute's-master, in whose gentle airs
He lost the day's heat and his own hot cares.
   Close in the covert of the leaves there stood
A nightingale, come from the neighboring wood
(The sweet inhabitant of each glad tree,
Their muse, their siren, harmless siren she) :
There stood she listening, and did entertain
The music's soft report, and mould the same
In her own murmurs; that whatever mood
His curious fingers lent, her voice made good.

    .   .   .   .   .

This lesson too

She gives them back; her supple breast thrills out

Sharp airs, and staggers in a warbling doubt
Of dallying sweetness, hovers o'er her skill,
And folds in waved notes, with a trembling bill,
The pliant series of her slippery song;
Then starts she suddenly into a throng
Of short thick sobs, whose thundering volleys
    float,
And roll themselves over her lubric throat
In panting murmurs, stilled out of her breast;
That ever-bubbling spring, the sugared nest
Of her delicious soul, that there does lie
Bathing in streams of liquid melody;
Music's best seed-plot; when in ripened airs
A golden-headed harvest fairly rears
His honey-dropping tops ploughed by her breath
Which there reciprocally laboreth.
In that sweet soil it seems a holy quire,
Sounded to the name of great Apollo's lyre;
Whose silver roof rings with the sprightly notes
Of sweet-lipped angel-imps, that swill their
    throats
In cream of morning Helicon, and then
Prefer soft anthems to the ears of men,
To woo them from their beds, still murmuring
That men can sleep while they their matins sing
(Most divine service), whose so early lay
Prevents the eyelids of the blushing day.
There might you hear her kindle her soft voice
In the close murmur of a sparkling noise;
And lay the groundwork of her hopeful song.
Still keeping in the forward stream so long,
Till a sweet whirlwind (striving to get out)
Heaves her soft bosom, wanders round about,

And makes a pretty earthquake in her breast,
Till the fledged notes at length forsake their nest,
Fluttering in wanton shoals, and to the sky,
Winged with their own wild echoes, prattling fly.
She opes the floodgate, and lets loose a tide
Of streaming sweetness, which in state doth ride
On the waved back of every swelling strain,
Rising and falling in a pompous train;
And while she thus discharges a shrill peal
Of flashing airs, she qualifies their zeal
With the cool epode of a graver note;
Thus high, thus low, as if her silver throat
Would reach the brazen voice of war's hoarse
　　　　bird;
Her little soul is ravished, and so poured
Into loose ecstasies, that she is placed
Above herself, music's enthusiast.

RICHARD CRASHAW.

PHILOMENA.

HARK! ah, the nightingale!
The tawny-throated!
Hark! from that moonlit cedar what a burst!
What triumph! hark,—what pain!
O wanderer from a Grecian shore,
Still,—after many years, in distant lands,—
Still nourishing in thy bewildered brain
That wild, unquenched, deep-sunken, Old-world
　　　　pain,—
　　　Say, will it never heal?
And can this fragrant lawn,
With its cool trees, and night,

And the sweet, tranquil Thames,
And the moonshine, and the dew,
To thy racked heart and brain
    Afford no balm?

    Dost thou to-night behold,
Here, through the moonlight on this English
    grass,
The unfriendly palace in the Thracian wild?
    Dost thou again peruse,
With hot cheeks and seared eyes,
The too clear web, and thy dumb sister's shame?
    Dost thou once more essay
Thy flight; and feel come over thee,
Poor fugitive! the feathery change
Once more; and once more make resound,
With love and hate, triumph and agony,
Lone Daulis, and the high Cephisian vale?
Listen, Eugenia,—
How thick the bursts come crowding through the
    leaves!
Again—thou hearest!
Eternal passion!
Eternal pain!

               MATTHEW ARNOLD.

UNMUSICAL BIRDS.

FROM "THE TASK," BOOK I.

TEN thousand warblers cheer the day, and one
The livelong night: nor these alone, whose notes
Nice-fingered Art must emulate in vain,
But cawing rooks, and kites that swim sublime

In still repeated circles, screaming loud,
The jay, the pie, and ev'n the boding owl,
That hails the rising moon, have charms for men.
Sounds inharmonious in themselves and harsh,
Yet heard in scenes where peace for ever reigns
And only there, please highly for their sake.

WILLIAM COWPER.

ROBERT OF LINCOLN.

MERRILY swinging on brier and weed,
    Near to the nest of his little dame,
Over the mountain-side or mead,
    Robert of Lincoln is telling his name:
        Bob-o'-link, bob-o'-link,
        Spink, spank, spink;
Snug and safe is that nest of ours,
Hidden among the summer flowers.
                    Chee, chee, chee.

Robert of Lincoln is gayly dressed,
    Wearing a bright black wedding coat;
White are his shoulders and white his crest,
    Hear him call in his merry note:
        Bob-o'-link, bob-o'-link,
        Spink, spank, spink;
Look, what a nice new coat is mine,
Sure there was never a bird so fine.
                    Chee, chee, chee.

Robert of Lincoln's Quaker wife,
    Pretty and quiet, with plain brown wings,

Passing at home a patient life,
  Broods in the grass while her husband sings:
    Bob-o'-link, bob-o'-link,
    Spink, spank, spink;
Brood, kind creature; you need not fear
Thieves and robbers while I am here.
              Chee, chee, chee.

Modest and shy as a nun is she,
  One weak chirp is her only note,
Braggart and prince of braggarts is he,
  Pouring boasts from his little throat:
    Bob-o'-link, bob-o'-link,
    Spink, spank, spink;
Never was I afraid of man;
Catch me, cowardly knaves, if you can.
              Chee, chee, chee.

Six white eggs on a bed of hay,
  Flecked with purple, a pretty sight!
There as the mother sits all day,
  Robert is singing with all his might:
    Bob-o'-link, bob-o'-link,
    Spink, spank, spink;
Nice good wife, that never goes out,
Keeping house while I frolic about.
              Chee, chee, chee.

Soon as the little ones chip the shell
  Six wide mouths are open for food;
Robert of Lincoln bestirs him well,
  Gathering seed for the hungry brood.
    Bob-o'-link, bob-o'-link,
    Spink, spank, spink;

This new life is likely to be
Hard for a gay young fellow like me.
                    Chee, chee, chee.

Robert of Lincoln at length is made
    Sober with work, and silent with care;
Off is his holiday garment laid,
    Half forgotten that merry air,
        Bob-o'-link, bob-o'-link,
        Spink, spank, spink;
Nobody knows but my mate and I
Where our nest and our nestlings lie.
                    Chee, chee, chee.

Summer wanes; the children are grown;
    Fun and frolic no more he knows;
Robert of Lincoln's a humdrum crone;
    Off he flies, and we sing as he goes:
        Bob-o'-link, bob-o'-link,
        Spink, spank, spink;
When you can pipe that merry old strain,
Robert of Lincoln, come back again.
                    Chee, chee, chee.
                    WILLIAM CULLEN BRYANT.

THE O'LINCOLN FAMILY.

A FLOCK of merry singing-birds were sporting in
    the grove·
Some were warbling cheerily, and some were
    making love:
There were Bobolincon, Wadolincon, Winter
    seeble, Conquedle,—

A livelier set was never led by tabor, pipe, or
    fiddle,—
Crying, " Phew, shew, Wadolincon, see, see, Bob-
    olincon,
Down among the tickletops, hiding in the butter-
    cups!
I know the saucy chap, I see his shining cap
Bobbing in the clover there,—see, see, see! "

Up flies Bobolincon, perching on an apple-tree,
Startled by his rival's song, quickened by his
    raillery;
Soon he spies the rogue afloat, curvetting in the
    air,
And merrily he turns about, and warns him to
    beware!
" 'T is you that would a-wooing go, down among
    the rushes O!
But wait a week, till flowers are cheery,—wait a
    week, and, ere you marry,
Be sure of a house wherein to tarry!
Wadolink, Whiskodink, Tom Denny, wait, wait,
    wait! "

Every one 's a funny fellow; every one 's a little
    mellow;
Follow, follow, follow, follow, o'er the hill and in
    the hollow!
Merrily, merrily, there they hie; now they rise
    and now they fly;
They cross and turn, and in and out, and down
    in the middle, and wheel about,—
With a " Phew, shew, Wadolincon! listen to me,
    Bobolincon!—

Happy 's the wooing that 's speedily doing, that 's
    speedily doing,
That 's merry and over with the bloom of the
    clover!
Bobolincon, Wadolincon, Winterseeble, follow,
    follow me!

WILSON FLAGG.

TO THE LAPLAND LONGSPUR.

I.

Oh, thou northland bobolink,
Looking over Summer's brink
Up to Winter, worn and dim,
Peering down from mountain rim,
Something takes me in thy note,
Quivering wing, and bubbling throat;
Something moves me in thy ways—
Bird, rejoicing in thy days,
In thy upward-hovering flight.
In thy suit of black and white,
Chestnut cape and circled crown,
In thy mate of speckled brown;
Surely I may pause and think
Of my boyhood's bobolink.

II.

Soaring over meadows wild
(Greener pastures never smiled);
Raining music from above,
Full of rapture, full of love;
Frolic, gay and debonair,

Yet not all exempt from care,
For thy nest is in the grass,
And thou worriest as I pass;
But nor hand nor foot of mine
Shall do harm to thee or thine;
I, musing, only pause to think
Of my boyhood's bobolink.

III.

But no bobolink of mine
Ever sang o'er mead so fine,
Starred with flowers of every hue,
Gold and purple, white and blue;
Painted-cup, anemone,
Jacob's-ladder, fleur-de-lis,
Orchid, harebell, shooting-star,
Crane's-bill, lupine, seen afar,
Primrose, poppy, saxifrage,
Pictured type on Nature's page—
These and others here unnamed,
In northland gardens, yet untamed,
Deck the fields where thou dost sing,
Mounting up on trembling wing;
While in wistful mood I think
Of my boyhood's bobolink.

IV.

On Unalaska's emerald lea,
On lonely isles in Bering Sea,
On far Siberia's barren shore,
On north Alaska's tundra floor,

At morn, at noon, in pallid night,
We heard thy song and saw thy flight,
While I, sighing, could but think
Of my boyhood's bobolink.

JOHN BURROUGHS.

THE BOBOLINKS.

WHEN Nature had made all her birds,
  With no more cares to think on,
She gave a rippling laugh, and out
  There flew a Bobolinkon.

She laughed again; out flew a mate;
  A breeze of Eden bore them
Across the fields of Paradise,
  The sunrise reddening o'er them.

Incarnate sport and holiday,
  They flew and sang forever;
Their souls through June were all in tune,
  Their wings were weary never.

Their tribe, still drunk with air and light,
  And perfume of the meadow,
Go reeling up and down the sky,
  In sunshine and in shadow.

One springs from out the dew-wet grass;
  Another follows after;
The morn is thrilling with their songs
  And peals of fairy laughter.

From out the marshes and the brook,
  They set the tall reeds swinging,
And meet and frolic in the air,
  Half prattling and half singing.

When morning winds sweep meadow-lands
  In green and russet billows,
And toss the lonely elm-tree's boughs,
  And silver all the willows,

I see you buffeting the breeze,
  Or with its motion swaying,
Your notes half drowned against the wind,
  Or down the current playing.

When far away o'er grassy flats,
  Where the thick wood commences,
The white-sleeved mowers look like specks
  Beyond the zigzag fences,

And noon is hot, and barn-roofs gleam
  White in the pale blue distance,
I hear the saucy minstrels still
  In chattering persistence.

When Eve her domes of opal fire
  Piles round the blue horizon,
Or thunder rolls from hill to hill
  A Kyrie Eleison,

Still merriest of the merry birds,
  Your sparkle is unfading,—
Pied harlequins of June,—no end
  Of song and masquerading.

What cadences of bubbling mirth,
  Too quick for bar and rhythm!
What ecstasies, too full to keep
  Coherent measure with them!

O could I share, without champagne
  Or muscadel, your frolic,
The glad delirium of your joy,
  Your fun unapostolic,

Your drunken jargon through the fields,
  Your bobolinkish gabble,
Your fine Anacreontic glee,
  Your tipsy reveller's babble!

Nay, let me not profane such joy
  With similes of folly;
No wine of earth could waken songs
  So delicately jolly!

O boundless self-contentment, voiced
  In flying air-born bubbles!
O joy that mocks our sad unrest,
  And drowns our earth-born troubles!

Hope springs with you: I dread no more
  Despondency and dulness;
For Good Supreme can never fail
  That gives such perfect fulness.

The life that floods the happy fields
  With song and light and color
Will shape our lives to richer states,
  And heap our measures fuller.

                    CHRISTOPHER PEARSE CRANCH.

THE MOCKING–BIRD.

He did n't know much music
    When first he come along;
An' all the birds went wonderin'
    Why he did n't sing a song.

They primped their feathers in the sun,
    An' sung their sweetest notes;
An' music jest come on the run
    From all their purty throats!

But still that bird was silent
    In summer time an' fall;
He jest set still an' listened,
    An' he would n't sing at all!

But one night when them songsters
    Was tired out an' still,
An' the wind sighed down the valley
    An' went creepin' up the hill;

When the stars was all a-tremble
    In the dreamin' fields o' blue,
An' the daisy in the darkness
    Felt the fallin' o' the dew,—

There come a sound o' melody
    No mortal ever heard,
An' all the birds seemed singin'
    From the throat o' one sweet bird!

Then the other birds went Mayin'
In a land too fur to call;
Fer there warn't no use in stayin'
When one bird could sing fer all!

FRANK LEBBY STANTON.

THE BLACKBIRD.

O BLACKBIRD! sing me something well:
 While all the neighbors shoot thee round,
 I keep smooth plats of fruitful ground,
Where thou may'st warble, eat, and dwell.

The espaliers and the standards all
 Are thine; the range of lawn and park:
 The unnetted black-hearts ripen dark;
All thine, against the garden wall.

Yet, tho' I spared thee all the spring,
 Thy sole delight is, sitting still,
 With that gold dagger of thy bill
To fret the summer jenneting.

A golden bill! the silver tongue,
 Cold February loved, is dry:
 Plenty corrupts the melody
That made thee famous once, when young

And in the sultry garden-squares,
 Now thy flute-notes are changed to coarse,

I hear thee not at all, or hoarse,
As when a hawker hawks his wares.

Take warning! he that will not sing
  When yon sun prospers in the blue,
  Shall sing for want, ere leaves are new,
Caught in the frozen palms of Spring.
             ALFRED, LORD TENNYSON.

THE EAGLE.

A FRAGMENT.

HE clasps the crag with hookèd hands;
Close to the sun in lonely lands,
Ringed with the azure world, he stands.

The wrinkled sea beneath him crawls;
He watches from his mountain walls,
And like a thunderbolt he falls.
             ALFRED, LORD TENNYSON.

THE OWL.

IN the hollow tree, in the old gray tower,
  The spectral owl doth dwell;
Dull, hated, despised, in the sunshine hour,
  But at dusk he 's abroad and well!
Not a bird of the forest e'er mates with him;
  All mock him outright by day;
But at night, when the woods grow still and dim,
  The boldest will shrink away!

21

O, when the night falls, and roosts the fowl,
Then, then, is the reign of the hornèd owl!

And the owl hath a bride, who is fond and bold,
　And loveth the wood's deep gloom;
And, with eyes like the shine of the moonstone
　　cold,
　She awaiteth her ghastly groom;
Not a feather she moves, not a carol she sings,
　As she waits in her tree so still;
But when her heart heareth his flapping wings,
　She hoots out her welcome shrill!
　　O, when the moon shines, and dogs do howl,
　　Then, then, is the joy of the hornèd owl!

Mourn not for the owl, nor his gloomy plight!
　The owl hath his share of good:
If a prisoner he be in the broad daylight,
　He is lord in the dark greenwood!
Nor lonely the bird, nor his ghastly mate,
　They are each unto each a pride;
Thrice fonder, perhaps, since a strange, dark fate
　Hath rent them from all beside!
　　So, when the night falls, and dogs do howl,
　　Sing, ho! for the reign of the hornèd owl!
　　　We know not alway
　　　Who are kings by day,
　　But the king of the night is the bold brown
　　　owl!

BRYAN WALLER PROCTER (*Barry Cornwall*).

THE DYING SWAN.

I.

THE plain was grassy, wild and bare,
Wide, wild and open to the air,
Which had built up everywhere
　　An under-roof of doleful gray.
With an inner voice the river ran,
Adown it floated a dying swan,
　　And loudly did lament.
It was the middle of the day.
Ever the weary wind went on,
　　And took the reed-tops as it went.

II.

Some blue peaks in the distance rose,
And white against the cold-white sky
Shone out their crowning snows.
　　One willow over the river wept,
And shook the wave as the wind did sigh;
Above in the wind was the swallow,
　　Chasing itself at its own wild will,
　　And far thro' the marish green and still
　　The tangled water-courses slept,
Shot over with purple, and green, and yellow.

III.

The wild swan's death-hymn took the soul
Of that waste place with joy
Hidden in sorrow: at first to the ear
The warble was low, and full and clear;

And floating about the under-sky,
Prevailing in weakness, the coronach stole
Sometimes afar, and sometimes anear;
But anon her awful jubilant voice,
With a music strange and manifold,
Flowed forth on a carol free and bold;
As when a mighty people rejoice
With shawms, and with cymbals, and harps of
      gold,
And the tumult of their acclaim is rolled
Thro' the open gates of the city afar,
To the shepherd who watcheth the evening star.
And the creeping mosses and clambering weeds,
And the willow-branches hoar and dank,
And the wavy swell of the soughing reeds,
And the wave-worn horns of the echoing bank,
And the silvery marish-flowers that throng
The desolate creeks and pools among,
Were flooded over with eddying song.

ALFRED, LORD TENNYSON.

THE HEATH–COCK.

Good morrow to thy sable beak
And glossy plumage dark and sleek,
Thy crimson moon and azure eye,
Cock of the heath, so wildly shy:
I see thee slyly cowering through
That wiry web of silvery dew,
That twinkles in the morning air,
Like casements of my lady fair.

A maid there is in yonder tower,
Who, peeping from her early bower,
Half shows, like thee, her simple wile,
Her braided hair and morning smile.
The rarest things, with wayward will,
Beneath the covert hide them still;
The rarest things to break of day
Look shortly forth, and shrink away.

A fleeting moment of delight
I sunned me in her cheering sight;
As short, I ween, the time will be
That I shall parley hold with thee.
Through Snowdon's mist red beams the day,
The climbing herd-boy chants his lay,
The gnat-flies dance their sunny ring,—
Thou art already on the wing.

JOANNA BAILLIE.

THE BELFRY PIGEON.

On the cross-beam under the Old South bell
The nest of a pigeon is builded well.
In summer and winter that bird is there,
Out and in with the morning air;
I love to see him track the street,
With his wary eye and active feet;
And I often watch him as he springs,
Circling the steeple with easy wings,
Till across the dial his shade has passed,
And the belfry edge is gained at last;
'T is a bird I love, with its brooding note,
And the trembling throb in its mottled throat;

There 's a human look in its swelling breast,
And the gentle curve of its lowly crest;
And I often stop with the fear I feel,—
He runs so close to the rapid wheel.

Whatever is rung on that noisy bell,—
Chime of the hour, or funeral knell,—
The dove in the belfry must hear it well.
When the tongue swings out to the midnight
  moon,
When the sexton cheerly rings for noon,
When the clock strikes clear at morning light,
When the child is waked with " nine at night,"
When the chimes play soft in the Sabbath air
Filling the spirit with tones of prayer,—
Whatever tale in the bell is heard,
He broods on his folded feet unstirred,
Or, rising half in his rounded nest,
He takes the time to smooth his breast,
Then drops again, with filmèd eyes,
And sleeps as the last vibration dies.

Sweet bird! I would that I could be
A hermit in the crowd like thee!
With wings to fly to wood and glen.
Thy lot, like mine, is cast with men;
And daily, with unwilling feet,
I tread, like thee, the crowded street,
But, unlike me, when day is o'er,
Thou canst dismiss the world, and soar:
Or, at a half-felt wish for rest,
Canst smooth the feathers on thy breast,
And drop, forgetful, to thy nest.

I would that in such wings of gold
I could my weary heart upfold;

I would I could look down unmoved
(Unloving as I am unloved),
And while the world throngs on beneath,
Smooth down my cares and calmly breathe;
And never sad with others' sadness,
And never glad with others' gladness,
Listen, unstirred, to knell or chime,
And, lapped in quiet, bide my time.

NATHANIEL PARKER WILLIS.

THE ENGLISH ROBIN.

SEE yon robin on the spray;
　Look ye how his tiny form
Swells, as when his merry lay
　Gushes forth amid the storm.

Though the snow is falling fast,
　Specking o'er his coat with white,—
Though loud roars the chilly blast,
　And the evening 's lost in night,—

Yet from out the darkness dreary
　Cometh still that cheerful note;
Praiseful aye, and never weary,
　Is that little warbling throat.

Thank him for his lesson's sake,
　Thank God's gentle minstrel there,
Who, when storms make others quake,
　Sings of days that brighter were.

HARRISON WEIR.

ASIAN BIRDS.

In this May-month, by grace
  of heaven, things shoot apace.
The waiting multitude
  of fair boughs in the wood,—
How few days have arrayed
  their beauty in green shade!

What have I seen or heard?
  it was the yellow bird
Sang in the tree: he flew
  a flame against the blue;
Upward he flashed. Again,
  hark! 't is his heavenly strain,

Another! Hush! Behold,
  many, like boats of gold,
From waving branch to branch
  their airy bodies launch.
What music is like this,
  where each note is a kiss?

The golden willows lift
  their boughs the sun to sift:
Their silken streamers screen
  the sky with veils of green,
To make a cage of song,
  where feathered lovers throng.

How the delicious notes
  come bubbling from their throats!

Full and sweet, how they are shed
 like round pearls from a thread,
The motions of their flight
 are wishes of delight.

Hearing their song, I trace
 the secret of their grace.
Ah, could I this fair time
 so fashion into rhyme,
The poem that I sing
 would be the voice of spring.

ROBERT SEYMOUR BRIDGES.

THE SCARLET TANAGER.

A BALL of fire shoots through the tamarack
In scarlet splendor, on voluptuous wings;
Delirious joy the pyrotechnist brings,
Who marks for us high summer's almanac.
How instantly the red-coat hurtles back!
No fiercer flame has flashed beneath the sky.
Note now the rapture in his cautious eye,
The conflagration lit along his track.
Winged soul of beauty, tropic in desire,
Thy love seems alien in our northern zone;
Thou giv'st to our green lands a burst of fire
And callest back the fables we disown.
The hot equator thou mightst well inspire,
Or stand above some Eastern monarch's throne.

JOEL BENTON.

THE WINGED WORSHIPPERS.

[Addressed to two swallows that flew into the Chauncy
Place Church during divine service.]

GAY, guiltless pair,
What seek ye from the fields of heaven?
Ye have no need of prayer;
Ye have no sins to be forgiven.

Why perch ye here,
Where mortals to their Maker bend?
Can your pure spirits fear
The God ye never could offend?

Ye never knew
The crimes for which we come to weep.
Penance is not for you,
Blessed wanderers of the upper deep.

To you 't is given
To wake sweet Nature's untaught lays;
Beneath the arch of heaven
To chirp away a life of praise.

Then spread each wing
Far, far above, o'er lakes and lands,
And join the choirs that sing
In yon blue dome not reared with hands.

Or, if ye stay,
To note the consecrated hour,

Teach me the airy way,
And let me try your envied power.

Above the crowd
On upward wings could I but fly,
    I 'd bathe in yon bright cloud,
And seek the stars that gem the sky.

    'T were heaven indeed
Through fields of trackless light to soar,
    On Nature's charms to feed,
And Nature's own great God adore.

CHARLES SPRAGUE.

THE DEPARTURE OF THE SWALLOW.

AND is the swallow gone?
        Who beheld it?
        Which way sailed it?
Farewell bade it none?

No mortal saw it go;—
        But who doth hear
        Its summer cheer
As it flitteth to and fro?

So the freed spirit flies!
        From its surrounding clay
        It steals away
Like the swallow from the skies.

Whither? wherefore doth it go?
        'T is all unknown;
        We feel alone
That a void is left below.

WILLIAM HOWITT.

THE FLIGHT OF THE GEESE.

I HEAR the low wind wash the softening snow,
The low tide loiter down the shore. The night,
Full filled with April forecast hath no light.
The salt wave on the sedge-flat pulses slow.
Through the hid furrows lisp in murmurous flow
The thaw's shy ministers; and hark! The height
Of heaven grows weird and loud with unseen
        flight
Of strong hosts prophesying as they go!
High through the drenched and hollow night
        their wings
Beat northward hard on winter's trail. The
        sound
Of their confused and solemn voices, borne
Athwart the dark to their long arctic morn,
Comes with a sanction and an awe profound,
A boding of unknown, foreshadowed things.

CHARLES G. D. ROBERTS.

LINES TO THE STORMY PETREL.

THE lark sings for joy in her own loved land,
In the furrowed field, by the breezes fanned;
        And so revel we
        In the furrowed sea,
As joyous and glad as the lark can be.

On the placid breast of the inland lake
The wild duck delights her pastime to take;

But the petrel braves
The wild ocean waves,
His wing in the foaming billow he laves.

The halcyon loves in the noontide beam
To follow his sport on the tranquil stream:
He fishes at ease
In the summer breeze,
But we go angling in stormiest seas.

No song-note have we but a piping cry,
That blends with the storm when the wind is high.
When the land-birds wail
We sport in the gale,
And merrily over the ocean we sail.

ANONYMOUS.

––––––––

ODE TO MOTHER CAREY'S CHICKEN.

ON SEEING A STORM-PETREL IN A CAGE ON A COTTAGE
WALL AND RELEASING IT.

GAZE not at me, my poor unhappy bird;
That sorrow is more than human in thine eye;
Too deep already is my spirit stirred
To see thee here, child of the sea and sky,
Cooped in a cage with food thou canst not eat,
Thy "snow-flake" soiled, and soiled those con-
quering feet
That walked the billows, while thy "*sweet-sweet-
sweet*"
Proclaimed the tempest nigh.

Bird whom I welcomed while the sailors cursed,
  Friend whom I blessed wherever keels may
    roam,
Prince of my childish dreams, whom mermaids
    nursed
  In purple of billows—silver of ocean-foam,
Abashed I stand before the mighty grief
That quells all other: Sorrow's king and chief:
To ride the wind and hold the sea in fief,
    Then find a cage for home!

From out thy jail thou seest yon heath and
    woods,
  But canst thou hear the birds or smell the
    flowers?
Ah, no! those rain-drops twinkling on the
    buds
  Bring only visions of the salt sea-showers.
" The sea! " the linnets pipe from hedge and
    heath;
" The sea! " the honeysuckles whisper and
    breathe;
And tumbling waves, where those wild-roses
    wreathe,
    Murmur from inland bowers.

These winds so soft to others,—how they burn!
  The mavis sings with gurgle and ripple and
    plash,
To thee yon swallow seems a wheeling tern.
  And when the rain recalls the briny lash,
Old Ocean's kiss thou lovest,—when thy sight
Is mocked with Ocean's horses—manes of white,

The long and shadowy flanks, the shoulders
    bright—
      Bright as the lightning's flash,—

When all these scents of heather and brier and
    whin,
  All kindly breaths of land-shrub, flower, and
    vine,
Recall the sea-scents, till thy feathered skin
  Tingles in answer to a dream of brine,—
When thou, remembering there thy royal birth,
Dost see between the bars a world of dearth,
Is there a grief—a grief on all the earth—
    So heavy and dark as thine?

But I can buy thy freedom—I (thank God!),
  Who loved thee more than albatross or gull,
Loved thee when on the waves thy footsteps trod,
  Dreamed of thee when, becalmed, we lay ahull—
'T is I thy friend who once, a child of six,
To find where Mother Carey fed her chicks,
Climbed up the stranded punt, and with two
    sticks
    Tried all in vain to scull,—

Thy friend who owed a Paradise of Storm,—
  The little dreamer of the cliffs and coves,
Who knew thy mother, saw her shadowy form
  Behind the cloudy bastions where she moves,
And heard her call: "Come! for the welkin
    thickens,
And tempests mutter and the lightning quick-
    ens!"

Then, starting from his dream, would find the
    chickens
       Were only blue rock-doves,—

Thy friend who owed another Paradise
    Of calmer air, a floating isle of fruit,
Where sang the Nereids on a breeze of spice
    While Triton, from afar, would sound salute:
There wast thou winging, though the skies were
    calm,
For marvellous strains, as of the morning's
    shalm,
Were struck by ripples round that isle of palm
       Whose shores were " Carey's lute."

And now to see thee here, my king, my king,
    Far-glittering memories mirrored in those eyes,
As if there shone within each iris-ring
    An orbèd world—ocean and hills and skies!—
Those black wings ruffled whose triumphant
    sweep
Conquered in sport!—yea, up the glimmering
    steep
Of highest billow, down the deepest deep,
       Sported with victories!

To see thee here!—a coil of wilted weeds
    Beneath those feet that danced on diamond
    spray,
Rider of sportive Ocean's reinless steeds—
    Winner in Mother Carey's sabbath-fray
When, stung by magic of the witch's chant,
They rise, each foamy-crested combatant—
They rise and fall and leap and foam and gallop
       and pant

Till albatross, sea-swallow, and cormorant
    Would flee like doves away!

And shalt thou ride no more where thou hast
    ridden,
  And feast no more in hyaline halls and caves,
Master of Mother Carey's secrets hidden,
  Master most equal of the wind and waves,
Who never, save in stress of angriest blast,
Asked ship for shelter,—never, till at last
The foam-flakes, hurled against the sloping masts,
    Slashed thee like whirling glaives!

Right home to fields no seamew ever kenned,
  Where scarce the great sea-wanderer fares with
    thee,
I come to take thee—nay, 't is I, thy friend—
  Ah, tremble not—I come to set thee free;
I come to tear this cage from off this wall,
And take thee hence to that fierce festival
Where billows march and winds are musical,
    Hymning the Victor-Sea!

.   .   .   .   .   .

Yea, lift thine eyes, my own can bear them now:
  Thou 'rt free! thou 'rt free. Ah, surely a bird
    can smile!
Dost know me, Petrel? Dost remember how
  I fed thee in the wake for many a mile,
Whilst thou wouldst pat the waves, then, rising,
    take
The morsel up and wheel about the wake?
Thou 'rt free, thou 'rt free, but for thine own dear
    sake
    I keep thee caged awhile.

22

Away to sea! no matter where the coast:
  The road that turns to home turns never wrong:
Where waves run high my bird will not be lost:
  His home I know: 't is where the winds are
      strong,—
Where, on her throne of billows, rolling hoary
And green and blue and splashed with sunny
     glory,
Far, far from shore—from farthest promontory—
The mighty Mother sings the triumphs of her
     story,
       Sings to my bird the song!

               THEODORE WATTS.

THE GRASSHOPPER AND CRICKET.

THE poetry of earth is never dead;
When all the birds are faint with the hot sun
And hide in cooling trees, a voice will run
From hedge to hedge about the new-mown mead.
That is the grasshopper's,—he takes the lead
In summer luxury,—he has never done
With his delights; for, when tired out with fun,
He rests at ease beneath some pleasant weed.
The poetry of earth is ceasing never.
On a lone winter evening, when the frost
Has wrought a silence, from the stove there
    shrills
The cricket's song, in warmth increasing ever,
And seems, to one in drowsiness half lost,
The grasshopper's among some grassy hills.

                JOHN KEATS.

TO THE GRASSHOPPER AND CRICKET.

GREEN little vaulter in the sunny grass,
Catching your heart up at the feel of June,—
Sole voice that 's heard amidst the lazy noon,
When even the bees lag at the summoning brass;
And you, warm little housekeeper, who class
With those who think the candles come too soon,
Loving the fire, and with your tricksome tune
Nick the glad silent moments as they pass!
O sweet and tiny cousins, that belong,
One to the fields, the other to the hearth,
Both have your sunshine; both, though small, are
  strong
At your clear hearts; and both seem given to
  earth
To sing in thoughtful ears this natural song,—
In doors and out, summer and winter, mirth.

       LEIGH HUNT.

A SOLILOQUY:

OCCASIONED BY THE CHIRPING OF A GRASSHOPPER.

  HAPPY insect! ever blest
  With a more than mortal rest,
  Rosy dews the leaves among,
  Humble joys, and gentle song!
  Wretched poet! ever curst
  With a life of lives the worst,
  Sad despondence, restless fears,
  Endless jealousies and tears.

In the burning summer thou
Warblest on the verdant bough,
Meditating cheerful play,
Mindless of the piercing ray;
Scorched in Cupid's fervors, I
Ever weep and ever die.

Proud to gratify thy will,
Ready Nature waits thee still;
Balmy wines to thee she pours,
Weeping through the dewy flowers,
Rich as those by Hebe given
To the thirsty sons of heaven.

Yet, alas, we both agree.
Miserable thou like me!
Each, alike, in youth rehearses
Gentle strains and tender verses;
Ever wandering far from home,
Mindless of the days to come
(Such as aged Winter brings
Trembling on his icy wings),
Both alike at last we die;
Thou art starved, and so am I!

WALTER HARTE.

TO AN INSECT.

I LOVE to hear thine earnest voice,
    Wherever thou art hid,
Thou testy little dogmatist,
    Thou pretty Katydid!
Thou mindest me of gentlefolks,—
    Old gentlefolks are they,—

Thou say'st an undisputed thing
  In such a solemn way.

Thou art a female, Katydid!
  I know it by the trill
That quivers through thy piercing notes,
  So petulant and shrill.
I think there is a knot of you
  Beneath the hollow tree,—
A knot of spinster Katydids,—
  Do Katydids drink tea?

O, tell me where did Katy live,
  And what did Katy do?
And was she very fair and young,
  And yet so wicked too?
Did Katy love a naughty man,
  Or kiss more cheeks than one?
I warrant Kitty did no more
  Than many a Kate has done.

OLIVER WENDELL HOLMES.

THE FLY.

OCCASIONED BY A FLY DRINKING OUT OF THE
AUTHOR'S CUP.

Busy, curious, thirsty fly,
Drink with me, and drink as I!
Freely welcome to my cup,
Couldst thou sip and sip it up:
Make the most of life you may;
Life is short and wears away!

Both alike, both mine and thine,
Hasten quick to their decline!
Thine's a summer; mine no more,
Though repeated to threescore!
Threescore summers, when they 're gone,
Will appear as short as one!

WILLIAM OLDYS.

TO THE HUMBLEBEE.

Burly, dozing humblebee!
Where thou art is clime for me;
Let me chase thy waving lines;
Far-off heats through seas to seek,
I will follow thee alone,
Thou animated torrid zone!
Zigzag steerer, desert cheerer,
Let me chase thy waving lines;
Keep me nearer, me thy hearer,
Singing over shrubs and vines.

Insect lover of the sun,
Joy of thy dominion!
Sailor of the atmosphere;
Swimmer through the waves of air,
Voyager of light and noon,
Epicurean of June!
Wait, I prithee, till I come
Within earshot of thy hum,—
All without is martyrdom.

When the south-wind, in May days,
With a net of shining haze

Silvers the horizon wall;
And, with softness touching all,
Tints the human countenance
With the color of romance;
And infusing subtle heats
Turns the sod to violets,—
Thou in sunny solitudes
Rover of the underwoods,
The green silence dost displace
With thy mellow breezy bass.

Hot midsummer's petted crone,
Sweet to me thy drowsy tone
Tells of countless sunny hours,
Long days, and solid banks of flowers;
Of gulfs of sweetness without bound,
In Indian wildernesses found;
Of Syrian peace, immortal leisure,
Firmest cheer, and birdlike pleasure.

Aught unsavory or unclean
Hath my insect never seen;
But violets, and bilberry bells,
Maple sap, and daffodels,
Grass with green flag half-mast high,
Succory to match the sky,
Columbine with horn of honey,
Scented fern, and agrimony,
Clover, catchfly, adder's-tongue,
And brier-rose, dwelt among:
All beside was unknown waste,
All was picture as he passed.

Wiser far than human seer,
Yellow-breeched philosopher,

Seeing only what is fair,
　Sipping only what is sweet,
Thou dost mock at fate and care,
　Leave the chaff and take the wheat.
When the fierce northwestern blast
Cools sea and land so far and fast,—
Thou already slumberest deep;
Woe and want thou canst outsleep;
Want and woe, which torture us,
Thy sleep makes ridiculous.

RALPH WALDO EMERSON.

WILD HONEY.

WHERE hints of racy sap and gum
Out of the old dark forest come;

Where birds their beaks like hammers wield,
And pith is pierced, and bark is peeled;

Where the green walnut's outer rind
Gives precious bitterness to the wind;—

There lurks the sweet creative power,
As lurks the honey in the flower.

In winter's bud that bursts in spring,
In nut of autumn's ripening,

In acrid bulb beneath the mold,
Sleeps the elixir, strong and old,

That Rosicrucians sought in vain,—
Life that renews itself again!

What bottled perfume is so good
As fragrance of split tulip-wood?

What fabled drink of god or Muse
Was rich as purple mulberry-juice?

And what school-polished gem of thought
Is like the rune from Nature caught?

He is a poet strong and true
Who loves wild thyme and honey-dew;

And like a brown bee works and sings,
With morning freshness on his wings,

And a gold burden on his thighs,—
The pollen-dust of centuries!

MAURICE THOMPSON.

A MORE ANCIENT MARINER.

THE swarthy bee is a buccaneer,
A burly velveted rover,
Who loves the booming wind in his ear
As he sails the seas of clover.

A waif of the goblin pirate crew,
With not a soul to deplore him,
He steers for the open verge of blue
With the filmy world before him.

His flimsy sails abroad on the wind
Are shivered with fairy thunder;
On a line that sings to the light of his wings
He makes for the lands of wonder.

He harries the ports of the Hollyhocks,
And levies on poor Sweetbrier;
He drinks the whitest wine of Phlox,
And the Rose is his desire.

He hangs in the Willows a night and a day;
He rifles the buckwheat patches;
Then battens his store of pelf galore
Under the tautest hatches.

He woos the Poppy and weds the Peach,
Inveigles Daffodilly,
And then like a tramp abandons each
For the gorgeous Canada Lily.

There's not a soul in the garden world
But wishes the day were shorter,
When Mariner B. puts out to sea
With the wind in the proper quarter.

Or, so they say! But I have my doubts;
For the flowers are only human,
And the valor and gold of a vagrant bold
Were always dear to woman.

He dares to boast, along the coast,
The beauty of Highland Heather,—
How he and she, with night on the sea,
Lay out on the hills together.

He pilfers from every port of the wind,
From April to golden autumn;
But the thieving ways of his mortal days
Are those his mother taught him.

His morals are mixed, but his will is fixed;
He prospers after his kind,
And follows an instinct, compass-sure,
The philosophers call blind.

And that is why, when he comes to die,
He 'll have an easier sentence
Than some one I know who thinks just so,
And then leaves room for repentance.

He never could box the compass round;
He does n't know port from starboard;
But he knows the gates of the Sundown Straits,
Where the choicest goods are harbored.

He never could see the Rule of Three,
But he knows a rule of thumb
Better than Euclid's, better than yours,
Or the teachers' yet to come.

He knows the smell of the hydromel
As if two and two were five;
And hides it away for a year and a day
In his own hexagonal hive.

Out in the day, hap-hazard, alone,
Booms the old vagrant hummer,
With only his whim to pilot him
Through the splendid vast of summer.

He steers and steers on the slant of the gale,
Like the fiend or Vanderdecken;
And there's never an unknown course to sail
But his crazy log can reckon.

He drones along with his rough sea-song
And the throat of a salty tar,
This devil-may-care, till he makes his lair
By the light of a yellow star.

He looks like a gentleman, lives like a lord,
And works like a Trojan hero;
Then loafs all winter upon his hoard,
With the mercury at zero.

BLISS CARMAN.

TO A LOUSE.

ON SEEING ONE ON A LADY'S BONNET AT CHURCH.

Ha! whare ye gaun, ye crawlin' ferlie?
Your impudence protects you sairly:
I canna say but ye strunt rarely
　　Owre gauze an' lace;
Though, faith! I fear ye dine but sparely
　　On sic a place.

Ye ugly, creepin', blastit wonner,
Detested, shunned by saunt an' sinner,
How dare you set your fit upon her,
　　Sae fine a lady?
Gae somewhere else, and seek your dinner
　　On some poor body.

Swith, in some beggar's haffet squattle;
There ye may creep and sprawl and sprattle
Wi' ither kindred, jumping cattle,
    In shoals and nations:
Whare horn nor bane ne'er daur unsettle
    Your thick plantations.

Now haud you there, ye're out o' sight,
Below the fatt'rels, snug an' tight;
Na, faith ye yet! ye'll no be right
    Till ye've got on it,
The very tapmost tow'ring height
    O' Miss's bonnet.

My sooth; right bauld ye set your nose out,
As plump and gray as ony grozet;
O for some rank, mercurial rozet,
    Or fell, red smeddum!
I'd gie you sic a hearty dose o't,
    Wad dress your droddum!

I wad na been surprised to spy
You on an auld wife's flannen toy;
Or aiblins some bit duddie boy,
    On's wyliecoat;
But Miss's fine Lunardi, fie!
    How daur ye do't?

O Jenny, dinna toss your head,
An' set your beauties a' abread!
Ye little ken what cursèd speed
    The blastie's makin'!
Thae winks and finger-ends, I dread,
    Are notice takin'!

O wad some power the giftie gie us
To see oursel's as others see us!
It wad frae monie a blunder free us,
     And foolish notion:
What airs in dress an' gait wad lea'e us,
     And ev'n devotion!

ROBERT BURNS.

TO A MOUSE.

ON TURNING HER UP IN HER NEST WITH THE PLOUGH,
NOVEMBER, 1785.

WEE, sleekit, cowerin', timorous beastie,
O, what a panic 's in thy breastie!
Thou needna start awa sae hasty,
     Wi' bickering brattle!
I wad be laith to rin an' chase thee,
     Wi' murdering pattle!

I 'm truly sorry man's dominion
Has broken nature's social union,
An' justifies that ill opinion
     Which makes thee startle
At me, thy poor earth-born companion,
     An' fellow-mortal!

I doubtna, whyles, but thou may thieve;
What then? poor beastie, thou maun live!
A daimen-icker* in a thrave †
     'S a sma' request;

  * An ear of corn.   † Twenty-four sheaves.

I 'll get a blessin' wi' the lave,
      And never miss 't!

Thy wee bit housie, too, in ruin!
Its silly wa's the win's are strewin'!
An' naething now to big a new ane
      O' foggage green!
An' bleak December's winds ensuin',
      Baith snell and keen!

Thou saw the fields laid bare an' waste,
An' weary winter comin' fast,
An' cozie here, beneath the blast,
      Thou thought to dwell,
Till, crash! the cruel coulter past
      Out through thy cell.

That wee bit heap o' leaves an' stibble
Has cost thee mony a weary nibble!
Now thou 's turned out, for a' thy trouble,
      But house or hald,
To thole the winter's sleety dribble,
      An' cranreuch * cauld!

But, Mousie, thou art no thy lane,
In proving foresight may be vain:
The best-laid schemes o' mice an' men
      Gang aft a-gley,
An' lea'e us naught but grief and pain,
      For promised joy.

Still thou art blest, compared wi' me!
The present only toucheth thee:

        * Hoar-frost.

But, och! I backward cast my e'e
  On prospects drear;
An' forward, though I canna see,
  I guess an' fear.

ROBERT BURNS.

THE HOUSEKEEPER.

THE frugal snail, with forecast of repose,
Carries his house with him where'er he goes;
Peeps out,—and if there comes a shower of rain,
Retreats to his small domicile again.
Touch but a tip of him, a horn,—'t is well,—
He curls up in his sanctuary shell.
He 's his own landlord, his own tenant; stay
Long as he will, he dreads no Quarter Day.
Himself he boards and lodges; both invites
And feasts himself; sleeps with himself o' nights.
He spares the upholsterer trouble to procure
Chattels; himself is his own furniture,
And his sole riches.   Wheresoe'er he roam,—
Knock when you will,—he 's sure to be at home.

CHARLES LAMB.

REMONSTRANCE WITH THE SNAILS.

Ye little snails,
With slippery tails,
Who noiselessly travel
Along this gravel,
By a silvery path of slime unsightly,
I learn that you visit my pea-rows nightly.

Felonious your visit, I guess!
  And I give you this warning,
  That, every morning,
    I 'll strictly examine the pods;
  And if one I hit on,
  With slaver or spit on,
    Your next meal will be with the gods.

I own you 're a very ancient race,
  And Greece and Babylon were amid;
You have tenanted many a royal dome,
  And dwelt in the oldest pyramid;
The source of the Nile!—O, you have been there!
  In the ark was your floodless bed;
On the moonless night of Marathon
  You crawled o'er the mighty dead;
    But still, though I reverence your ancestries,
    I don't see why you should nibble my peas.

The meadows are yours,—the hedgerow and
      brook,
  You may bathe in their dews at morn;
By the agèd sea you may sound your *shells*,
  On the mountains erect your *horn;*
The fruits and the flowers are your rightful
      dowers.
    Then why—in the name of wonder—
Should my six pea-rows be the only cause
  To excite your midnight plunder?

I have never disturbed your slender shells;
  You have hung round my agèd walk;
And each might have sat, till he died in his fat,
  Beneath his own cabbage-stalk:
  23

But now you must fly from the soil of your sires;
　Then put on your liveliest crawl,
And think of your poor little snails at home,
　Now orphans or emigrants all.

Utensils domestic and civil and social
　I give you an evening to pack up;
But if the moon of this night does not rise on
　　your flight,
　To-morrow I 'll hang each man Jack up.
You 'll think of my peas and your thievish tricks,
With tears of slime, when crossing the *Styx*.

ANONYMOUS.

THE TIGER.

TIGER! Tiger! burning bright,
In the forests of the night;
What immortal hand or eye
Could frame thy fearful symmetry?

In what distant deeps or skies
Burned the fire of thine eyes?
On what wings dare he aspire?
What the hand dare seize the fire?

And what shoulder, and what art,
Could twist the sinews of thine heart?
And when thy heart began to beat,
What dread hand? and what dread feet?

What the hammer, what the chain?
In what furnace was thy brain?

What the anvil? what dread grasp
Dare its deadly terrors clasp?

When the stars threw down their spears,
And watered heaven with their tears,
Did he smile his work to see?
Did He, who made the Lamb, make thee!

Tiger! Tiger! burning bright,
In the forests of the night,
What immortal hand or eye
Dare frame thy fearful symmetry?

WILLIAM BLAKE.

THE LION'S RIDE.

The lion is the desert's king; through his domain
    so wide
Right swiftly and right royally this night he
    means to ride.
By the sedgy brink, where the wild herds drink,
    close couches the grim chief;
The trembling sycamore above whispers with
    every leaf.

At evening, on the Table Mount, when ye can see
    no more
The changeful play of signals gay; when the
    gloom is speckled o'er
With kraal fires; when the Caffre wends home
    through the lone karroo;
When the boshbok in the thicket sleeps, and by
    the stream the gnu;

Then bend your gaze across the waste,—what see
    ye? The giraffe,
Majestic, stalks towards the lagoon, the turbid
    lymph to quaff;
With outstretched neck and tongue adust, he
    kneels him down to cool
His hot thirst with a welcome draught from the
    foul and brackish pool.

A rustling sound, a roar, a bound,—the lion sits
    astride
Upon his giant courser's back. Did ever king so
    ride?
Had ever king a steed so rare, caparisons of state
To match the dappled skin whereon that rider sits
    elate?

In the muscles of the neck his teeth are plunged
    with ravenous greed;
His tawny mane is tossing round the withers of
    the steed.
Up leaping with a hollow yell of anguish and
    surprise,
Away, away, in wild dismay, the cameleopard
    flies.

His feet have wings; see how he springs across the
    moonlit plain!
As from their sockets they would burst, his glar-
    ing eyeballs strain;
In thick black streams of purling blood, full fast
    his life is fleeting;
The stillness of the desert hears his heart's tu-
    multuous beating.

Like the cloud that, through the wilderness, the
    path of Israel traced,—
Like an airy phantom, dull and wan, a spirit of
    the waste,—
From the sandy sea uprising, as the water-spout
    from ocean,
A whirling cloud of dust keeps pace with the
    courser's fiery motion.

Croaking companion of their flight, the vulture
    whirs on high;
Below, the terror of the fold, the panther fierce
    and sly,
And hyenas foul, round graves that prowl, join
    in the horrid race;
By the footprints wet with gore and sweat, their
    monarch's course they trace.

They see him on his living throne, and quake with
    fear, the while
With claws of steel he tears piecemeal his
    cushion's painted pile.
On! on! no pause, no rest, giraffe, while life and
    strength remain!
The steed by such a rider backed may madly
    plunge in vain.

Reeling upon the desert's verge, he falls, and
    breathes his last;
The courser, stained with dust and foam, is the
    rider's fell repast.
O'er Madagascar, eastward far, a faint flush is
    descried:—
Thus nightly, o'er his broad domain, the king of
    beasts doth ride.

From the German of FERDINAND FREILIGRATH.

FODDER–TIME.

FROM " SONGS OF TOIL."

How sweet the manger smells! The cows all
    listen
    With outstretched necks, and with impatient
      lowing;
    They greet the clover, their content now show-
      ing—
And how they lick their noses till they glisten!

The velvet-coated beauties do not languish
    Beneath the morning's golden light that 's
      breaking,
    The unexhausted spring of life awaking,
Their golden eyes of velvet full of anguish.

They patiently endure their pains. Bestowing
    Their sympathy, the other cows are ruing
    Their unproductive udders, and renewing
At milking-time their labor and their lowing.

And now I must deceive the darling bossy,—
    With hand in milk must make it suck my finger.
    Its tender lips cling close like joys that linger,
And feel so warm with dripping white and flossy.

This very hand my people with devotion
    Do kiss,—which paints and plays and writes,
      moreover,—
    I would it had done naught but pile the clover
To feed the kine that know no base emotion!

From the German of CARMEN SYLVA, Queen of Roumania.
Translation of JOHN ELIOT BOWEN.

THE OX.

FROM THE "POESIE."

I LOVE thee, pious ox; a gentle feeling
  Of vigor and of peace thou giv'st my heart.
  How solemn, like a monument, thou art!
Over wide fertile fields thy calm gaze stealing,
Unto the yoke with grave contentment kneeling,
    To man's quick work thou dost thy strength
      impart.
  He shouts and goads, and answering thy smart,
Thou turn'st on him thy patient eyes appealing.
From thy broad nostrils, black and wet, arise
  Thy breath's soft fumes; and on the still air
    swells,
Like happy hymn, thy lowing's mellow strain.
In the grave sweetness of thy tranquil eyes
  Of emerald, broad and still reflected dwells
All the divine green silence of the plain.

From the Italian of GIOSUÉ CARDUCCI.

Translation of FRANK SEWALL.

FOLDING THE FLOCKS.

SHEPHERDS all, and maidens fair,
Fold your flocks up; for the air
'Gins to thicken, and the sun
Already his great course hath run.
See the dew-drops, how they kiss
Every little flower that is;
Hanging on their velvet heads,

Like a string of crystal beads.
See the heavy clouds low falling
And bright Hesperus down calling
The dead night from underground;
At whose rising, mists unsound,
Damps and vapors, fly apace,
And hover o'er the smiling face
Of these pastures; where they come,
Striking dead both bud and bloom.
Therefore from such danger lock
Every one his lovèd flock;
And let your dogs lie loose without,
Lest the wolf come as a scout
From the mountain, and ere day,
Bear a lamb or kid away;
Or the crafty, thievish fox,
Break upon your simple flocks.
To secure yourself from these,
Be not too secure in ease;
So shall you good shepherds prove,
And deserve your master's love.
Now, good night! may sweetest slumbers
And soft silence fall in numbers
On your eyelids.   So farewell:
Thus I end my evening knell.

BEAUMONT AND FLETCHER.

BETH GÊLERT.

THE spearmen heard the bugle sound,
    And cheerily smiled the morn;
And many a brach, and many a hound,
    Obeyed Llewellyn's horn.

And still he blew a louder blast,
  And gave a lustier cheer,
" Come, Gêlert, come, wert never last
  Llewellyn's horn to hear.

" O, where does faithful Gêlert roam,
  The flower of all his race;
So true, so brave,—a lamb at home,
  A lion in the chase? "

In sooth, he was a peerless hound,
  The gift of royal John;
But now no Gêlert could be found,
  And all the chase rode on.

That day Llewellyn little loved
  The chase of hart and hare;
And scant and small the booty proved,
  For Gêlert was not there.

Unpleased, Llewellyn homeward hied,
  When, near the portal seat,
His truant Gêlert he espied,
  Bounding his lord to greet.

But, when he gained his castle-door,
  Aghast the chieftain stood;
The hound all o'er was smeared with gore;
  His lips, his fangs, ran blood.

Llewellyn gazed with fierce surprise;
  Unused such looks to meet,
His favorite checked his joyful guise,
  And crouched, and licked his feet.

Onward, in haste, Llewellyn passed,
　　And on went Gêlert too;
And still, where'er his eyes he cast,
　　Fresh blood-gouts shocked his view.

O'erturned his infant's bed he found,
　　With blood-stained covert rent;
And all around the walls and ground
　　With recent blood besprent.

He called his child,—no voice replied,—
　　He searched with terror wild;
Blood, blood he found on every side,
　　But nowhere found his child.

"Hell-hound! my child's by thee devoured,"
　　The frantic father cried;
And to the hilt his vengeful sword
　　He plunged in Gêlert's side.

Aroused by Gêlert's dying yell,
　　Some slumberer wakened nigh:
What words the parent's joy could tell
　　To hear his infant's cry!

Concealed beneath a tumbled heap
　　His hurried search had missed,
All glowing from his rosy sleep,
　　The cherub boy he kissed.

Nor scathe had he, nor harm, nor dread,
　　But, the same couch beneath,
Lay a gaunt wolf, all torn and dead,
　　Tremendous still in death.

Ah, what was then Llewellyn's pain!
  For now the truth was clear;
His gallant hound the wolf had slain
  To save Llewellyn's heir.

WILLIAM ROBERT SPENCER.

TO A DOG'S MEMORY.

THE gusty morns are here,
When all the reeds ride low with level spear;
And on such nights as lured us far of yore,
Down rocky alleys yet, and thro' the pine,
The Hound-star and the pagan Hunter shine:
But I and thou, ah, field-fellow of mine,
Together roam no more.

Soft showers go laden now
With odors of the sappy orchard-bough,
And brooks begin to brawl along the march;
The late frost steams from hollow sedges high;
The finch is come, the flame-blue dragon-fly,
The cowslip's common gold that children spy,
The plume upon the larch.

There is a music fills
The oaks of Belmont and the Wayland hills
Southward to Dewing's little bubbly stream,
The heavenly weather's call! Oh, who alive
Hastes not to start, delays not to arrive,
Having free feet that never felt a gyve
Weigh, even in a dream?

But thou, instead, hast found
The sunless April uplands underground,
And still, wherever thou art, I must be.
My beautiful! arise in might and mirth,
For we were tameless travellers from our birth;
Arise against thy narrow door of earth,
And keep the watch for me.

                    LOUISE IMOGEN GUINEY.

HELVELLYN.

[In the spring of 1805, a young gentleman of talents,
and of a most amiable disposition, perished by losing his
way on the mountain Helvellyn. His remains were not
discovered till three months afterwards, when they were
found guarded by a faithful terrier, his constant atten-
dant during frequent solitary rambles through the wilds
of Cumberland and Westmoreland.]

I CLIMBED the dark brow of the mighty Helvellyn,
    Lakes and mountains beneath me gleamed misty
        and wide:
All was still, save, by fits, when the eagle was
        yelling,
    And starting around me the echoes replied.
On the right, Striden Edge round the Red Tarn
        was bending,
And Catchedicam its left verge was defending,
One huge nameless rock in the front was ascend-
        ing,
    When I marked the sad spot where the wan-
        derer had died.

Dark green was that spot mid the brown moun-
        tain heather,

Where the Pilgrim of Nature lay stretched in
decay.
Like the corpse of an outcast abandoned to
weather,
Till the mountain winds wasted the tenantless
clay;
Not yet quite deserted, though lonely extended,
For, faithful in death, his mute favorite attended,
The much-loved remains of her master defended,
And chased the hill-fox and the raven away.

How long didst thou think that his silence was
slumber?
When the wind waved his garment, how oft
didst thou start?
How many long days and long nights didst thou
number
Ere he faded before thee, the friend of thy
heart?
And, O, was it meet that—no requiem read o'er
him,
No mother to weep, and no friend to deplore him,
And thou, little guardian, alone stretched before
him—
Unhonored the Pilgrim from life should depart?

When a prince to the fate of the peasant has
yielded,
The tapestry waves dark round the dim-lighted
hall,
With 'scutcheons of silver the coffin is shielded,
And pages stand mute by the canopied pall:
Through the courts, at deep midnight, the torches
are gleaming;

In the proudly arched chapel the banners are
     beaming;
Far adown the long aisle sacred music is stream-
     ing,
  Lamenting a Chief of the People should fall.

But meeter for thee, gentle lover of nature,
  To lay down thy head like the meek mountain
    lamb,
When, wildered, he drops from some cliff huge in
    stature,
  And draws his last sob by the side of his dam.
And more stately thy couch by this desert lake
    lying,
Thy obsequies sung by the gray plover flying,
With one faithful friend but to witness thy dying,
  In the arms of Helvellyn and Catchedicam.

SIR WALTER SCOTT.

THE ARAB TO HIS FAVORITE STEED.

My beautiful! my beautiful! that standest meekly
    by,
With thy proudly arched and glossy neck, and
    dark and fiery eye,
Fret not to roam the desert now, with all thy
    wingèd speed;
I may not mount on thee again,—thou 'rt sold,
    my Arab steed!
Fret not with that impatient hoof,—snuff not the
    breezy wind,—
The farther that thou fliest now, so far am I be-
    hind;

The stranger hath thy bridle-rein,—thy master
    hath *his* gold,—
Fleet-limbed and beautiful, farewell; thou 'rt
    sold, my steed, thou 'rt sold.

Farewell! those free, untired limbs full many a
    mile must roam,
To reach the chill and wintry sky which clouds
    the stranger's home;
Some other hand, less fond, must now thy corn
    and bed prepare,
Thy silky mane, I braided once, must be another's
    care!
The morning sun shall dawn again, but never-
    more with thee
Shall I gallop through the desert paths, where we
    were wont to be;
Evening shall darken on the earth, and o'er the
    sandy plain
Some other steed, with slower step, shall bear me
    home again.

Yes, thou must go! the wild, free breeze, the bril-
    liant sun and sky,
Thy master's house,—from all of these my exiled
    one must fly;
Thy proud dark eye will grow less proud, thy step
    become less fleet,
And vainly shalt thou arch thy neck, thy mas-
    ter's hand to meet.
Only in sleep shall I behold that dark eye, glan-
    cing bright;—
Only in sleep shall hear again that step so firm
    and light;

And when I raise my dreaming arm to check or
cheer thy speed,
Then must I, starting, wake to feel,—thou 'rt
sold, my Arab steed!

Ah! rudely then, unseen by me, some cruel hand
may chide,
Till foam-wreaths lie, like crested waves, along
thy panting side:
And the rich blood that 's in thee swells, in thy
indignant pain,
Till careless eyes, which rest on thee, may count
each starting vein.
Will they ill-use thee? If I thought—but no, it
cannot be,—
Thou art so swift, yet easy curbed; so gentle, yet
so free:
And yet, if haply, when thou 'rt gone, my lonely
heart should yearn,—
Can the hand which casts thee from it now command thee to return?

Return! alas! my Arab steed! what shall thy
master do,
When thou, who wast his all of joy, hast vanished
from his view?
When the dim distance cheats mine eye, and
through the gathering tears
Thy bright form, for a moment, like the false
mirage appears;
Slow and unmounted shall I roam, with weary
step alone,
Where, with fleet step and joyous bound, thou
oft hast borne me on;

And sitting down by that green well, I 'll pause
 and sadly think,
" It was here he bowed his glossy neck when last
 I saw him drink! "

When last I saw thee drink!—Away! the fevered
 dream is o'er,—
I could not live a day, and *know* that we should
 meet no more!
They tempted me, my beautiful!—for hunger's
 power is strong,—
They tempted me, my beautiful! but I have loved
 too long.
Who said that I had given thee up? who said that
 thou wast sold?
'T is false,—'t is false, my Arab steed! I fling
 them back their gold!
Thus, *thus*, I leap upon thy back, and scour the
 distant plains;
Away! who overtakes us now shall claim thee for
 his pains!

    CAROLINE ELIZABETH SARAH NORTON.

THE BLOOD HORSE.

GAMARRA is a dainty steed,
Strong, black, and of a noble breed,
Full of fire, and full of bone,
With all his line of fathers known;
Fine his nose, his nostrils thin,
But blown abroad by the pride within!
His mane is like a river flowing,
And his eyes like embers glowing

24

In the darkness of the night,
And his pace as swift as light.

Look,—how round his straining throat
Grace and shifting beauty float;
Sinewy strength is in his reins,
And the red blood gallops through his veins:
Richer, redder, never ran
Through the boasting heart of man.
He can trace his lineage higher
Than the Bourbon dare aspire,—
Douglas, Guzman, or the Guelph,
Or O'Brien's blood itself!

He, who hath no peer, was born
Here, upon a red March morn.
But his famous fathers dead
Were Arabs all, and Arab-bred,
And the last of that great line
Trod like one of a race divine!
And yet,—he was but friend to one
Who fed him at the set of sun
By some lone fountain fringed with green;
With him, a roving Bedouin,
He lived (none else would he obey
Through all the hot Arabian day),
And died untamed upon the sands
Where Balkh amidst the desert stands.

BRYAN WALLER PROCTER (*Barry Cornwall*).

THE CHARIOT OF CUCHULLIN.*

FROM " THE BREACH OF THE PLAIN OF MUIRHEVNEY."

THE car, light-moving, I behold,
Adorned with gems and studs of gold;
Ruled by the hand of skilful guide,
Swiftly—and swiftly—see it glide!

.   .   .   .   .   .

Comes thundering on, unmatched in speed,
The gallant gray, high-bounding steed;
His four firm hoofs, at every bound,
Scarce seem to touch the solid ground,
Outflashing from their flinty frame
Flash upon flash of ruddy flame.
The other steed, of equal pace,
Well shaped to conquer in the race;
Of slender limb, firm-knit, and strong,
    His small, light head he lifts on high,
Impetuous as he scours along;
    Red lightning glances from his eye;
Flung on his curved neck and chest,
Toss his crisped manes like warrior's crest;
Of the wild chafer's dark-brown hues,
The color that his flanks imbues.

ANONYMOUS.   From the Ancient Irish.
Translation of W. H. DRUMMOND.

CHIQUITA.

BEAUTIFUL! Sir, you may say so. Thar isn't
   her match in the county,—

* A legendary Irish hero.

Is thar, old gal? Chiquita, my darling, my
  beauty!
Feel of that neck, sir,—thar's velvet! Whoa!
  Steady—ah, will you? you vixen!
Whoa! I say. Jack, trot her out; let the gentle-
  man look at her paces.

Morgan!—She ain't nothin' else, and I've got the
  papers to prove it.
Sired by Chippewa Chief, and twelve hundred dol-
  lars won't buy her.
Briggs of Tuolumne owned her. Did you know
  Briggs of Tuolumne?—
Busted hisself in White Pine, and blew out his
  brains down in 'Frisco.

Hedn't no savey,—hed Briggs. Thar, Jack!
  that 'll do,—quit that foolin'!
Nothin' to what she kin do when she's got her
  work cut out before her.
Hosses is hosses, you know, and likewise, too,
  jockeys is jockeys;
And 'tain't every man as' can ride as knows what
  a hoss has got in him.

Know the old ford on the Fork, that nearly got
  Flanigan's leaders?
Nasty in daylight, you bet, and a mighty rough
  ford in low water!
Well, it ain't six weeks ago that me and the Jedge,
  and his nevey,
Struck for that ford in the night, in the rain, and
  the water all round us;

Up to our flanks in the gulch, and Rattlesnake
  Creek just a bilin',

Not a plank left in the dam, and nary a bridge on
    the river.
I had the gray, and the Jedge had his roan, and
    his nevey, Chiquita;
And after us trundled the rocks jest loosed from
    the top of the cañon.

Lickity, lickity, switch, we came to the ford, and
    Chiquita
Buckled right down to her work, and afore I could
    yell to her rider,
Took water jest at the ford, and there was the
    Jedge and me standing,
And twelve hundred dollars of hoss-flesh afloat,
    and a driftin' to thunder!

Would ye b'lieve it, that night, that hoss,—that
    ar' filly,—Chiquita,—
Walked herself into her stall, and stood there
    all quiet and dripping!
Clean as a beaver or rat, with nary a buckle of
    harness,
Just as she swam the Fork,—that hoss, that ar'
    filly, Chiquita.

That 's what I call a hoss! and—what did you
    say? O, the nevey?
Drownded, I reckon,—leastways, he never kem
    back to deny it.
Ye see the derned fool had no seat,—ye could
    n't have made him a rider;
And then, ye know, boys will be boys, and hosses
    —well, hosses is hosses!

                      BRET HARTE.

VII.

THE SEA.

THE SEA.

> BEHOLD the Sea,
> The opaline, the plentiful and strong,
> Yet beautiful as is the rose in June,
> Fresh as the trickling rainbow of July:
> Sea full of food, the nourisher of kinds,
> Purger of earth, and medicine of men;
> Creating a sweet climate by my breath,
> Washing out harms and griefs from memory,
> And, in my mathematic ebb and flow,
> Giving a hint of that which changes not.
> Rich are the sea-gods:—who gives gifts but they?
> They grope the sea for pearls, but more than
>   pearls:
> They pluck Force thence, and give it to the wise.
> For every wave is wealth to Dædalus,
> Wealth to the cunning artist who can work
> This matchless strength. Where shall he find, O
>   waves!
> A load your Atlas shoulders cannot lift?
>   I with my hammer pounding evermore
> The rocky coast, smite Andes into dust,
> Strewing my bed, and, in another age,

Rebuild a continent of better men.
Then I unbar the doors: my paths lead out
The exodus of nations: I disperse
Men to all shores that front the hoary main.

RALPH WALDO EMERSON.

THE SEA.

FROM " CHILDE HAROLD," CANTO IV.

THERE is a pleasure in the pathless woods,
There is a rapture on the lonely shore,
There is society where none intrudes
By the deep sea, and music in its roar:
I love not man the less, but nature more,
From these our interviews, in which I steal
From all I may be, or have been before,
To mingle with the universe, and feel
What I can ne'er express, yet cannot all conceal.

Roll on, thou deep and dark blue Ocean,—roll!
Ten thousand fleets sweep over thee in vain;
Man marks the earth with ruin,—his control
Stops with the shore;—upon the watery plain
The wrecks are all thy deed, nor doth remain
A shadow of man's ravage, save his own,
When, for a moment, like a drop of rain,
He sinks into thy depths with bubbling groan,
Without a grave, unknelled, uncoffined, and un-
knffodown.

His steps are not upon thy paths,—thy fields
Are not a spoil for him,—thou dost arise

And shake him from thee; the vile strength he
    wields
For earth's destruction thou dost all despise,
Spurning him from thy bosom to the skies,
And send'st him, shivering in thy playful spray
And howling, to his gods, where haply lies
His petty hope in some near port or bay,
And dashest him again to earth:—there let him
    lay.

The armaments which thunderstrike the walls
Of rock-built cities, bidding nations quake
And monarchs tremble in their capitals,
The oak leviathans, whose huge ribs make
Their clay creator the vain title take
Of lord of thee and arbiter of war,—
These are thy toys, and, as the snowy flake,
They melt into thy yeast of waves, which mar
Alike the Armada's pride or spoils of Trafalgar.

Thy shores are empires, changed in all save
    thee;
Assyria, Greece, Rome, Carthage, what are
    they?
Thy waters wasted them while they were free,
And many a tyrant since; their shores obey
The stranger, slave, or savage; their decay
Has dried up realms to deserts: not so thou;
Unchangeable save to thy wild waves' play,
Time writes no wrinkles on thine azure brow;
Such as creation's dawn beheld, thou rollest now.

Thou glorious mirror, where the Almighty's
    form
Glasses itself in tempests; in all time,

Calm or convulsed,—in breeze, or gale, or
    storm,
Icing the pole, or in the torrid clime
Dark-heaving; boundless, endless, and sublime,
The image of Eternity,—the throne
Of the Invisible! even from out thy slime
The monsters of the deep are made; each zone
Obeys thee; thou goest forth, dread, fathomless,
    alone.

And I have loved thee, Ocean! and my joy
Of youthful sports was on thy breast to be
Borne, like thy bubbles, onward; from a boy
I wantoned with thy breakers,—they to me
Were a delight; and if the freshening sea
Made them a terror, 't was a pleasing fear;
For I was as it were a child of thee,
And trusted to thy billows far and near,
And laid my hand upon thy mane,—as I do here.

LORD BYRON.

THE SEA.

BEAUTIFUL, sublime, and glorious;
    Mild, majestic, foaming, free,—
Over time itself victorious,
    Image of eternity!

Sun and moon and stars shine o'er thee,
    See thy surface ebb and flow,
Yet attempt not to explore thee
    In thy soundless depths below.

Whether morning's splendors steep thee
With the rainbow's glowing grace,
Tempests rouse, or navies sweep thee,
   'T is but for a moment's space.

Earth,—her valleys and her mountains,
   Mortal man's behests obey;
The unfathomable fountains
   Scoff his search and scorn his sway.

Such art thou, stupendous Ocean!
   But, if overwhelmed by thee,
Can we think, without emotion,
   What must thy Creator be?

BERNARD BARTON.

THE DISAPPOINTED LOVER.

FROM " THE TRIUMPH OF TIME."

I WILL go back to the great sweet mother—
   Mother and lover of men, the Sea.
I will go down to her, I and none other,
   Close with her, kiss her, and mix her with me;
Cling to her, strive with her, hold her fast.
O fair white mother, in days long past
Born without sister, born without brother,
   Set free my soul as thy soul is free.

O fair green-girdled mother of mine,
   Sea, that are clothed with the sun and the rain,
Thy sweet hard kisses are strong like wine,
   Thy large embraces are keen like pain.

Save me and hide me with all thy waves,
Find me one grave of thy thousand graves,
Those pure cold populous graves of thine,—
    Wrought without hand in a world without
      stain.

I shall sleep, and move with the moving ships,
    Change as the winds change, veer in the tide;
My lips will feast on the foam of thy lips,
    I shall rise with thy rising, with thee subside;
Sleep, and not know if she be, if she were,—
Filled full with life to the eyes and hair,
As a rose is full filled to the rose-leaf tips
    With splendid summer and perfume and pride.

This woven raiment of nights and days,
    Were it once cast off and unwound from me,
Naked and glad would I walk in thy ways,
    Alive and aware of thy waves and thee;
Clear of the whole world, hidden at home,
Clothed with the green, and crowned with the
      foam,
A pulse of the life of thy straits and bays,
    A vein in the heart of the streams of the Sea.
              ALGERNON CHARLES SWINBURNE.

OCEAN.

FROM "THE COURSE OF TIME," BOOK I.

GREAT Ocean! strongest of creation's sons,
Unconquerable, unreposed, untired,
That rolled the wild, profound, eternal bass
In nature's anthem, and made music such

As pleased the ear of God! original,
Unmarred, unfaded work of Deity!
And unburlesqued by mortal's puny skill;
From age to age enduring, and unchanged,
Majestical, inimitable, vast,
Loud uttering satire, day and night, on each
Succeeding race, and little pompous work
Of man; unfallen, religious, holy sea!
Thou bowedest thy glorious head to none, fearedst
     none,
Heardst none, to none didst honor, but to God
Thy Maker, only worthy to receive
Thy great obeisance.

                              ROBERT POLLOK.

THE SEA.

THE sea! the sea! the open sea!
The blue, the fresh, the ever free!
Without a mark, without a bound,
It runneth the earth's wide regions round;
It plays with the clouds; it mocks the skies;
Or like a cradled creature lies.

I 'm on the sea! I 'm on the sea!
I am where I would ever be;
With the blue above, and the blue below,
And silence wheresoe'er I go;
If a storm should come and wake the deep,
What matter? *I* shall ride and sleep.

I love, O, *how* I love to ride
On the fierce, foaming, bursting tide,

When every mad wave drowns the moon,
Or whistles alóft his tempest tune,
And tells how goeth the world below,
And why the sou'west blasts do blow.

I never was on the dull, tame shore,
But I loved the great sea more and more,
And backwards flew to her billowy breast,
Like a bird that seeketh its mother's nest;
And a mother she *was*, and *is*, to me;
For I was born on the open sea!

The waves were white, and red the morn,
In the noisy hour when I was born;
And the whale it whistled, the porpoise rolled,
And the dolphins bared their backs of gold;
And never was heard such an outcry wild
As welcomed to life the ocean child!

I 've lived since then, in calm and strife,
Full fifty summers, a sailor's life,
With wealth to spend and a power to range,
But never have sought nor sighed for change;
And Death, whenever he comes to me,
Shall come on the wild, unbounded sea!

        BRYAN WALLER PROCTER (*Barry Cornwall*).

ADDRESS TO THE OCEAN.

O THOU vast Ocean! ever-sounding Sea!
Thou symbol of a drear immensity!
Thou thing that windest round the solid world
Like a huge animal, which, downward hurled

From the black clouds, lies weltering and alone,
Lashing and writhing till its strength be gone!
Thy voice is like the thunder, and thy sleep
Is as a giant's slumber, loud and deep.
Thou speakest in the east and in the west
At once, and on thy heavily laden breast
Fleets come and go, and shapes that have no life
Or motion, yet are moved and meet in strife.
The earth has naught of this: no chance or change
Ruffles its surface, and no spirits dare
Give answer to the tempest-wakened air;
But o'er its wastes the weakly tenants range
At will, and wound its bosom as they go:
Ever the same, it hath no ebb, no flow:
But in their stated rounds the seasons come,
And pass like visions to their wonted home;
And come again, and vanish; the young Spring
Looks ever bright with leaves and blossoming;
And Winter always winds his sullen horn,
When the wild Autumn, with a look forlorn,
Dies in his stormy manhood; and the skies
Weep, and flowers sicken, when the summer flies.
O, wonderful thou art, great element,
And fearful in thy spleeny humors bent,
And lovely in repose! thy summer form
Is beautiful, and when thy silver waves
Make music in earth's dark and winding caves,
I love to wander on thy pebbled beach,
Marking the sunlight at the evening hour,
And hearken to the thoughts thy waters teach,—
Eternity—Eternity—and Power.

                    BRYAN WALLER PROCTER (*Barry Cornwall*).

THE GRAVEDIGGER.

Oh, the shambling sea is a sexton old,
And well his work is done.
With an equal grave for lord and knave,
He buries them every one.

Then hoy and rip, with a rolling hip,
He makes for the nearest shore;
And God, who sent him a thousand ship,
Will send him a thousand more;
But some he 'll save for a bleaching grave,
And shoulder them in to shore,—
Shoulder them in, shoulder them in,
Shoulder them in to shore.

Oh, the ships of Greece and the ships of Tyre
Went out, and where are they?
In the port they made, they are delayed
With the ships of yesterday.

He followed the ships of England far,
As the ships of long ago;
And the ships of France they led him a dance,
But he laid them all arow.

Oh, a loafing, idle lubber to him
Is the sexton of the town;
For sure and swift, with a guiding lift,
He shovels the dead men down.

But though he delves so fierce and grim,
His honest graves are wide,

As well they know who sleep below
The dredge of the deepest tide.

Oh, he works with a rollicking stave at lip,
And loud is the chorus skirled;
With the burly note of his rumbling throat
He batters it down the world.

He learned it once in his father's house,
Where the ballads of eld were sung;
And merry enough is the burden rough,
But no man knows the tongue.

Oh, fair they say, was his bride to see,
And wilful she must have been,
That she could bide at his gruesome side
When the first red dawn came in.

And sweet, they say, is her kiss to those
She greets to his border home;
And softer than sleep her hand's first sweep
That beckons, and they come.

Oh, crooked is he, but strong enough
To handle the tallest mast;
From the royal barque to the slaver dark,
He buries them all at last.

Then hoy and rip, with a rolling hip,
He makes for the nearest shore;
And God, who sent him a thousand ship,
Will send him a thousand more;

But some he'll save for a bleaching grave,
And shoulder them in to shore,—
Shoulder them in, shoulder them in,
Shoulder them in to shore.

BLISS CARMAN.

THE TREASURES OF THE DEEP.

WHAT hid'st thou in thy treasure-caves and cells?
  Thou hollow-sounding and mysterious main!—
Pale glistening pearls and rainbow-colored shells,
    Bright things which gleam unrecked of and in
        vain!—
Keep, keep thy riches, melancholy sea!
    We ask not such from thee.

Yet more, the depths have more!—what wealth
       untold,
  Far down, and shining through their stillness
     lies!
Thou hast the starry gems, the burning gold,
  Won from ten thousand royal argosies!—
Sweep o'er thy spoils, thou wild and wrathful
     main!
    Earth claims not *these* again.

Yet more, the depths have more!—thy waves have
     rolled
  Above the cities of a world gone by!
Sand hath filled up the palaces of old,
  Sea-weed o'ergrown the halls of revelry.

25

Dash o'er them, Ocean, in thy scornful play!
  Man yields them to decay.

Yet more, the billows and the depths have more!
  High hearts and brave are gathered to thy
      breast!
They hear not now the booming waters roar,
  The battle-thunders will not break their rest.—
Keep thy red gold and gems, thou stormy grave!
  Give back the true and brave!

Give back the lost and lovely!—those for whom
  The place was kept at board and hearth so
      long!
The prayer went up through midnight's breath-
      less gloom,
  And the vain yearning woke midst festal song!
Hold fast thy buried isles, thy towers o'er-
      thrown,—
    But all is not thine own.

To thee the love of woman hath gone down,
  Dark flow thy tides o'er manhood's noble head,
O'er youth's bright locks, and beauty's flowery
      crown;
  Yet must thou hear a voice,—Restore the dead!
Earth shall reclaim her precious things from
      thee!—
    Restore the dead, thou sea!

                            FELICIA HEMANS.

FLOTSAM AND JETSAM.

THE sea crashed over the grim gray rocks,
  It thundered beneath the height,
It swept by reef and sandy dune,
It glittered beneath the harvest moon,
  That bathed it in yellow light.

Shell, and sea-weed, and sparkling stone,
  It flung on the golden sand.
Strange relics torn from its deepest caves,
Sad trophies of wild victorious waves,
  It scattered upon the strand.

Spars that had looked so strong and true,
  At many a gallant launch,
Shattered and broken, flung to the shore,
While the tide in its wild triumphant roar
  Rang a dirge for the vessel stanch.

Petty trifles that lovers had brought
  From many a foreign clime,
Snatched by the storm from the clinging clasp
Of hands that the lonely will never grasp,
  While the world yet measures time.

Back, back to its depths went the ebbing tide,
  Leaving its stores to rest,
Unsought and unseen in the silent bay,
To be gathered again, ere close of day,
  To the ocean's mighty breast.

Kinder than man art thou, O sea;
  Frankly we give our best,
Truth, and hope, and love, and faith,
Devotion that challenges time and death
  Its sterling worth to test.

We fling them down at our darling's feet,
  Indifference leaves them there.
The careless footstep turns aside,
Weariness, changefulness, scorn, or pride,
  Bring little of thought or care.

No tide of human feeling turns;
  Once ebbed, love never flows;
The pitiful wreckage of time and strife,
The flotsam and jetsam of human life,
  No saving reflux knows.

ANONYMOUS.

A FORSAKEN GARDEN.

IN a coign of the cliff between lowland and high-
      land,
  At the sea-down's edge between windward and
      lee,
Walled round with rocks as an inland island,
  The ghost of a garden fronts the sea.
A girdle of brushwood and thorn encloses
  The steep, square slope of the blossomless bed
Where the weeds that grew green from the graves
      of its roses
          Now lie dead.

The fields fall southward, abrupt and broken,
  To the low last edge of the long lone land.
If a step should sound or a word be spoken,
  Would a ghost not rise at the strange guest's
    hand?
So long have the gray, bare walks lain guestless,
  Through branches and briers if a man make
    way,
He shall find no life but the sea-wind's, restless
  Night and day.

The dense, hard passage is blind and stifled
  That crawls by a track none turn to climb
To the strait waste place that the years have
    rifled
  Of all but the thorns that are touched not of
    Time.
The thorns he spares when the rose is taken;
  The rocks are left when he wastes the plain.
The wind that wanders, the weeds wind-shaken,
    These remain.

Not a flower to be pressed of the foot that falls
    not;
  As the heart of a dead man the seed-plots are
    dry;
From the thicket of thorns whence the nightin-
    gale calls not,
  Could she call, there were never a rose to reply.
Over the meadows that blossom and wither
  Rings but the note of a sea-bird's song;
Only the sun and the rain come hither
    All year long.

The sun burns sere and the rain dishevels
  One gaunt bleak blossom of scentless breath.
Only the wind here hovers and revels
  In a round where life seems barren as death.
Here there was laughing of old, there was weep-
      ing,
Haply, of lovers none ever will know,
  Whose eyes went seaward a hundred sleeping
      Years ago.

Heart handfast in heart as they stood, "Look
      thither,"
  Did he whisper? " Look forth from the flowers
      to the sea;
For the foam-flowers endure when the rose-blos-
      soms wither,
  And men that love lightly may die—but we?"
And the same wind sang and the same waves
      whitened,
  And or ever the garden's last petals were shed,
In the lips that had whispered, the eyes that had
      lightened,
      Love was dead.

Or they loved their life through, and then went
      whither?
  And were one to the end—but what end who
      knows?
Love deep as the sea as a rose must wither,
  As the rose-red seaweed that mocks the rose.
Shall the dead take thought for the dead to love
      them?
  What love was ever as deep as a grave?

They are loveless now as the grass above them
    Or the wave.

All are at one now, roses and lovers,
    Not known of the cliffs and the fields and the
        sea.
Not a breath of the time that has been hovers
    In the air now soft with a summer to be.
Not a breath shall there sweeten the seasons here-
        after
    Of the flowers or the lovers that laugh now or
        weep,
When, as they that are free now of weeping and
        laughter,
        We shall sleep.

Here death may deal not again forever;
    Here change may come not till all change end.
From the graves they have made they shall rise
        up never,
    Who have left nought living to ravage and
        rend.
Earth, stones, and thorns of the wild ground
        growing,
    While the sun and the rain live, these shall be;
Till a last wind's breath upon all these blowing
        Roll the sea.

Till the slow sea rise and the sheer cliff crumble,
    Till terrace and meadow the deep gulfs drink,
Till the strength of the waves of the high tides
        humble
    The fields that lessen, the rocks that shrink,

Here now in his triumph where all things falter,
  Stretched out on the spoils that his own hand
    spread,
As a god self-slain on his own strange altar,
  Death lies dead.

ALGERNON CHARLES SWINBURNE.

GULF–WEED.

A WEARY weed, tossed to and fro,
  Drearily drenched in the ocean brine,
Soaring high and sinking low,
  Lashed along without will of mine;
Sport of the spume of the surging sea;
  Flung on the foam, afar and anear,
Mark my manifold mystery,—
  Growth and grace in their place appear.

I bear round berries, gray and red,
  Rootless and rover though I be;
My spangled leaves, when nicely spread,
  Arboresce as a trunkless tree;
Corals curious coat me o'er,
  White and hard in apt array;
Mid the wild waves' rude uproar
  Gracefully grow I, night and day.

Hearts there are on the sounding shore,
  Something whispers soft to me,
Restless and roaming forevermore,
  Like this weary weed of the sea;

Bear they yet on each beating breast
    The eternal type of the wondrous whole,
Growth unfolding amidst unrest,
    Grace informing with silent soul.

CORNELIUS GEORGE FENNER.

SEA–WEED.

WHEN descends on the Atlantic
    The gigantic
Storm-wind of the equinox,
Landward in his wrath he scourges
    The toiling surges,
Laden with sea-weed from the rocks:

From Bermuda's reefs; from edges
    Of sunken ledges,
In some far-off, bright Azore;
From Bahama, and the dashing,
    Silver flashing
Surges of San Salvador;

From the tumbling surf, that buries
    The Orkneyan skerries,
Answering the hoarse Hebrides;
And from wrecks of ships, and drifting
    Spars, uplifting
On the desolate, rainy seas;—

Ever drifting, drifting, drifting
    On the shifting
Currents of the restless main;

Till in sheltered coves, and reaches
    Of sandy beaches,
All have found repose again.

So when storms of wild emotion
    Strike the ocean
Of the poet's soul, erelong,
From each cave and rocky fastness
    In its vastness,
Floats some fragment of a song:

From the far-off isles enchanted
    Heaven has planted
With the golden fruit of Truth;
From the flashing surf, whose vision
    Gleams Elysian
In the tropic clime of Youth;

From the strong Will, and the Endeavor
    That forever
Wrestles with the tides of Fate;
From the wreck of Hopes far-scattered,
    Tempest-shattered,
Floating waste and desolate;—

Ever drifting, drifting, drifting
    On the shifting
Currents of the restless heart;
Till at length in books recorded,
    They, like hoarded
Household words, no more depart.

          HENRY WADSWORTH LONGFELLOW.

THE CORAL INSECT.

TOIL on! toil on! ye ephemeral train,
Who build in the tossing and treacherous main;
Toil on! for the wisdom of man ye mock,
With your sand-based structure and domes of
     rock,
Your columns the fathomless fountains' cave,
And your arches spring up to the crested wave;
Ye 're a puny race thus to boldly rear
A fabric so vast in a realm so drear.

Ye bind the deep with your secret zone,—
The ocean is sealed, and the surge a stone;
Fresh wreaths from the coral pavement spring,
Like the terraced pride of Assyria's king;
The turf looks green where the breakers rolled;
O'er the whirlpool ripens the rind of gold;
The sea-snatched isle is the home of men,
And mountains exult where the wave hath been.

But why do ye plant, 'neath the billows dark,
The wrecking reef for the gallant bark?
There are snares enough on the tented field,
Mid the blossomed sweets that the valleys yield;
There are serpents to coil ere the flowers are up,
There 's a poison drop in man's purest cup.
There are foes that watch for his cradle breath,
And why need ye sow the floods with death?

With mouldering bones the deeps are white,
From the ice-clad pole to the tropics bright;

The mermaid hath twisted her fingers cold
With the mesh of the sea-boy's curls of gold,
And the gods of the ocean have frowned to see
The mariner's bed in their halls of glee;
Hath earth no graves, that ye thus must spread
The boundless sea for the thronging dead?

Ye build—ye build—but ye enter not in,
Like the tribes whom the desert devoured in
    their sin;
From the land of promise ye fade and die
Ere its verdure gleams forth on your weary eye:
As the kings of the cloud-crowned pyramid,
Their noiseless bones in oblivion hid,
Ye slumber unmarked mid the desolate main,
While the wonder and pride of your works re-
    main.

LYDIA HUNTLEY SIGOURNEY.

THE CORAL REEF.

FROM "THE PELICAN ISLAND."

                                    EVERY one,
By instinct taught, performed its little task,—
To build its dwelling and its sepulchre,
From its own essence exquisitely modelled;
There breed, and die, and leave a progeny,
Still multiplied beyond the reach of numbers,
To frame new cells and tombs; then breed and die
As all their ancestors had done,—and rest,
Hermetically sealed, each in its shrine,
A statue in this temple of oblivion!

Millions of millions thus, from age to age,
With simplest skill and toil unweariable,
No moment and no movement unimproved,
Laid line on line, on terrace terrace spread,
To swell the heightening, brightening, gradual
    mound,
By marvellous structure climbing towards the
    day.

    .   .   .   .   .   .

                    A point at first
It peered above those waves; a point so small
I just perceived it, fixed where all was floating;
And when a bubble crossed it, the blue film
Expanded like a sky above the speck;
That speck became a hand-breadth; day and
    night
It spread, accumulated, and erelong
Presented to my view a dazzling plain,
White as the moon amid the sapphire sea;
Bare at low water, and as still as death,
But when the tide came gurgling o'er the surface
'T was like a resurrection of the dead:
From graves innumerable, punctures fine
In the close coral, capillary swarms
Of reptiles, horrent as Medusa's snakes,
Covered the bald-pate reef;

    .   .   .   .   .   .

Erelong the reef o'ertopt the spring-flood's height,
And mocked the billows when they leapt upon it,
Unable to maintain their slippery hold,
And falling down in foam-wreaths round its
    verge.
Steep were the flanks, with precipices sharp,

Descending to their base in ocean gloom.
Chasms few and narrow and irregular
Formed harbors, safe at once and perilous,—
Safe for defence, but perilous to enter.
A sea-lake shone amidst the fossil isle,
Reflecting in a ring its cliffs and caverns,
With heaven itself seen like a lake below.

JAMES MONTGOMERY.

THE CHAMBERED NAUTILUS.

THIS is the ship of pearl, which, poets feign,
 Sails the unshadowed main,—
 The venturous bark that flings
On the sweet summer wind its purpled wings
In gulfs enchanted, where the Siren sings,
 And coral reefs lie bare,
Where the cold sea-maids rise to sun their stream-
  ing hair.

Its webs of living gauze no more unfurl;
 Wrecked is the ship of pearl!
 And every chambered cell,
Where its dim dreaming life was wont to dwell,
As the frail tenant shaped his growing shell,
 Before thee lies revealed,—
Its irised ceiling rent, its sunless crypt unsealed!

Year after year beheld the silent toil
 That spread his lustrous coil;
 Still, as the spiral grew,
He left the past year's dwelling for the new,

Stole with soft step its shining archway through,
  Built up its idle door,
Stretched in his last-found home, and knew the
    old no more.

Thanks for the heavenly message brought by thee,
  Child of the wandering sea,
  Cast from her lap, forlorn!
From thy dead lips a clearer note is born
Than ever Triton blew from wreathèd horn!
  While on mine ear it rings,
Through the deep caves of thought I hear a voice
    that sings:—

Build thee more stately mansions, O my soul,
  As the swift seasons roll!
  Leave thy low-vaulted past!
Let each new temple, nobler than the last,
Shut thee from heaven with a dome more vast,
  Till thou at length art free,
Leaving thine outgrown shell by life's unresting
    sea!

OLIVER WENDELL HOLMES.

————

A WET SHEET AND A FLOWING SEA.

A WET sheet and a flowing sea,—
  A wind that follows fast,
And fills the white and rustling sail,
  And bends the gallant mast,—
And bends the gallant mast, my boys,
  While, like the eagle free,

Away the good ship flies, and leaves
Old England on the lee.

O for a soft and gentle wind!
I heard a fair one cry;
But give to me the snoring breeze
And white waves heaving high,—
And white waves heaving high, my boys,
The good ship tight and free;
The world of waters is our home,
And merry men are we.

There 's tempest in yon hornèd moon,
And lightning in yon cloud;
And hark the music, mariners!
The wind is piping loud,—
The wind is piping loud, my boys,
The lightning flashing free;
While the hollow oak our palace is,
Our heritage the sea.

ALLAN CUNNINGHAM.

SONG OF THE EMIGRANTS IN BERMUDA.

WHERE the remote Bermudas ride
In the ocean's bosom unespied,
From a small boat that rowed along
The listening winds received this song:
"What should we do but sing His praise
That led us through the watery maze
Where he the huge sea monsters wracks,
That lift the deep upon their backs,

Unto an isle so long unknown,
And yet far kinder than our own?
He lands us on a grassy stage,
Safe from the storms, and prelate's rage;
He gave us this eternal spring
Which here enamels everything,
And sends the fowls to us in care
On daily visits through the air.
He hangs in shades the orange bright
Like golden lamps in a green night.
And does in the pomegranates close
Jewels more rich than Ormus shows:
He makes the figs our mouths to meet,
And throws the melons at our feet;
But apples, plants of such a price,
No tree could ever bear them twice.
With cedars chosen by his hand
From Lebanon he stores the land;
And makes the hollow seas that roar
Proclaim the ambergris on shore.
He cast (of which we rather boast)
The Gospel's pearl upon our coast;
And in these rocks for us did frame
A temple where to sound his name.
O, let our voice his praise exalt
Till it arrive at heaven's vault,
Which then perhaps rebounding may
Echo beyond the Mexique bay!"—
Thus sung they in the English boat
A holy and a cheerful note;
And all the way, to guide their chime,
With falling oars they kept the time.

ANDREW MARVELL.

MY BRIGANTINE.

FROM " THE WATER WITCH."

Just in thy mould and beauteous' in thy form,
Gentle in roll and buoyant on the surge,
Light as the sea-fowl rocking in the storm,
In breeze and gale thy onward course we urge,
     My water-queen!
     Lady of mine,
More light and swift than thou none thread the
         sea
With surer keel or steadier on its path,
We brave each waste of ocean-mystery
And laugh to hear the howling tempest's wrath,
     For we are thine.
     My brigantine!
Trust to the mystic power that points thy way,
Trust to the eye that pierces from afar;
Trust the red meteors that around thee play,
And, fearless, trust the Sea-Green Lady's star,
     Thou bark divine!
             JAMES FENIMORE COOPER.

THE HEAVING OF THE LEAD.

For England when with favoring gale
  Our gallant ship up channel steered,
And, scudding under easy sail,
  The high blue western land appeared;
To heave the lead the seaman sprung,
And to the pilot cheerly sung,
     " By the deep—nine!"

And bearing up to gain the port,
   Some well-known object kept in view,—
An abbey-tower, a harbor-fort,
   Or beacon to the vessel true;
While oft the lead the seaman flung,
And to the pilot cheerly sung,
             " By the mark—seven!"

And as the much-loved shore we near,
   With transport we behold the roof
Where dwelt a friend or partner dear,
   Of faith and love a matchless proof.
The lead once more the seaman flung,
And to the watchful pilot sung,
             " Quarter less—five!"

Now to her berth the ship draws nigh:
   We shorten sail,—she feels the tide,—
" Stand clear the cable " is the cry,—
   The anchor 's gone; we safely ride.
The watch is set, and through the night
We hear the seamen with delight
             Proclaim,—" All 's well!"
                CHARLES DIBDIN.

THE MINUTE-GUN.

WHEN in the storm on Albion's coast,
The night-watch guards his weary post,
   From thoughts of danger free,
He marks some vessel's dusky form,
And hears, amid the howling storm,
   The minute-gun at sea.

Swift on the shore a hardy few
The life-boat man with a gallant crew
  And dare the dangerous wave;
Through the wild surf they cleave their way,
Lost in the foam, nor know dismay,
  For they go the crew to save.

But O, what rapture fills each breast
Of the hopeless crew of the ship distressed!
Then, landed safe, what joy to tell
Of all the dangers that befell!
  Then is heard no more,
  By the watch on shore,
    The minute-gun at sea.

R. S. SHARPE.

ALL 'S WELL.

FROM " THE BRITISH FLEET."

DESERTED by the waning moon,
When skies proclaim night's cheerless noon,
On tower, or fort, or tented ground
The sentry walks his lonely round;
And should a footstep haply stray
Where caution marks the guarded way,
" Who goes there? Stranger, quickly tell! "
" A friend! " " The word? " " Good-night; " all 's
    well.

Or, sailing on the midnight deep,
When weary messmates soundly sleep,
The careful watch patrols the deck,
To guard the ship from foes or wreck;

And while his thoughts oft homewards veer,
Some friendly voice salutes his ear,—
"What cheer? Brother, quickly tell;
Above,—below." Good-night; all 's well.

THOMAS DIBDIN.

THE BAY OF BISCAY.

LOUD roared the dreadful thunder,
　The rain a deluge showers,
The clouds were rent asunder
　By lightning's vivid powers;
The night both drear and dark,
Our poor devoted bark,
Till next day, there she lay,
In the Bay of Biscay, O!

Now dashed upon the billow,
　Her opening timbers creak,
Each fears a watery pillow,
　None stops the dreadful leak;
To cling to slippery shrouds
Each breathless seaman crowds,
As she lay, till the day,
In the Bay of Biscay, O!

At length the wished-for morrow
　Broke through the hazy sky,
Absorbed in silent sorrow,
　Each heaved a bitter sigh;
The dismal wreck to view
Struck horror to the crew,
As she lay, on that day,
In the Bay of Biscay, O!

Her yielding timbers sever,
  Her pitchy seams are rent,
When Heaven, all bounteous ever,
  Its boundless mercy sent,—
A sail in sight appears!
We hail her with three cheers;
Now we sail, with the gale,
From the Bay of Biscay, O!

ANDREW CHERRY.

TOM BOWLING.

HERE, a sheer hulk, lies poor Tom Bowling,
  The darling of our crew;
No more he 'll hear the tempest howling,
  For death has broached him to.
His form was of the manliest beauty,
  His heart was kind and soft;
Faithful, below, he did his duty;
  But now he 's gone aloft.

Tom never from his word departed,
  His virtues were so rare,
His friends were many and true-hearted,
  His Poll was kind and fair:
And then he 'd sing, so blithe and jolly,
  Ah, many 's the time and oft!
But mirth is turned to melancholy,
  For Tom is gone aloft.

Yet shall poor Tom find pleasant weather,
  When He who all commands
Shall give, to call life's crew together,
  The word to " pipe all hands."

Thus Death, who kings and tars despatches,
    In vain Tom's life has doffed;
For though his body 's under hatches,
    His soul has gone aloft.

                              CHARLES DIBDIN.

_____

YE MARINERS OF ENGLAND.

Ye mariners of England!
That guard our native seas;
Whose flag has braved, a thousand years,
The battle and the breeze!
Your glorious standard launch again
To match another foe!
And sweep through the deep,
While the stormy winds do blow;
While the battle rages loud and long,
And the stormy winds do blow.

The spirits of your fathers
Shall start from every wave!—
For the deck it was their field of fame,
And ocean was their grave:
Where Blake and mighty Nelson fell,
Your manly hearts shall glow,
As ye sweep through the deep,
While the stormy winds do blow;
While the battle rages loud and long,
And the stormy winds do blow.

Britannia needs no bulwarks,
No towers along the steep;
Her march is o'er the mountain-waves,
Her home is on the deep.

With thunders from her native oak,
She quells the floods below,—
As they roar on the shore,
When the stormy winds do blow;
When the battle rages loud and long
And the stormy winds do blow.

The meteor flag of England
Shall yet terrific burn;
Till danger's troubled night depart,
And the star of peace return.
Then, then, ye ocean warriors!
Our song and feast shall flow
To the fame of your name,
When the storm has ceased to blow;
When the fiery fight is heard no more,
And the storm has ceased to blow.

THOMAS CAMPBELL.

THE WHITE SQUALL.

THE sea was bright, and the bark rode well;
The breeze bore the tone of the vesper bell;
'T was a gallant bark with a crew as brave
As ever launched on the heaving wave.
She shone in the light of declining day,
And each sail was set, and each heart was gay.

They neared the land where in beauty smiles
The sunny shore of the Grecian Isles;
All thought of home, of that welcome dear
Which soon should greet each wanderer's ear;
And in fancy joined the social throng
In the festive dance and the joyous song.

A white cloud glides through the azure sky,—
What means that wild despairing cry?
Farewell the visioned scenes of home!
That cry is " Help," where no help can come;
For the White Squall rides on the surging wave,
And the bark is 'gulfed in an ocean grave.

BRYAN WALLER PROCTER (Barry Cornwall).

OUR BOAT TO THE WAVES.

OUR boat to the waves go free,
    By the bending tide, where the curled wave
      breaks,
    Like the track of the wind on the white snow-
      flakes:
Away, away!   'T is a path o'er the sea.

Blasts may rave,—spread the sail,
    For our spirits can wrest the power from the
      wind,
    And the gray clouds yield to the sunny mind,
Fear not we the whirl of the gale.

WILLIAM ELLERY CHANNING.

A LIFE ON THE OCEAN WAVE.

A LIFE on the ocean wave,
    A home on the rolling deep;
Where the scattered waters rave,
    And the winds their revels keep!
Like an eagle caged I pine
    On this dull, unchanging shore:

O, give me the flashing brine,
  The spray and the tempest's roar!

Once more on the deck I stand,
  Of my own swift-gliding craft:
Set sail! farewell to the land;
  The gale follows fair abaft.
We shoot through the sparkling foam,
  Like an ocean-bird set free,—
Like the ocean-bird, our home
  We'll find far out on the sea.

The land is no longer in view,
  The clouds have begun to frown;
But with a stout vessel and crew,
  We'll say, Let the storm come down!
And the song of our hearts shall be,
  While the winds and the waters rave,
A home on the rolling sea!
  A life on the ocean wave!

EPES SARGENT.

TO SEA!

To sea! to sea! the calm is o'er,
  The wanton water leaps in sport,
And rattles down the pebbly shore,
  The dolphin wheels, the sea-cows snort,
And unseen mermaid's pearly song
Comes bubbling up, the weeds among.
Fling broad the sail, dip deep the oar:
To sea! to sea! the calm is o'er.

To sea! to sea! our white-winged bark
  Shall billowing cleave its watery way,
And with its shadow, fleet and dark,
  Break the caved Triton's azure day,
Like mountain eagle soaring light
O'er antelopes on Alpine height.
The anchor heaves! The ship swings free!
Our sails swell full! To sea! to sea!
THOMAS LOVELL BEDDOES.

TWILIGHT AT SEA.

THE twilight hours, like birds, flew by,
  As lightly and as free,
Ten thousand stars were in the sky,
  Ten thousand on the sea;
For every wave, with dimpled face,
  That leaped upon the air,
Had caught a star in its embrace,
  And held it trembling there.
AMELIA B. WELBY.

TACKING SHIP OFF SHORE.

THE weather-leech of the topsail shivers,
  The bowlines strain, and the lee-shrouds slacken,
The braces are taut, the lithe boom quivers,
  And the waves with the coming squall-cloud
    blacken.

Open one point on the weather-bow,
  Is the light-house tall on Fire Island Head?
There's a shade of doubt on the captain's brow,
  And the pilot watches the heaving lead.

I stand at the wheel, and with eager eye
  To sea and to sky and to shore I gaze,
Till the muttered order of " Full and by ! "
  Is suddenly changed for " Full for stays ! "

The ship bends lower before the breeze,
  As her broadside fair to the blast she lays;
And she swifter springs to the rising seas,
  As the pilot calls, " Stand by for stays ! "

It is silence all, as each in his place,
  With the gathered coil in his hardened hands,
By tack and bowline, by sheet and brace,
  Waiting the watchword impatient stands.

And the light on Fire Island Head draws near,
  As, trumpet-winged, the pilot's shout
From his post on the bowsprit's heel I hear,
  With the welcome call of " Ready!   About ! "

No time to spare!   It is touch and go;
  And the captain growls, " Down, helm! hard
    down ! "
As my weight on the whirling spokes I throw,
  While heaven grows black with the storm-
    cloud's frown.

High o'er the knight-heads flies the spray,
  As we meet the shock of the plunging sea;
And my shoulder stiff to the wheel I lay,
  As I answer, " Ay, ay, sir!   Ha-a-rd a-lee ! "

With the swerving leap of a startled steed
  The ship flies fast in the eye of the wind,

The dangerous shoals on the lee recede,
　　And the headland white we have left behind.

The topsails flutter, the jibs collapse,
　　And belly and tug at the groaning cleats;
The spanker slats, and the mainsail flaps;
　　And thunders the order, " Tacks and sheets!"

'Mid the rattle of blocks and the tramp of the crew,
　　Hisses the rain of the rushing squall:
The sails are aback from clew to clew,
　　And now is the moment for, " Mainsail, haul!"

And the heavy yards, like a baby's toy,
　　By fifty strong arms are swiftly swung:
She holds her way, and I look with joy
　　For the first white spray o'er the bulwarks flung.

" Let go, and haul!"   'T is the last command,
　　And the head-sails fill to the blast once more:
Astern and to leeward lies the land,
　　With its breakers white on the shingly shore.

What matters the reef, or the rain, or the squall?
　　I steady the helm for the open sea;
The first mate clamors, " Belay, there, all!"
　　And the captain's breath once more comes free.

And so off shore let the good ship fly;
　　Little care I how the gusts may blow,
In my fo'castle bunk, in a jacket dry,
　　Eight bells have struck, and my watch is below.

　　　　　　　　　　WALTER MITCHELL.

THE STORM.

CEASE, rude Boreas, blustering railer!
  List, ye landsmen, all to me,
Messmates, hear a brother sailor
  Sing the dangers of the sea;

From bounding billows, first in motion,
  When the distant whirlwinds rise,
To the tempest-troubled ocean,
  Where the seas contend with skies.

Hark! the boatswain hoarsely bawling,
  By topsail sheets and halyards stand!
Down top-gallants quick be hauling!
  Down your stay-sails, hand, boys, hand!

Now it freshens, set the braces,
  Quick the topsail sheets let go;
Luff, boys, luff! don't make wry faces,
  Up your topsails nimbly clew.

Round us roars the tempest louder,
  Think what fear our minds inthralls!
Harder yet, it yet blows harder,
  Now again the boatswain calls.

The topsail yard point to the wind, boys,
  See all clear to reef each course;
Let the fore sheet go, don't mind, boys,
  Though the weather should be worse.

Fore and aft the sprit-sail yard get,
  Reef the mizzen, see all clear;
Hands up! each preventive brace set!
  Man the fore yard, cheer, lads, cheer!

Now the dreadful thunder 's roaring
  Peal on peal contending clash,
On our heads fierce rain falls pouring,
  In our eyes blue lightnings flash.

One wide water all around us,
  All above us one black sky;
Different deaths at once surround us:
  Hark! what means that dreadful cry?

The foremast 's gone, cries every tongue out,
  O'er the lee twelve feet 'bove deck;
A leak beneath the chest-tree 's sprung out,
  Call all hands to clear the wreck.

Quick the lanyards cut to pieces;
  Come, my hearts, be stout and bold;
Plumb the well,—the leak increases,
  Four feet water in the hold!

While o'er the ship wild waves are beating,
  We our wives and children mourn;
Alas! from hence there 's no retreating,
  Alas! to them there 's no return!

Still the leak is gaining on us!
  Both chain-pumps are choked below:
Heaven have mercy here upon us!
  For only that can save us now.

O'er the lee-beam is the land, boys,
  Let the guns o'erboard be thrown;
To the pumps call every hand, boys,
  See! our mizzen-mast is gone.

The leak we 've found, it cannot pour fast;
  We 've lighted her a foot or more;
Up and rig a jury foremast,
  She rights! she rights, boys! we 're off shore.
                    GEORGE ALEXANDER STEVENS.

THE WRECK.

FROM "DON JUAN," CANTO II.

THEN rose from sea to sky the wild farewell—
  Then shrieked the timid, and stood still the
    brave,—
Then some leaped overboard with dreadful yell,
  As eager to anticipate their grave;
And the sea yawned around her like a hell,
  And down she sucked with her the whirling
    wave,
Like one who grapples with his enemy,
And strives to strangle him before he die.

And first one universal shriek there rushed,
  Louder than the loud ocean, like a crash
Of echoing thunder; and then all was hushed,
  Save the wild wind and the remorseless dash
Of billows; but at intervals there gushed,
  Accompanied with a convulsive splash,
A solitary shriek, the bubbling cry
Of some strong swimmer in his agony.
                    LORD BYRON.

THE SHIPWRECK.

In vain the cords and axes were prepared,
For now the audacious seas insult the yard;
High o'er the ship they throw a horrid shade,
And o'er her burst in terrible cascade.
Uplifted on the surge, to heaven she flies,
Her shattered top half buried in the skies,
Then headlong plunging thunders on the ground;
Earth groans! air trembles! and the deeps re-
    sound!
Her giant-bulk the dread concussion feels,
And quivering with the wound in torment reels.
So reels, convulsed with agonizing throes,
The bleeding bull beneath the murderer's blows.
Again she plunges! hark! a second shock
Tears her strong bottom on the marble rock:
Down on the vale of death, with dismal cries,
The fated victims, shuddering, roll their eyes
In wild despair; while yet another stroke,
With deep convulsion, rends the solid oak;
Till like the mine, in whose infernal cell
The lurking demons of destruction dwell,
At length asunder torn her frame divides,
And, crashing, spreads in ruin o'er the tides.
  O, were it mine with tuneful Maro's art
To wake to sympathy the feeling heart;
Like him the smooth and mournful verse to dress
In all the pomp of exquisite distress,
Then too severely taught by cruel fate,
To share in all the perils I relate,

27

Then might I with unrivalled strains deplore
The impervious horrors of a leeward shore!

As o'er the surge the stooping mainmast hung,
Still on the rigging thirty seamen clung;
Some, struggling, on a broken crag were cast,
And there by oozy tangles grappled fast.
Awhile they bore the o'erwhelming billows' rage,
Unequal combat with their fate to wage;
Till, all benumbed and feeble, they forego
Their slippery hold, and sink to shades below.
Some, from the main-yard-arm impetuous thrown
On marble ridges, die without a groan.
Three with Palemon on their skill depend,
And from the wreck on oars and rafts descend.
Now on the mountain wave on high they ride,
Then downward plunge beneath the involving tide,
Till one, who seems in agony to strive,
The whirling breakers heave on shore alive;
The rest a speedier end of anguish knew,
And pressed the stony beach, a lifeless crew!

WILLIAM FALCONER.

THE ROCK AND THE SEA.

The Rock.

I AM the Rock, presumptuous Sea!
I am set to encounter thee.
Angry and loud, or gentle and still,
I am set here to limit thy power, and I will—
     I am the Rock!

I am the Rock. From age to age
I scorn thy fury and dare thy rage.

Scarred by frost and worn by time,
Brown with weed and green with slime,
Thou mayst drench and defile me and spit in my
    face,
But while I am here thou keep'st thy place!
      I am the Rock!

I am the Rock, beguiling Sea!
I know thou art fair as fair can be,
With golden glitter and silver sheen,
And bosom of blue and garments of green.
Thou mayst pat my cheek with baby hands,
And lap my feet in diamond sands,
And play before me as children play;
But plead as thou wilt, I bar the way!
      I am the Rock!

I am the Rock. Black midnight falls;
The terrible breakers rise like walls;
With curling lips and gleaming teeth
They plunge and tear at my bones beneath.
Year upon year they grind and beat
In storms of thunder and storms of sleet—
Grind and beat and wrestle and tear,
But the rock they beat on is always there!
      I am the Rock!

THE SEA.

I am the Sea. I hold the land
As one holds an apple in his hand.
Hold it fast with sleepless eyes,
Watching the continents sink and rise.
Out of my bosom the mountains grow,

Back to its depths they crumble' slow:
The earth is a helpless child to me—
      I am the Sea!

I am the Sea. When I draw back
Blossom and verdure follow my track,
And the land I leave grows proud and fair,
For the wonderful race of man is there;
And the winds of heaven wail and cry
While the nations rise and reign and die—
Living and dying in folly and pain,
While the laws of the universe thunder in vain.
What is the folly of man to me?
      I am the Sea!

I am the Sea. The earth I sway;
Granite to me is potter's clay;
Under the touch of my careless waves
It rises in turrets and sinks in caves;
The iron cliffs that edge the land
I grind to pebbles and sift to sand,
And beach-grass bloweth and children play
In what were the rocks of yesterday;
It is but a moment of sport to me—
      I am the Sea!

I am the Sea. In my bosom deep
Wealth and Wonder and Beauty sleep;
Wealth and Wonder and Beauty rise
In changing splendor of sunset skies,
And comfort the earth with rains and snows
Till waves the harvest and laughs the rose.
Flower and forest and child of breath

With me have life—without me, death.
What if the ships go down in me?—
I am the Sea!

CHARLOTTE PERKINS GILMAN.

THE POLAR QUEST.

UNCONQUERABLY, men venture on the quest
And seek an ocean amplitude unsailed,
Cold, virgin, awful. Scorning ease and rest,
And heedless of the heroes who have failed,
They face the ice floes with a dauntless zest.

The polar quest! Life's offer to the strong!
To pass beyond the pale, to do and dare,
Leaving a name that stirs us like a song.
And making captive some strange Otherwhere,
Though grim the conquest, and the labor long.

Forever courage kindles, faith moves forth
To find the mystic floodway of the North.

RICHARD BURTON.

THE SHORE.

FROM "ARIADNE."

HUNG like a rich pomegranate o'er the sea
The ripened moon; along the trancèd sand
The feather-shadowed ferns drooped dreamfully;
The solitude's evading harmony
Mingled remotely over sea and land;
A light wind woke and whispered warily,
And myriad ripples tinkled on the strand.

CHARLES G. D. ROBERTS.

THE KEARSARGE.

In the gloomy ocean bed
Dwelt a formless thing, and said,
In the dim and countless eons long ago,
" I will build a stronghold high,
Ocean's power to defy,
And the pride of haughty man to lay low."

Crept the minutes for the sad,
Sped the cycles for the glad,
But the march of time was neither less nor more;
While the formless atom died,
Myriad millions by its side,
And above them slowly lifted Roncador.

Roncador of Caribee,
Coral dragon of the sea,
Ever sleeping with his teeth below the wave;
Woe to him who breaks the sleep!
Woe to them who sail the deep!
Woe to ship and man that fear a shipman's grave!

Hither many a galleon old,
Heavy-keeled with guilty gold,
Fled before the hardy rover smiting sore;
But the sleeper silent lay
Till the preyer and his prey
Brought their plunder and their bones to Ronca-
dor.

Be content, O conqueror!
Now our bravest ship of war,

War and tempest who had often braved before,
    All her storied prowess past,
    Strikes her glorious flag at last
To the formless thing that builded Roncador.

                    JAMES JEFFREY ROCHE.

THE BUOY-BELL.

How like the leper, with his own sad cry
Enforcing his own solitude, it tolls!
That lonely bell set in the rushing shoals,
To warn us from the place of jeopardy!
O friend of man! sore-vexed by ocean's power,
The changing tides wash o'er thee day by day;
Thy trembling mouth is filled with bitter spray,
Yet still thou ringest on from hour to hour;
High is thy mission, though thy lot is wild—
To be in danger's realm a guardian sound;
In seamen's dreams a pleasant part to bear,
And earn their blessing as the year goes round,
And strike the key-note of each grateful prayer,
Breathed in their distant homes by wife or child!

                  CHARLES TENNYSON TURNER.

DOVER BEACH.

THE sea is calm to-night.
The tide is full, the moon lies fair
Upon the straits;—on the French coast the light
Gleams and is gone; the cliffs of England stand,
Glimmering and vast, out in the tranquil bay.
Come to the window, sweet is the night-air!

Only, from the long line of spray
Where the sea meets the moon-blanched sand,
Listen! you hear the grating roar
Of pebbles which the waves draw back, and fling,
At their return, up the high strand,
Begin, and cease, and then again begin,
With tremulous cadence slow, and bring
The eternal note of sadness in.

Sophocles long ago
Heard it on the Ægæan, and it brought
Into his mind the turbid ebb and flow
Of human misery; we
Find also in the sound a thought,
Hearing it by this distant northern sea.

The sea of faith
Was once, too, at the full, and round earth's shore
Lay like the folds of a bright girdle furled.
But now I only hear
Its melancholy, long, withdrawing roar,
Retreating, to the breath
Of the night-winds, down the vast edges drear
And naked shingles of the world.

Ah, love, let us be true
To one another! for the world, which seems
To lie before us like a land of dreams,
So various, so beautiful, so new,
Hath really neither joy, nor love, nor light,
Nor certitude, nor peace, nor help for pain;
And we are here as on a darkling plain
Swept with confused alarms of struggle and flight,
Where ignorant armies clash by night.

MATTHEW ARNOLD.

WITH A NANTUCKET SHELL.

I SEND a shell from the ocean beach;
But listen thou well, for my shell hath speech.
Hold to thine ear,
And plain thou 'lt hear
Tales of ships
That were lost in the rips,
Or that sunk on the shoals
Where the bell-buoy tolls,
And ever and ever its iron tongue rolls
In a ceaseless lament for the poor lost souls.

And a song of the sea
Has my shell for thee:
The melody in it
Was hummed at Wauwinet,
And caught at Coatue
By the gull that flew
Outside to the ships with its perishing crew.
But the white wings wave
Where none may save,
And there's never a stone to mark a grave.

See, its sad heart bleeds
For the sailor's needs;
But it bleeds again
For more mortal pain,
More sorrow and woe,
Than is theirs who go
With shuddering eyes and whitening lips
Down in the sea in their shattered ships.

Thou fearest the sea?
And a tyrant is he,—
A tyrant as cruel as tyrant may be;
But though winds fierce blow,
And the rocks lie low,
And the coast be lee,
This I say to thee:
Of Christian souls more have been wrecked on
shore
Than ever were lost at sea!

CHARLES HENRY WEBB.

────────

THE SEA SHELL.

FROM "THE EXCURSION," BOOK IV.

I HAVE seen
A curious child, who dwelt upon a tract
Of inland ground, applying to his ear
The convolutions of a smooth-lipped shell;
To which, in silence hushed, his very soul
Listened intensely; and his countenance soon
Brightened with joy; for from within were heard
Murmurings, whereby the monitor expressed
Mysterious union with its native sea.
Even such a shell the universe itself
Is to the ear of Faith; and there are times,
I doubt not, when to you it doth impart
Authentic tidings of invisible things;
Of ebb and flow, and ever-during power;
And central peace, subsisting at the heart
Of endless agitation.

WILLIAM WORDSWORTH.

THE SHELL.

FROM " GEBIR," BOOK I.

I AM not daunted, no; I will engage.
But first, said she, what wager will you lay?
A sheep, I answered, add whate'er you will.
I cannot, she replied, make that return:
Our hided vessels in their pitchy round
Seldom, unless from rapine, hold a sheep.
But I have sinuous shells of pearly hue
Within, and they that lustre have imbibed
In the Sun's palace-porch, where when unyoked
His chariot-wheel stands midway in the wave:
Shake one and it awakens, then apply
Its polisht lips to your attentive ear
And it remembers its august abodes,
And murmurs as the ocean murmurs there.

WALTER SAVAGE LANDOR.

HAMPTON BEACH.

THE sunlight glitters keen and bright,
        Where, miles away,
Lies stretching to my dazzled sight
A luminous belt, a misty light,
Beyond the dark pine bluffs and wastes of sandy
        gray.

The tremulous shadow of the Sea!
        Against its ground

Of silvery light, rock, hill, and tree,
Still as a picture, clear and free,
With varying outline mark the coast for miles
    around.

On—on—we tread with loose-flung rein
        Our seaward way,
    Through   dark-green   fields   and   blossoming
        grain,
    Where the wild brier-rose skirts the lane,
And bends above our heads the flowering locust
        spray.

Ha! like a kind hand on my brow
        Comes this fresh breeze,
    Cooling its dull and feverish glow,
    While through my being seems to flow
The breath of a new life,—the healing of the seas!

Now rest we, where this grassy mound
        His feet hath set
    In the great waters, which have bound
    His granite ankles greenly round
With long and tangled moss, and weeds with cool
        spray wet.

Good-bye to pain and care! I take
        Mine ease to-day;
    Here, where the sunny waters break,
    And ripples this keen breeze, I shake
All burdens from the heart, all weary thoughts
        away.

I draw a freer breath—I seem
    Like all I see—
Waves in the sun—the white-winged gleam
Of sea-birds in the slanting beam—
And far-off sails which flit before the south-wind
    free.

So when Time's veil shall fall asunder,
    The soul may know
No fearful change, nor sudden wonder,
Nor sink the weight of mystery under,
But with the upward rise, and with the vastness
    grow.

And all we shrink from now may seem
    No new revealing,—
Familiar as our childhood's stream,
Or pleasant memory of a dream,
The loved and cherished Past upon the new life
    stealing.

Serene and mild, the untried light
    May have its dawning;
And, as in summer's northern night
The evening and the dawn unite,
The sunset hues of Time blend with the soul's
    new morning.

I sit alone; in foam and spray
    Wave after wave
Breaks on the rocks which, stern and gray,
Shoulder the broken tide away,
Or murmurs hoarse and strong through mossy
    cleft and cave.

What heed I of the dusty land
　　And noisy town?
I see the mighty deep expand
From its white line of glimmering sand
To where the blue of heaven on bluer waves shuts
　　　down!

In listless quietude of mind,
　　　I yield to all
The change of cloud and wave and wind;
And passive on the flood reclined,
I wander with the waves, and with them rise and
　　　fall.

But look, thou dreamer!—wave and shore
　　　In shadow lie;
The night-wind warns me back once more
To where, my native hill-tops o'er,
Bends like an arch of fire the glowing sunset sky!

So then, beach, bluff, and wave, farewell!
　　　I bear with me
No token stone nor glittering shell,
But long and oft shall Memory tell
Of this brief thoughtful hour of musing by the
　　　Sea.

　　　　　　JOHN GREENLEAF WHITTIER.

_____

AMONG THE ROCKS.

Oh, good gigantic smile o' the brown old earth,
　This autumn morning! How he sets his bones
To bask i' the sun, and thrusts out knees and feet

For the ripple to run over in its mirth;
  Listening the while, where on the heap of stones
The white breast of the sea-lark twitters sweet.

That is the doctrine, simple, ancient, true;
  Such is life's trial, as old earth smiles and
    knows.
If you loved only what were worth your love,
Love were clear gain, and wholly well for you:
  Make the low nature better by your throes!
Give earth yourself, go up for gain above!
                ROBERT BROWNING.

THE INCHCAPE ROCK.

No stir in the air, no stir in the sea,—
The ship was as still as she could be;
Her sails from heaven received no motion;
Her keel was steady in the ocean.

Without either sign or sound of their shock,
The waves flowed over the Inchcape rock;
So little they rose, so little they fell,
They did not move the Inchcape bell.

The holy Abbot of Aberbrothok
Had placed that bell on the Inchcape rock;
On a buoy in the storm it floated and swung,
And over the waves its warning rung.

When the rock was hid by the surges' swell,
The mariners heard the warning bell;
And then they knew the perilous rock,
And blessed the Abbot of Aberbrothok.

The sun in heaven was shining gay,—
All things were joyful on that day;
The sea-birds screamed as they wheeled around,
And there was joyance in their sound.

The buoy of the Inchcape bell was seen,
A darker speck on the ocean green;
Sir Ralph, the rover, walked his deck,
And he fixed his eye on the darker speck.

He felt the cheering power of spring,—
It made him whistle, it made him sing;
His heart was mirthful to excess;
But the rover's mirth was wickedness.

His eye was on the bell and float:
Quoth he, " My men, put out the boat;
And row me to the Inchcape rock,
And I 'll plague the priest of Aberbrothok."

The boat is lowered, the boatmen row,
And to the Inchcape rock they go;
Sir Ralph bent over from the boat,
And cut the warning bell from the float.

Down sank the bell with a gurgling sound;
The bubbles rose, and burst around.
Quoth Sir Ralph, " The next who comes to the
  rock
Will not bless the Abbot of Aberbrothok."

Sir Ralph, the rover, sailed away,—
He scoured the seas for many a day;

And now, grown rich with plundered store,
He steers his course to Scotland's shore.

So thick a haze o'erspreads the sky
They cannot see the sun on high;
The wind hath blown a gale all day;
At evening it hath died away.

On the deck the rover takes his stand;
So dark it is they see no land.
Quoth Sir Ralph, " It will be lighter soon,
For there is the dawn of the rising moon."

" Canst hear," said one, " the breakers roar?
For yonder, methinks, should be the shore.
Now where we are I cannot tell,
But I wish we could hear the Inchcape bell."

They hear no sound; the swell is strong;
Though the wind hath fallen, they drift along;
Till the vessel strikes with a shivering shock,—
O Christ! it is the Inchcape rock!

Sir Ralph, the rover, tore his hair;
He cursed himself in his despair.
The waves rush in on every side;
The ship is sinking beneath the tide.

But ever in his dying fear
One dreadful sound he seemed to hear,—
A sound as if with the Inchcape bell
The Devil below was ringing his knell.

ROBERT SOUTHEY.

28

HOW'S MY BOY?

"Ho, sailor of the sea!
How's my boy—my boy?"
"What's your boy's name, good wife,
And in what ship sailed he?"

"My boy John—
He that went to sea—
What care I for the ship, sailor?
My boy's my boy to me.

"You come back from sea,
And not know my John?
I might as well have asked some landsman,
Yonder down in the town.
There's not an ass in all the parish
But he knows my John.

"How's my boy—my boy?
And unless you let me know,
I'll swear you are no sailor,
Blue jacket or no,
Brass buttons or no, sailor,
Anchor and crown or no!
Sure his ship was the 'Jolly Briton'"—
"Speak low, woman, speak low!"

"And why should I speak low, sailor,
About my own boy John?
If I was loud as I am proud

I 'd sing him over the town!
Why should I speak low, sailor?"
" That good ship went down."

" How 's my boy—my boy?
What care I for the ship, sailor?
I was never aboard her.
Be she afloat or be she aground,
Sinking or swimming, I 'll be bound
Her owners can afford her!
I say, how 's my John?"
" Every man on board went down,
Every man aboard her."

" How 's my boy—my boy?
What care I for the men, sailor?
I 'm not their mother—
How 's my boy—my boy?
Tell me of him and no other!
How 's my boy—my boy?"

SYDNEY DOBELL.

THE SAILOR'S CONSOLATION.

ONE night came on a hurricane,
   The sea was mountains rolling,
When Barney Buntline turned his quid,
   And said to Billy Bowling:
" A strong nor'wester 's blowing, Bill;
   Hark! don't ye hear it roar now?
Lord help 'em, how I pities them
   Unhappy folks on shore now!

" Foolhardy chaps who live in towns,
　　What danger they are all in,
And now lie quaking in their beds,
　　For fear the roof shall fall in :
Poor creatures! how they envies us,
　　And wishes, I 've a notion,
For our good luck, in such a storm,
　　To be upon the ocean!

" And as for them who 're out all day
　　On business from their houses,
And late at night are coming home,
　　To cheer their babes and spouses,—
While you and I, Bill, on the deck
　　Are comfortably lying,
My eyes! what tiles and chimney-pots
　　About their heads are flying!

" And very often have we heard
　　How men are killed and undone
By overturns of carriages,
　　By thieves and fires in London.
We know what risks all landsmen run,
　　From noblemen to tailors;
Then, Bill, let us thank Providence
　　That you and I are sailors."

　　　　　　　　　　WILLIAM PITT.

POOR JACK.

Go, patter to lubbers and swabs, do ye see,
　　'Bout danger, and fear, and the like;
A tight-water boat and good sea-room give me,
　　And it a'n't to a little I 'll strike.

Though the tempest topgallant-masts smack
    smooth should smite,
  And shiver each splinter of wood,—
Clear the deck, stow the yards, and bouse every-
    thing tight,
  And under reefed foresail we 'll scud:
Avast! nor don't think me a milksop so soft
  To be taken for trifles aback;
For they say there 's a Providence sits up aloft,
  To keep watch for the life of poor Jack!

I heard our good chaplain palaver one day
  About souls, heaven, mercy, and such;
And, my timbers! what lingo he 'd coil and belay;
  Why, 't was just all as one as High Dutch;
For he said how a sparrow can't founder, d' ye
    see,
  Without orders that come down below;
And a many fine things that proved clearly to me
  That Providence takes us in tow:
" For," says he, do you mind me, " let storms e'er
    so oft
  Take the topsails of sailors aback,
There 's a sweet little cherub that sits up aloft,
  To keep watch for the life of poor Jack! "

I said to our Poll,—for, d' ye see, she would
    cry,—
  When last we weighed anchor for sea,
" What argufies snivelling and piping your eye?
  Why, what a blamed fool you must be!
Can't you see, the world 's wide, and there 's room
    for us all,
  Both for seamen and lubbers ashore?

And if to old Davy I should go, friend Poll,
  You never will hear of me more.
What then?   All 's a hazard: come, don't be so
      soft:
  Perhaps I may laughing come back;
For, d' ye see, there 's a cherub sits smiling aloft,
  To keep watch for the life of poor Jack!"

D' ye mind me, a sailor should be every inch
  All as one as a piece of the ship,
And with her brave the world, not offering to
      flinch
  From the moment the anchor 's a-trip.
As for me, in all weathers, all times, sides, and
      ends,
  Naught 's a trouble from duty that springs,
For my heart is my Poll's, and my rhino 's my
      friend's,
  And as for my will, 't is the king's.
Even when my time comes, ne'er believe me so
      soft
  As for grief to be taken aback;
For the same little cherub that sits up aloft
  Will look out a good berth for poor Jack!

                              CHARLES DIBDIN.

THE MARINER'S DREAM.

In slumbers of midnight the sailor-boy lay;
  His hammock swung loose at the sport of the
      wind;
But watch-worn and weary, his cares flew away,
  And visions of happiness danced o'er his mind.

He dreamt of his home, of his dear native bowers,
  And pleasures that waited on life's merry morn,
While Memory stood sideways, half covered with
    flowers,
  And restored every rose, but secreted its thorn.

Then Fancy her magical pinions spread wide,
  And bade the young dreamer in ecstasy rise;
Now far, far behind him the green waters glide,
  And the cot of his forefathers blesses his eyes.

The jessamine clambers in flowers o'er the thatch,
  And the swallow chirps sweet from her nest in
    the wall;
All trembling with transport he raises the latch,
  And the voices of loved ones reply to his call.

A father bends o'er him with looks of delight;
  His cheek is impearled with a mother's warm
    tear;
And the lips of the boy in a love-kiss unite
  With the lips of the maid whom his bosom
    holds dear.

The heart of the sleeper beats high in his breast;
  Joy quickens his pulse, all his hardships seem
    o'er;
And a murmur of happiness steals through his
    rest,—
  "O God! thou hast blest me,—I ask for no
    more."

Ah! whence is that flame which now bursts on
    his eye?
  Ah! what is that sound which now larums his
    ear?

'T is the lightning's red glare, painting hell on
the sky!
'T is the crash of the thunder, the groan of the
sphere!

He springs from his hammock, he flies to the
deck;
Amazement confronts him with images dire;
Wild winds and mad waves drive the vessel a
wreck;
The masts fly in splinters; the shrouds are on
fire.

Like mountains the billows tremendously swell;
In vain the lost wretch calls on mercy to save;
Unseen hands of spirits are ringing his knell,
And the death-angel flaps his broad wing o'er
the wave!

O sailor-boy, woe to thy dream of delight!
In darkness dissolves the gay frost-work of
bliss.
Where now is the picture that Fancy touched
bright,—
Thy parents' fond pressure, and love's honeyed
kiss?

O sailor-boy! sailor-boy! never again
Shall home, love, or kindred thy wishes repay;
Unblessed and unhonored, down deep in the main,
Full many a fathom, thy frame shall decay.

No tomb shall e'er plead to remembrance for thee,
Or redeem form or fame from the merciless
surge;

But the white foam of waves shall thy winding-
    sheet be,
And winds in the midnight of winter thy dirge!

On a bed of green sea-flowers thy limbs shall be
    laid,—
  Around thy white bones the red coral shall
    grow;
Of thy fair yellow locks threads of amber be
    made,
And every part suit to thy mansion below.

Days, months, years, and ages shall circle away,
  And still the vast waters above thee shall roll;
Earth loses thy pattern forever and aye,—
  O sailor-boy! sailor-boy! peace to thy soul!

                    WILLIAM DIMOND.

THE SEA-LIMITS.

CONSIDER the sea's listless chime:
  Time's self it is, made audible—
  The murmur of the earth's own shell.
Secret continuance sublime
  Is the sea's end: our sight may pass
  No furlong further. Since time was,
This sound hath told the lapse of time.

No quiet, which is death's—it hath
  The mournfulness of ancient life,
  Enduring always at dull strife.
As the world's heart of rest and wrath,
  Its painful pulse is in the sands.
  Last utterly, the whole sky stands,
Gray and not known, along its path.

Listen alone beside the sea,
　　Listen alone among the woods;
　　Those voices of twin solitudes
Shall have one sound alike to thee:
　　Hark where the murmurs of thronged men,
　　Surge and sink back and surge again—
Still the one voice of wave and tree.

Gather a shell from the strown beach
　　And listen at its lips: they sigh
　　The same desire and mystery,
The echo of the whole sea's speech.
　　And all mankind is thus at heart
　　Not any thing but what thou art:
And Earth, Sea, Man, are all in each.

DANTE GABRIEL ROSSETTI.

INDEX: AUTHORS AND TITLES.

VOL. V.   443

INDEX OF AUTHORS AND TITLES.

For occupation, nativity, etc., of Authors, and the American publishers of American poetical works, see General Index of Authors, Volume X.

ALDRICH, THOMAS BAILEY.   PAGE.
After the Rain 123
Before the Rain 117

ARISTOPHANES.
Cloud Chorus, The (*Lang's Translation*)........... 131

ARNOLD, GEORGE.
September 147

ARNOLD, MATTHEW.
Dover Beach 423
Early June 252
Oxus, The (*Sohrab and Rustum*) 207
Philomela 308

AVERILL, ANNA BOYNTON.
Birch Stream, The 199

BAILLIE, JOANNA.
Heath-Cock, The 324
Morning Song 39

BARTON, BERNARD.
Sea, The 377

BEATTIE, JAMES.
Morning (*The Minstrel*) 42

BEAUMONT AND FLETCHER.
Folding the Flocks 359

BEDDOES, THOMAS LOVELL.
To Sea 410

BENNETT, WILLIAM COX.
Invocation to Rain in Summer 113

BENTON, JOEL.   PAGE.
  December 175
  Scarlet Tanager, The 329

BLAKE, WILLIAM.
  Tiger, The 354

BLUNT, WILFRED SCAWEN.
  Oasis of Sidi Khaled, The 44
  Old Squire, The 165

BOWEN, JOHN ELIOT.
  Fodder-Time (*German of Carmen Sylva*) 358

BOWLES, WILLIAM LISLE.
  "Come to these scenes of peace" 17
  On the Rhine 207

BRAINARD, JOHN GARDINER CALKINS.
  Fall of Niagara, The 208

BRIDGES, ROBERT SEYMOUR.
  Asian Birds 328
  Sea Poppy, The 285

BROOKS, CHARLES TIMOTHY.
  Harvest Song (*German of Hölty*) 150
  Winter (*German of Claudius*) 172
  Winter Song (*German of Hölty*) 186

BROWNE, WILLIAM.
  Hunted Squirrel, The (*Britannia's Pastorals*) 157

BROWNING, ROBERT.
  Among the Rocks 430
  God in Nature   6
  Home Thoughts from Abroad 83

BRYANT, JOHN HOWARD.
  Valley Brook, The 193
  Winter 183

BRYANT, WILLIAM CULLEN.
  Death of the Flowers, The 255
  Evening Wind, The 54
  Forest Hymn, A 223
  Fringed Gentian, To the 284
  June 102
  Planting of the Apple Tree, The 232
  Robert of Lincoln 310
  Snow-Shower, The 178
  Waterfowl, To a 304

BURNS, ROBERT.   PAGE.
  Afton Water 202
  Louse, To a 348
  Mountain Daisy, To a 277
  Mouse, To a 350

BURROUGHS, JOHN.
  Lapland Longspur, To the 314

BURTON, RICHARD.
  Polar Quest, The 421

BYRON, GEORGE NOEL GORDON, LORD.
  Calm on Lake Leman (*Childe Harold*) 211
  Evening (*Don Juan*) 57
  Night (*Childe Harold*) 65
  Sea, The (*Childe Harold*) 375
  Storm in the Alps (*Childe Harold*) 213
  Swimming (*Two Foscari*) 141
  Wreck, The (*Don Juan*) 416

CAMPBELL, THOMAS.
  Evening Star, To the 54
  " Ye mariners of England " 407

CARDUCCI, GIOSUÈ.
  Ox, The (*Sewall's Translation*) 359

CAREW, THOMAS.
  " Sweetly breathing, vernal air " 82

CARMAN, BLISS.
  Gravedigger, The 383
  More Ancient Mariner, A 345

CHALKHILL, JOHN.
  Angler, The 139

CHANNING, WILLIAM ELLERY.
  " Our boat to the waves " 409

CHAPMAN, GEORGE.
  Camp at Night, The (*Greek of Homer*) 62

CHAUCER, GEOFFREY.
  Daisy, The (*Legend of Good Women*) 275
  Morning in May 89

CHERRY, ANDREW.
  Bay of Biscay, The 405

CHORLEY, HENRY FOTHERGILL.
  Brave old Oak, The 220

CLARE, JOHN.   PAGE.
  Summer Moods 136

CLAUDIUS, MATTHIAS.
  Winter (*Brooks' Translation*) 172

COLERIDGE, HARTLEY.
  Summer Rain 43

COLERIDGE, SAMUEL TAYLOR.
  Fancy in Nubibus 50

COOKE, PHILIP PENDLETON.
  Life in the Autumn Woods 151

COOKE, ROSE TERRY.
  Trailing Arbutus 250

COOLBRITH, INA DONNA.
  Copa de Oro 281
  Mariposa Lily, The 280

COOPER, JAMES FENIMORE.
  My Brigantine (*The Water Witch*) 402

COWLEY, ABRAHAM.
  Hymn to Light, From the 35

COWPER, WILLIAM.
  Unmusical Birds (*The Task*) 309
  Winter Morning (*The Task*) 186

CRANCH, CHRISTOPHER PEARSE.
  Bobolinks, The 316

CRASHAW, RICHARD.
  Nightingale's Song, The (*Music's Duel*) 306

CROSS, MARY ANN EVANS LEWES (*George Eliot*).
  "Day is dying" (*Spanish Gypsy*) 50

CUNNINGHAM, ALLAN.
  "A wet sheet and a flowing sea" 399

CUNNINGHAM, JOHN.
  Morning 40

DANA, RICHARD HENRY.
  Little Beach Bird, The 302
  Pleasure-Boat, The 142

DANIEL, SAMUEL.
  Delia, To 61

DARLEY, GEORGE.   PAGE.
  Song of the Summer Winds 99

DAVIES, SIR JOHN.
  Dancing of the Air, The 125

DIBDIN, CHARLES.
  Heaving of the Lead, The 402
  Poor Jack 436
  Tom Dowling 406

DIBDIN, THOMAS JOHN.
  All's Well (*The British Fleet*) 404

DICKENS, CHARLES.
  Ivy Green, The 263

DIMOND, WILLIAM.
  Mariner's Dream, The 438

DOBELL, SYDNEY THOMPSON.
  " How's my boy " 434

DODGE, MARY ELIZABETH MAPES.
  Snowflakes 176

DRUMMOND, WILLIAM HAMILTON.
  Chariot of Cuchullin, The (*From the Irish*) 371

EASTMAN, CHARLES GAMAGE.
  Snow-Storm, A 180

EASTMAN, ELAINE GOODALE.
  Goldenrod 285

ELIZABETH, QUEEN OF ROUMANIA (*Carmen Sylva*).
  Fodder-Time (*Bowen's Translation*) 358

ELLIOTT, EBENEZER.
  Spring 88

EMERSON, RALPH WALDO.
  Each and All.................................. 9
  Humblebee, To the............................ 342
  Rhodora, The 252
  Sea, The 374
  Snow-Storm, The 176

EURIPIDES.
  Choral Song (*Milman's Translation*) 215

FALCONER, WILLIAM.
  Shipwreck, The 417

FENNER, CORNELIUS GEORGE.   PAGE.
  Gulf-Weed 392

FIELDING, HENRY.
  " A-hunting we will go "........................ 158

FLAGG, WILSON.
  O'Lincoln Family, The 312

FOSDICK, WILLIAM WHITEMAN.
  Maize, The 267

FOSTER, WILLIAM PRESCOTT.
  Silence of the Hills, The 213

FREILIGRATH, FERDINAND.
  Lion's Ride, The (*Translation*)................... 355

GALE, NORMAN.
  Country Faith, The 10

GEOGHEGAN, ARTHUR GERALD.
  Mountain Fern, The 264

GILDER, RICHARD WATSON.
  Dawn (*Five Books of Song*) 38
  " Great nature is an army gay " (*Five Books of
    Song*) 16

GILMAN, CHARLOTTE PERKINS STETSON.
  Rock and the Sea, The 418

GOODALE, DORA READ.
  Twilight Fancy, A 53

GRAY, DAVID.
  " Die down, O dismal day " 88
  " O winter! wilt thou never go "................. 191

GRAY, THOMAS.
  Pleasure Arising from Vicissitude, Ode on the 18
  Spring 79

GUINEY, LOUISE IMOGEN.
  To a Dog's Memory 363

HARDINGE, WILLIAM M.
  Wreath, The (*Greek of Meleager*) 255

HARPUR, CHARLES.
  Midsummer's Noon in the Australian Forest, A..... 44

HARTE, [FRANCIS] BRET.
  Chiquita 371

PAGE.

HARTE, WALTER.
  Soliloquy, A 339

HAYNE, PAUL HAMILTON.
  Storm in the Distance, A 123

HEMANS, FELICIA DOROTHEA BROWNE.
  Treasures of the Deep, The 385

HENLEY, WILLIAM ERNEST.
  Ballade of Midsummer Days and Nights 112

HERRICK, ROBERT.
  Blossoms, To 279
  Daffodils, To 246
  Violets, To 253

HEYWOOD, THOMAS.
  " Pack clouds away " 41

HIGGINSON, THOMAS WENTWORTH.
  " The snowing of the pines " 180

HOGG, JAMES.
  Skylark, The 301

HOLMES, OLIVER WENDELL.
  Chambered Nautilus, The 398
  Insect, To an 340
  Ploughman, The 94

HÖLTY, LUDWIG HEINRICH CHRISTOPH.
  Harvest Song (*Brooks' Translation*) 150
  Winter Song (*Brooks' Translation*) 186

HOMER.
  Camp at Night, The (*Chapman's Translation*) 62

HOOD, THOMAS.
  Flowers 282
  No 167

HORNE, RICHARD HENRY HENGIST.
  Plough, The 96

HOVEY, RICHARD.
  Faun, The 26

HOWITT, MARY.
  Use of Flowers, The 241

HOWITT, WILLIAM.
  Departure of the Swallow, The 331
  Summer Noon, A 46

HUME, ALEXANDER.   PAGE.
   Story of a Summer Day, The 104

HUNT, LEIGH.
   Grasshopper and the Cricket, To the 339

JENNER, DR. EDWARD.
   Signs of Rain 118

JOHNSON, ROBERT UNDERWOOD.
   September Violet, A (*Poems*) 254

JONES, EBENEZER.
   Rain 124

KEATS, JOHN.
   Autumn, To 149
   Grasshopper and the Cricket, The 338

KINGSLEY, CHARLES.
   Song of the River 201

KRUMMACHER, FRIEDRICH WILHELM.
   Moss Rose, The (*Translation*) 281

LAMB, CHARLES.
   Housekeeper, The 352

LAMPMAN, ARCHIBALD.
   Evening 52

LANDOR, WALTER SAVAGE.
   Life of Flowers, The 244
   Shell, The (*Gebir*) 427

LANG, ANDREW.
   Cloud Chorus, The (*Greek of Aristophanes*) 131

LANIER, SIDNEY.
   Sunrise: A Hymn of the Marshes 257

LEYDEN, JOHN.
   Noontide 46

LOGAN, JOHN.
   Cuckoo, To the 289

LONGFELLOW, HENRY WADSWORTH.
   Daybreak 37
   Flowers 238
   Hymn to the Night 68
   Moonlight on the Prairie (*Evangeline*) 59
   Primeval Forest, The (*Evangeline*) 218
   Rain in Summer 114
   Sea-Weed 393
   Snowflakes 174

LOWELL, JAMES RUSSELL. PAGE.
Dandelion, To the 248
Summer Storm 119

MacCARTHY, DENIS FLORENCE.
Summer Longings 81

MacDONALD, ELIZABETH ROBERTS.
Song of Seasons, A 191

MacDONALD, GEORGE.
Light 32

MARVELL, ANDREW.
Drop of Dew, A 100
Song of the Emigrants in Bermuda 400

MELEAGER.
Wreath, The (*Hardinge's Translation*) 255

MEREDITH, GEORGE.
Lark Ascending, The 292

MILTON, JOHN.
Evening in Paradise (*Paradise Lost*) 56
Invocation to Light (*Paradise Lost*) 30
Light (*Paradise Lost*) 32
Nightingale, To the 305
Song: On May Morning 85

MILMAN, HENRY HART.
Choral Song (*Greek of Euripides*) 215

MITCHELL, WALTER.
Tacking Ship Off-Shore 411

MONTGOMERY, JAMES.
Birds (*The Pelican Island*) 288
Coral Reef, The (*The Pelican Island*) 396

MOORE, THOMAS.
" 'Tis the last rose of summer " 283

MÖRIKE, EDUARD.
My River (*Translation*) 205

MORRIS, WILLIAM.
March 74

MOTHERWELL, WILLIAM.
" They come! the merry summer months " 97

NASH, THOMAS.
" Spring, the sweet spring " 77

PAGE.

NORTON, CAROLINE E. S. SHERIDAN (LADY STIRLING-MAXWELL).
Arab to his Favorite Steed, The 366

OLDYS, WILLIAM.
Fly, The 341

PECK, SAMUEL MINTURN.
Sassafras 274

PERCIVAL, JAMES GATES.
Seneca Lake, To 209

PETTEE, G. W.
Sleigh Song 189

PITT, WILLIAM.
Sailor's Consolation, The 435

POLLOK, ROBERT.
Ocean (*The Course of Time*) 379

PROCTER, BRYAN WALLER (*Barry Cornwall*).
Address to the Ocean 381
Blood Horse, The 369
Hunter's Song, The 156
Owl, The 321
Sea, The 380
White Squall, The 408

RILEY, JAMES WHITCOMB.
First Blue-Bird, The 287
" Knee-deep in June "............................ 108
" When the frost is on the punkin " 168

ROBERTS, CHARLES GEORGE DOUGLAS.
Flight of the Geese, The 332
" In the wide awe and wisdom of the night " 69
Shore, The (*Ariadne*) 421
Solitary Woodsman, The 145

ROBERTS, SARAH.
Voice of the Grass, The 237

ROCHE, JAMES JEFFREY.
Kearsarge, The 422

ROGERS, SAMUEL.
Alpine Descent, An 216

RONSARD, PIERRE DE.
Return of Spring (*Translation*) 78

ROSSETTI, DANTE GABRIEL.   PAGE.
Sea-Limits, The 441
Woodspurge, The 251

SANGSTER, CHARLES.
Snows, The 203

SARGENT, EPES.
"A life on the ocean wave" 409

SAVAGE-ARMSTRONG, GEORGE FRANCIS.
Wicklow Winds (*Wicklow*) 127

SCOTT, CLEMENT WILLIAM.
Rus in Urbe 25

SCOTT, DUNCAN CAMPBELL.
End of the Day, The 51

SCOTT, SIR WALTER.
Helvellyn 364
Hunting Song 154
Stag Hunt, The (*Lady of the Lake*) 159

SEWALL, FRANK.
Ox, The (*Italian of Carducci*) 359

SHAKESPEARE, WILLIAM.
Dover Cliff (*King Lear*) 214
Greenwood Tree, The 219
"Hark, hark! the lark" (*Cymbeline*) 292
"When icicles hang by the wall" (*Love's Labor's Lost*) 171

SHARPE, R. S.
Minute-Gun, The 403

SHELLEY, PERCY BYSSHE.
Autumn: A Dirge 170
Cloud, The 133
Earth, Ocean, Air (*Alastor*) 4
Mont Blanc, From 217
Night (*Queen Mab*) 66
Night, To 63
Question, The 272
Skylark, The 297
Sunset (*Queen Mab*) 48
West Wind, Ode to the 128

SIGOURNEY, LYDIA HUNTLEY.
Coral Insects, The 395

SILL, EDWARD ROWLAND.
Among the Redwoods 234

SIMMS, WILLIAM GILMORE.
                                    PAGE.
  Grape-Vine Swing, The 231
  Shaded Water, The ...., ... 196
SMITH, HORACE.
  Hymn to the Flowers 242
SOUTHEY, ROBERT.
  Holly-Tree, The 221
  Inchcape Rock, The 431
SPENCER, WILLIAM ROBERT.
  Beth Gêlert 360
SPRAGUE, CHARLES.
  Winged Worshippers, The 330
STANTON, FRANK LEBBY.
  Mocking-Bird, The 319
STEDMAN, EDMUND CLARENCE.
  Betrothed Anew 92
STERLING, JOHN.
  Beautiful Day, On a 6
STEVENS, GEORGE ALEXANDER.
  Storm, The 414
SWINBURNE, ALGERNON CHARLES.
  Disappointed Lover, The 378
  Forsaken Garden, A 388
  " When the hounds of spring "................... 75
TABB, JOHN BANISTER.
  Indian Summer 167
  Water-Lily, The 280
TANNAHILL, ROBERT.
  " The midges dance aboon the burn " 47
TAYLOR, BAYARD.
  Arab to the Palm, The 227
TAYLOR, BENJAMIN FRANKLIN.
  Northern Lights, The 34
TAYLOR, SIR HENRY.
  Wind and the Pine-Tree, The (*Edwin the Fair*) 219
TENNYSON, ALFRED, LORD.
  Blackbird, The 320
  Bugle, The (*The Princess*) 210
  Dying Swan, The 323
  Eagle, The 321
  Farewell, A 199
  Song of the Brook (*The Brook: an Idyl*) 194
  Spring (*In Memoriam*) 91

THAXTER, CELIA LAIGHTON. PAGE.
May Morning 84
Sandpiper, The 303

THOMAS, EDITH MATILDA.
Frost 173

THOMPSON, [JAMES] MAURICE.
Wild Honey 344

THOMSON, JAMES.
Hymn, A (*The Seasons*) 70
Stag Hunt, The (*The Seasons*) 163
Winter Scenes (*The Seasons*) 184

TIMROD, HENRY.
Spring in Carolina 86

TURNER, CHARLES TENNYSON.
Buoy-Bell, The 423

VERY, JONES.
Latter Rain, The 148
Nature 20

WALTON, IZAAK (See also JOHN CHALKHILL).
Angler's Wish, The 138

WATTS-DUNTON, THEODORE.
Ode to Mother Carey's Chicken.................. 333

WEBB, CHARLES HENRY (*John Paul*).
With a Nantucket Shell 425

WEIR, HARRISON WILLIAM.
English Robin, The 327

WELBY, AMELIA B. COPPUCK.
Twilight at Sea 411

WETHERALD, ETHELWYN.
Snow Storm, The 177

WHITE, HENRY KIRKE.
Early Primrose, The 245

WHITE, JOSEPH BLANCO.
Night 64

WHITTIER, JOHN GREENLEAF.
Hampton Beach 427
Palm-Tree, The 229
Pumpkin, The 270

WILLIS, NATHANIEL PARKER.   PAGE.
  Belfry Pigeon, The 325

WORDSWORTH, WILLIAM.
  Cuckoo, To the 290
  Daffodils 247
  Influence of Natural Objects (*The Prelude*)....... 20
  March 77
  "My heart leaps up" 8
  Sea Shell, The (*The Excursion*) 426
  Skylark, To the 296
  Tables Turned, The 23
  "The world is too much with us" 3
  Tintern Abbey 11

WOTTON, SIR HENRY.
  In Praise of Angling 136

YEATS, WILLIAM BUTLER.
  Indian Song, An 22
  Lake Isle of Innisfree, The 211

ANONYMOUS.
  Cuckoo Song 90
  Flotsam and Jetsam 387
  Our Skater Belle 190
  Remonstrance with the Snails 352
  Stormy Petrel, Lines to the 332